Mastering
*the**SAT**®
Critical Reading
Test

Mastering *the* **SAT**® Critical Reading Test

Thomas R. Davenport

BICENTENNIAL
1807
WILEY
2007
BICENTENNIAL

Wiley Publishing, Inc.

About the Author

Thomas R. Davenport, M. A., is with the English Department at Barron Collier High School. He teaches SAT Prep, ACT Prep, and AP English Prep. He is a member of the Florida Department of Education's Reading Content Advisory Committee.

Publisher's Acknowledgments

Editorial

Project Editor: Kelly Dobbs Henthorne

Acquisitions Editor: Greg Tubach

Composition

Proofreader: Betty Kish

Wiley Indianapolis Composition Services

Mastering the ˚SAT® Critical Reading Test

Published by:
Wiley Publishing, Inc.
111 River Street
Hoboken, NJ 07030-5774
www.wiley.com

Copyright © 2007 Wiley, Hoboken, NJ

Published by Wiley, Hoboken, NJ
Published simultaneously in Canada

ISBN-13: 978-0-470-04201-4

ISBN-10: 0-470-04201-X

Printed in the United States of America

10 9 8 7 6 5 4 3 2

1O/QS/RR/QW/IN

Library of Congress Cataloging-in-Publication Data

Davenport, Thomas R., 1949–
  Mastering the SAT critical reading test / by Thomas R. Davenport.
  ISBN-13: 978-0-470-04201-4
  ISBN-10: 0-470-04201-X
  1. SAT (Educational test)—Study guides. 2. Reading comprehension—Examinations—Study guides. I. Title.
LB2353.57.D38 2007
378.1'662—dc22

2006029061

WILEY

Table of Contents

PART I: SENTENCE COMPLETION

PART II: READING COMPREHENSION

PART III: PRACTICE TESTS

Dedication

I would like to dedicate this book to the memory of my father, James Edward Davenport. Although I could write more pages than contained in this book singing his praises, there simply are no words to express my love, admiration, and respect for him. Let it suffice to say, he walked on this earth, but was not of this earth. . .

Preface

The College Board administered the new SAT for the first time in March, 2005. Although the author has worked with College Board on specific projects, he has learned much about the Critical Reading portion of the examination since this first actual testing window. This book contains the most up-to-date information needed to ensure the best results possible on the Critical Reading section.

The absolute best way to prepare for the SAT (and any other college entrance exam), is to take arduous, challenging coursework in high school, read extensively, and write often. If you have not employed these practices to this point, it is likely too late to ready yourself in this way. It is, however, possible for you to greatly improve your performance by adopting the strategies provided in this book. Familiarity with the style of the test, the type of problems you will face, and proven test-taking strategies will serve to increase your scores appreciably.

This guide is written to enhance student performance. It is written for the student in an easy-to-understand format with in-depth information to promote better understanding of each of the components of the Critical Reading portion of the SAT. These strategies are used across the country in courses presented by some of the best test preparation services and at leading colleges and universities.

Mastering the SAT Critical Reading Test provides you with the following:

- Complete familiarity with the format of the Critical Reading section
- In-depth analysis of answer choices for both correct and incorrect answers
- Various approaches to all sections contained within the Critical Reading section
- Sample Critical Reading section tests
- Instructional guidelines to help increase your overall Critical Reading score

Each of the three Critical Reading sections begins with specific information and individual strategies, followed by a series of skill sets complete with explanations for each correct answer and each incorrect answer selection. Finally, two practice Critical Reading tests are included to help you practice taking the Critical Reading portion of the SAT under self-timed conditions. These tests are followed by answer keys and complete analyses to help hone your overall skills.

Remember, you **can** improve your scores through realistic practice, analysis, and evaluation of your individual performance areas. *Mastering the SAT Critical Reading Test* is the most up-to-date, effective tool to maximize your performance in a reasonable time frame.

Introduction

The Critical Reading section of the SAT is often referred to as the most difficult in which to adequately prepare. This is partially due to the uncertainty surrounding the materials. Unlike the math section that tests your understanding of skills against learned formulas, the Critical Reading section tests vocabulary, literary analysis, comprehension, and a variety of fairly subtle interpretative skills based on a host of authors using complex writing styles. This book shows you concrete and proven methodologies to address all of the areas tested in the Critical Reading sections of the SAT. Specific strategies regarding the Sentence Completion section will prepare you to effectively analyze even the most subtle connotations to improve your scores. In-depth discussions regarding the Short and Long Reading sections specifically show you what you will see on the SAT and will help you develop an individualized strategy based on proven, results-oriented methods to improve your score in each of these vital areas. By working through the Skill Sets in this book and taking the practice tests, you will gain the knowledge necessary to perform your best and achieve the highest scores possible.

Most colleges and universities require applicants to take some form of a college entrance examination. In fact, more than two million students take the SAT each year. Many students find it advantageous to take the test multiple times, lessening their levels of anxiety with each undertaking. Spending time with *Mastering the SAT Critical Reading* is one of the best ways to familiarize yourself with the format and strategies proven to increase scores on the SAT. Standardized college entrance examinations are generally designed to measure critical thinking skills and, therefore, serve as a general predictor of your chances of success in a higher learning environment. Certainly, colleges look at more than just an individual test score when considering students for admission. They look at your overall academic record, especially the rigor of your high school curriculum, your involvement in school and community activities, letters of recommendation, and your overall presentation contained within the application.

The SAT is divided into three major sections. The following table reflects the major sections and components of each:

Section	Question Type	Apprx. Number	Time Allotted
Critical Reading	Sentence Completion	19	
	Short and Extended Passage	48	
	Total Critical Reading	67	70 minutes consisting of two 25-minute and one 20-minute section
Writing	Identifying Sentence Errors	18	
	Improving Sentences	25	
	Improving Paragraphs	6	
	Essay Writing	1 Essay	25 minutes
	Total Writing	49 plus Essay	60 minutes consisting of two 25-minute and one 10-minute section
Math	Multiple-choice	44	
	Student-produced (grid)	10	
	Total Math	54	70 minutes consisting of two 25-minute and one 20-minute section

A total time of 3 hours and 45 minutes is allocated to complete the test.

One of the sections is called a variable section. It will be included in either critical reading, writing, or math for which 25 minutes is allocated. This section is generally included on all standardized tests. This section is sometimes referred to as an *equating* section or a *pilot test*. Regardless of nomenclature, it is designed to assist test makers in ensuring that the questions are performance ready and appropriate for inclusion on the standardized test in question. Even though this section will not count toward your score, you won't be able to determine which section is being piloted so do your best on every section. Each question goes through an exacting review at least 12 times before appearing on an actual live test. Because you will not know which of the sections is included in the variable section, it is imperative that you do your best on all sections of the test. To learn more about the structure and design of the test and to gain additional valuable information regarding such things as test sites, dates of administration, and so on, it is highly recommended that you visit the College Board website at www.collegeboard.com.

Although specific strategies and information regarding the Critical Reading section of the test are covered later in this book, some general information and test-taking strategies are important to know. Becoming familiar with the types and format of questions you will face on the test will help you save time when you do actually take the SAT. A simple review on test day will help you remain at ease and help eliminate careless errors. You have probably been told throughout your educational career to get plenty of sleep and have a good, healthy breakfast before the test. You may even have been told to devour some mints to help stimulate the brain and keep you sharp during the test. Although well intentioned, some advice is best not followed. Adventuring well outside your normal patterns of behavior will generally do more harm than good. Recent research suggests that going to bed more than two hours before normal may upset your body's internal clock and cause you to become more out of sync than to enhance performance. And, if you are used to a small breakfast consisting of a piece of fruit and toast, steak and eggs with a side of hash browns, complete with biscuits and gravy, will tend to throw your metabolism into shock and result in bodily functions that are less than superbly conducive for test taking. As far as the mint goes, about the worst thing that could happen is that you have fresh breath.

During the test, you will want to read and think carefully and clearly. Understanding the form and format of questions you will face will help in this regard. Consider all of the answer choices and do not fall into the trap of selecting the first answer choice that appears to fulfill the requirements of the question. Remember, test writers place four distractors with one correct answer. **Distractors** are answer choices that seems viable but are incorrect. Be sure you know exactly what the question is asking before selecting an answer choice.

As the SAT is a timed test, be sure to give yourself ample time in each section. Keep track of the time and allocate a sufficient amount to answer the greatest number of questions correctly. Remember, each correct answer is of the same raw value whether the question is rated easy or hard. Don't lose points because you were trying to hurry through the easier questions to have more time to figure out the hard ones. If a question baffles you when you first read it, and it doesn't make any more sense on the second reading, skip it, and return to it if time permits. Be sure to indicate which question you are skipping and will need to return to in your test booklet. When it comes to reading passages, short or long, making margin notes or underlining key words and phrases may help you focus as you read. Although the test booklet is your own domain—meaning you can mark it up any way you see fit—the answer sheet is not. Circling the number of the question on your answer sheet is a good way to indicate that this question needs further attention. *Caution:* Be sure to erase these marks even if you don't have time to actually answer the questions.

Knowing how the questions are presented will help you determine what is appropriate when it comes to pacing. Although ranking questions in terms of degrees of difficulty is a subjective endeavor at best, generally speaking the questions in the SAT are arranged as follows:

Generally Arranged Easiest to Hardest	
Section	*Type*
Math	Multiple Choice Student–Produced Grid
Critical Reading	Sentence Completion
Writing	Sentence Errors Improving Sentences

NOT Arranged Easiest to Hardest	
Section	**Type**
Critical Reading	Short Passage Comprehension
	Long Passage Comprehension
Writing	Improving Paragraphs
	Essay Writing

Remember that SAT is a timed test and will be over when time is up, not when you are finished. Although some people will finish the test, this has very little to do with final scoring. Don't let someone who is flipping pages more quickly than you distract you. Keep mindful of the time in relation to where you are in a particular section. You are not allowed to work ahead in another section, so use the time allocated completely for each section. If areas that you know are generally arranged in a progressively more difficult series, plan accordingly. Also keep in mind that the further along you are into a section that is progressive, the obvious or most easily recognized *correct* answer bears reconsideration. Within each section, clues are given in the stem or base of the question that will help lead you to the right answer. Those clues will be discussed within each section later in the book.

In sections that are not progressively arranged, remember to still work at a steady pace. Don't get so involved in trying to figure out any individual question such as to negatively limit the time you might have to answer the questions of lesser difficulty. Obviously, you won't know whether the next question will be easier or more difficult for you. Generally speaking, if you don't get a good sense or feeling about a question on the first or second reading, it may be better to skip it and come back to it. Naturally, this depends greatly upon your particular strategy and strengths. If, for example, you are working in the long passage comprehension section and you come to a seemingly impossible question, you may want to address this question not in sequence but before you go back to an alternate passage. Simple reasoning suggests that you are more familiar with the passage after having read and answered some questions about it than you will be after reading a different passage and focusing on those questions.

Each test taker has particular strengths. After taking the sample tests, analyze your particular strengths and use this information to help you on test day. Address the questions aligned with your particular strengths before trying to deal with questions requiring more time and focus. This will help build confidence, generate the most number of points, and allocate more time for sorting information on the more difficult questions as they relate to your personal strengths. Remember, you may work in any order as long as you stay within the section being tested. Again, be very careful when answering questions out of sequence. It is recommended that you indicate which questions have been skipped on your answer sheet and that you verify you are answering the same number question on the answer sheet as you are reading in the test booklet. This cannot be overstressed. Many students are thrown into an absolute panic when they realize they are working on the next to the last question in the test booklet but have three answer slots left on the answer sheet.

Educated guessing is a term often used when discussing any testing. Actually, we make educated guesses in all walks of life every day. When a recipe calls for a pinch of salt, the baker makes an educated guess as to how much salt to add. Without much conscious effort, the baker reasons that using the forefinger and thumb will produce a more accurate representation than using the little finger and thumb. In this example, there is also physical reasoning. It is simply more practical to use the thumb and forefinger. Educated guessing is really an alternative term for *reasoning*. If we reason that at least one distractor, or answer choice, is incorrect, then we can reason which is the most likely correct answer choice. It may be a subtle difference like whether you consider writing fiction to be writing an untruth, but it's a valuable tool when it comes to test taking. And when it comes to the SAT, subtleties can make a significant difference in scores. After all, the SAT is designed to measure one's ability to differentiate between two seemingly correct answer choices based upon both experiential and vicarious historical knowledge.

The first step in reasoning is to eliminate any answer choice you know to be incorrect. Obviously, the more known incorrect answers you can eliminate, the better your chances of reasoning the correct answer. In order to dissuade test takers from pure random guessing, there is a quarter point penalty for each incorrect answer. So, for every four incorrect answers, one correct answer is taken away. This is a change from most tests taken in high school. Even the so-called high stakes tests given in most states don't use a penalty system. Don't give this penalty system more consideration than it deserves. Remember, if you can eliminate just one of the answer choices, you should go ahead and reason an answer choice. You may then reason that if you cannot eliminate even one of the answer choices, it is probably best to leave the question unanswered.

An example of reasoning as it relates to Sentence Completion follows:

> **1.** She was _____ student, but in her personal life she was kind, giving, and _____.
>   - **A.** a serious . . . egotistical
>   - **B.** a competitive . . . warm
>   - **C.** an amiable . . . loving
>   - **D.** a respected . . . demanding
>   - **E.** a successful . . . cordial

Now, let's do some reasoning. We'll start with the second blank because the question gives us some clues as to what kind of word is needed. Since the words *kind* and *giving* are used in a series with the needed word, we know the correct answer must be a positive. We can eliminate Choices A and D because those second word choices are negative, *egotistical* and *demanding*, respectfully. This leaves Choices B, C, and E as possible correct choices. A further clue to help us reason is the fact that the word *but* is indicative of a change from negative to the positive series; therefore, we are looking for a more negative choice for the first blank. As first word choices in C and E, *amiable* and *successful*, are positive, this leaves Choice **B,** *a competitive . . . warm,* which is correct. Even without the second reasoning, it would have been prudent to make a reasoned guess based on the elimination of answer Choices A and D.

As you can mark in your test booklet, it is wise to put a diagonal slash through any answer choice you have reasoned cannot be correct. This will leave you with only plausible answer choices from which to choose. Even if you decide to skip the question after you have eliminated an answer choice, marking through an incorrect answer will save you time when you return to re-reason an answer choice.

Another test-taking tactic is to indicate a further degree of measurement on questions you have decided to skip. If a question makes absolutely no sense to you and reasoning seems likely to produce no appreciable help, you may wish to indicate this by placing a minus sign (–) beside the question number on your answer sheet. If the question seems reasonable in terms of eliminating a wrong choice or possibly working out an answer, you may wish to place a plus (+) beside the number on your answer sheet. This way, when you return to questions you've skipped, you will have some idea of which questions to attack first.

It is also important to avoid misreading a question and selecting an answer choice that would be correct if the question actually read as it was interpreted by you. This typically happens when a question has one of the following terms: EXCEPT or NOT. The question may also ask for an alternative to the expected or anticipated question. For example, a math question may ask you to select the value of $x + 2$ instead of simply the value of $x,$ which obviously changes the correct answer choice. Indeed, when the question states that "All of the following EXCEPT help develop the main idea," the correct answer selection will not be the first choice that actually does help develop the main idea. The same general thought methodology applies for questions that use the term NOT.

Some answer selections will actually be a set of multiple answers. These questions are sometimes referred to as the "multiple-multiple choice" format. Although they may appear more daunting than the straightforward (A, B, C, D, E) multiple-choice problems, they can actually be easier. The best way to address these answer choices is to judge each variable individually. Then the combination becomes easy. A rather elementary example follows:

1. If x is a positive integer, then which of the following must be true?

    I. $x > 0$

    II. $x = 0$

  III. $x < 1$

    A.   I only

    B.   II only

    C.   III only

    D.   I and II only

    E.   I and III only

Because x is a positive integer, it must be a counting number. As such, possible values for x could be 1, 2, 3, and so on. Statement I, $x > 0$ is always true and must be used in any combination of answer choices. As statement I is not contained in Choices B or C, they cannot be correct. Since II is incorrect, any choice that contains II as part of the answer choice cannot be correct, thereby further eliminating Choice D. Finally, as x must be greater than 0, III must be incorrect, thus alleviating Choice E. This leaves answer Choice **A,** which is correct.

Finally, remember to keep the SAT test in proper perspective. No one test will determine whether or not you will attend college. Indeed, it is but one factor indicating your readiness for college admission. Becoming as familiar with the experience before the actual test will help quell any anxiety related to the unknown. Studying the information contained in this book and taking the sample tests contained herein will prepare you as much as possible for the Critical Reading section of the SAT.

SAT Critical Reading Overview and General Strategies

The Critical Reading section of the SAT used to be called the Verbal Reasoning section for good reason—it tests your ability to reason words. This is a critical concept as it requires reasoning abilities in addition to a rudimentary knowledge of word meaning. Indeed, good reasoning skills widely contribute to higher scores above those achieved with simply a good working vocabulary.

Although SAT no longer tests analogies *per se,* we must remember that the sentence completion, and to some degree, the reading passage questions are, in fact, analogies. By way of explanation, previously SATs may have asked you to select the best analogy in the following question:

1. OBSESSIVE:INDIFFERENT. . .

    A.   meticulous:sloppy

    B.   insatiable:hungry

    C.   gregarious:abject

    D.   evanescent:fleeting

    E.   forgetful:reminiscent

Effectively, this analogy question is asking you to differentiate between the positive *obsessive* and the negative *indifferent* and then to pick a suitable pair of antonyms in comparison. As *meticulous* is opposite to *sloppy*, answer Choice **A** would have been correct.

Now let's take a sample sentence completion question:

> **1.** Although a ___~~✗~~___ dresser, her dwellings exposed her ___⌒___ side.
>
> ⓐ **A.** meticulous . . . sloppy
> **B.** fashionable . . . expensive
> **C.** slovenly . . . miscreant
> ✗ **D.** boring . . . tasteless
> ✗ **E.** weird . . . eclectic

In kindred spirit to the analogy, the sentence completion question asks you to identify and reason that the term *although* indicates that an opposite pair is needed to correctly complete the sentence. As *meticulous* and *sloppy* are the only pair of opposites that best complement the meaning of the sentence, answer Choice **A** is correct.

The Critical Reading section is composed of two types of multiple choice questions:

- **Sentence Completion** questions are designed to test your vocabulary and your ability to relate parts of the sentence for comprehension and meaning. Sentences will be split between those with one blank and those with two blanks for which you must select the answer or pair to fill in the blank(s).
- **Short and Long Passage Comprehension** questions are based on passages that range from 100 to 850 words in length. Selections are made from social studies, natural sciences, literary fiction, and the humanities.

The reason that the College Board, and colleges, focus on verbal acuity is because reading skills are the basis for academic success. Since academic success at the college level depends largely on independent study skills, your ability to reason as you read and to think critically as new concepts and ideas are presented, will, in large measure, foretell your degree of comprehension and success. The two types of questions used by the College Board on the SAT measure your vocabulary, ability to understand complex sentences and passages, and ability to reason appropriately in those situations in which an answer choice is not easily determined. Just as reading a lot helps improve vocabulary, analyzing questions helps you reason a correct answer choice. The ability to reason a correct answer is one of the most valuable skills you can possess, and this book will help you develop that skill set.

All three sources of questions in the Critical Reading section of this book are followed with detailed explanations as to how to understand the question, apply this analysis to help eliminate distractors, and provide an understanding of factors that will help you select the correct answer. Through practice, you will be able to apply this methodology to all types of questions, whether it be in verbal, math, or writing sections when multiple-choice questions are presented.

Although you will develop your own approach to taking the Critical Reading test, most agree the following approach is perhaps the most practical:

1. Attempt sentence completion questions first. You will find that about a third of the questions in the Critical Reading section of the SAT are sentence completion questions. Remember that sentence completion questions are arranged from easiest to most difficult. Although the sentence completion questions take less time, remember to save enough time to attend to the passage-based questions.

   Read the sentence completion question and mark your booklet indicating any key words such as *but, however, although, on the other hand, albeit, conversely, notwithstanding,* and *except,* or words of similar meaning. These are important clue words and indicate a shift in tone, meaning, choice, or definition.

   Before reading the answer choices, predict the type word or words that would fit. Your prediction should follow the overall tone of the sentence. If the sentence were upbeat, you wouldn't predict something morose. This is not an exercise to hone your extra sensory perception skills, it is just to front-load your brain with plausible information to help narrow your selection process.

   Perform a simple comparison between your prediction and the answer choices given. This may be more easily done with single versus multiple blanks, but the process works well with both styles. Don't rush to judgment. Review all selections before deciding on a single answer choice. Remember, the SAT reviewers want the *best* answer choice in all instances. Just because an answer choice could fit doesn't mean it is the *best* fit.

If you get to a point where you aren't sure between two choices, read the sentence with both answer choices plugged into the blank(s). Which one sounds the best? Sometimes your ear is the best judge of correctness. After all, you've been listening since before birth. Use this tool to your advantage.

Only one choice will be the *best*. Only one choice will make overall sense and keep the total meaning of the sentence.

2. If you come to a question that you cannot seem to reason in short order, mark that question on your test booklet and indicate that you need to come back to that question on your answer sheet by marking either a (+) or a (−) next to that number. The (+) indicates a skipped question you believe you can reason given time. A (−) indicates a question you don't believe you will be able to reason unless you gain some inspiration along the way.

3. Before moving on to the passage-based questions, go back and take another look at those skipped questions marked with a (+). If you can eliminate one distractor, go ahead and make a *reasoned guess* at an answer.

4. Move on to the passage-based questions. As both short and extended reading passage multiple-choice questions require the same skill set, the methodology for selecting an answer choice is the same. It is best to front load your mind by reading the title of the passage, if there is one. Otherwise, quickly peruse the passage. This is not time for deep reading or pleasure reading. Mark the passage by underlining key words and phrases. Indicate key ideas as a one- or two-word margin note. Again, don't rewrite the paragraph, but a margin note can help you follow a pattern of development in the passage.

Read the question most carefully and be sure that you understand exactly what is being asked. Just as with the sentence completion questions, watch for keywords contained within the question. Remember, many questions will actually help point you to the correct answer. Each explanations section in this book will present ways to help identify those clues.

Locate the area of content addressing the question. Reread the section that most likely pertains to the question being addressed.

Predict a correct answer. Don't make this your primary focus. Just quickly try to answer the question as you read the passage.

Review the answer choices to find a match to your prediction. Remember to read all distractors as the SAT reviewers will want the *best* answer choice. Eliminate answer choices you identify as incorrect by crossing them out with a slash through the letter in your test booklet. If you find a match to your prediction, however, you can be fairly certain of a correct choice.

5. Finally, don't forget to employ your prior knowledge. The vocabulary within both the text and questions may give you initial pause. In fact, you may not know the meaning of a key word contained in the question. Try to identify its meaning by association. If you have heard the word in a phrase, try to associate the phrase with the context in which you heard it or it is generally used. For example, you may not remember the term *annul* but may remember the phrase when someone "annuls their marriage" and can at least know that this is likely not to be a positive, uplifting answer selection. Naturally, you must keep in mind the overall tone of the passage.

There is one more aspect of preparation that most students fail to adopt. Prepare to be unsure more often than with other types of tests. Remember, a good score on the SAT will come from answering somewhere in the vicinity of 50+ percent correctly. So don't let it concern you when you put many more (+) and (−) indicators on your answer sheet than you expected. This is normal and expected.

By this stage in your educational career, you undoubtedly have developed certain personal strategies and preferences you use when taking tests. As you work through the skill sets and take the practice sets in this book, try to utilize those suggestions presented here and those you have previously developed. The goal is to end up with a set of tools that work for you. The more you practice, the better these tools will feel.

Strategies for the SAT Vocabulary

Simply put, if you haven't developed a broad usable vocabulary to this point, you likely won't before the test. The only proven way to truly develop a working vocabulary is to read, read, and read some more. Given the fact that there is probably insufficient time for that to happen before you take the SAT, you are left with only certain vocabulary development exercises that will help increase your score. One methodology is to present you with a list of words most used over the past several tests for you to memorize. A second exercise is to give you a list of most anticipated words you'll encounter on the test, along with definitions for you to study. A third possibility would be to give you a group of flash cards with definitions on the back to cram for the test. But, unless you see the words in context and take special note of those with which you have difficulty, search the in-context meaning, and review them with applied definition, you will not effectively master the contextual meaning. Additionally, you needn't waste time passing over lists containing words you have already mastered.

With this in mind, both the sentence completion and passage review questions in this book are designed to use identified SAT words in the actual question, or as answer choices. When you come across a word you are not familiar with, simply write it down or mark it for follow-up. When convenient, look up the word and select the definition most befitting the meaning as used in context. This reduces the risk of learning a single definition of a word and attempting to force that definition when the word is used in any context. We all know that many words have different meanings predicated upon how they are used in context. This is why we prefer to use the words in context rather than simply provide you with a flash card approach.

Indeed, a "hot potato," "hot tomato," "hot spot," and a "hot time" all convey variations as to the meaning of "hot" and may not have anything to do with the weather.

One proven, and relatively simple, method to improve your chances regarding reasoning a definition to an unknown word is to understand the meaning of the prefix and/or suffix appended to the unknown root. Spending time with the following common prefixes and suffixes will help you at least eliminate some answer choices and allow you to reason an answer and improve your score.

Prefixes

Prefix	Meaning	Sample Word
ad-	to, toward	advance
anti-	against	antidote
bi-	two	bicycle
co-	together	coincide
com-	together, with	composite
de-	away, off, down, from	descend
dis-	not	distasteful
epi-	upon	epilogue
equi-	equal, equally	equivalent
ex-	out of	expel
homo-	same, equal, like	homogenized
hyper-	over, too much	hyperactive
hypo-	under, too little	hypodermic
in-	not	insufficient
in-	into	instruct
inter-	between	interstate

Prefix	Meaning	Sample Word
mal-	bad	malfunction
mid-	middle	midnight
mis-	wrong	mistake
mono-	alone, one	monolith
multi-	many	multilayered
non-	not	nonentity
ob-	against	objection
omni-	all, everyone	omniscient
over-	above	overbearing
poly-	many	polymorphous
pre-	before	prefix
pro-	forward	propel
re-	back, again	regress
retro-	backward	retrograde
semi-	half, partly	semicircle
sub-	under, below average	submarine
trans-	across, beyond	transcend
un-	not, opposite of	unneeded
-able, -ible	able to	usable
-en	to make happen, made of	waxen
-er, -or	one who does	competitor
-ful	full of	harmful
-fy	to make	dignify
-ish	like	childish
-ism	the practice of	rationalism
-ist	one who is occupied with	feminist
-ize	cause to become	dramatize
-less	without, lacking	meaningless
-like	resembling	ladylike

Prefix	Meaning	Sample Word
-logue	a particular kind of speaking or writing	prologue
-ment	state of being	astonishment
-ness	the quality of	aggressiveness
-ship	the art or skill of	statesmanship
-tude	the state of	rectitude
-ward	in the direction of	inward
-y	resembling	frosty

PART I

SENTENCE COMPLETION

Strategies for the Sentence Completion Section

Of the three Critical Reading sections, the Sentence Completion section of the SAT is most obviously designed to measure your knowledge of college-level vocabulary. Although vocabulary building books are available, the best way to develop a good working vocabulary is to read. Reading a variety of authors in a variety of genres will help you develop not only a good vocabulary but will help you understand the structure of sentences, which in turn will help you comprehend not only what you are reading, but the subtleties hidden to surface readers. Obviously, the more widely read you are, the better you will score on the SAT. Notwithstanding, some clues will help improve your scores when you learn to identify them and how to use them to your advantage. Clues and techniques specifically designed for the Sentence Completion portion will be presented throughout this section and in the answers and explanations sections.

This section tests your ability to understand the composition of a sentence and select the correct word or two words that best complete and complement the overall meaning of the sentence, while retaining the structure and style. Although the sentences generally will be about familiar topics, you need not necessarily know the definitions of all words to correctly answer these questions. In some ways, this section is a warm up, if you will, to the reading passage questions. The Sentence Completion section will front-load your brain with a variety of sentence structures and styles you may well see in the Reading Comprehension sections.

The College Board tells us that instructions for the Sentence Completion section of the SAT will be something like the following:

Each sentence below has one or two blanks, each blank indicating that something has been omitted. Beneath the sentence are five words or sets of words labeled A through E. Choose the word or set of words that, when inserted in the sentence, *best* fits the meaning of the sentence as a whole.

Before looking at a sample set of questions, let's make sure that we understand the instructions. By asking that we choose the word or set of words that "best" fit the meaning of the sentence, we are being warned that there may be more than one word or set of words that actually fit the meaning of the sentence. In other words, do not select the first word or set of words that make sense when inserted into the sentence. Rather, read all answer choices, marking out the ones that do not fit, and then select the one that *best* fits the meaning of the sentence "as a whole." Although this may seem rather rudimentary, the subtleties of tone, mood, and direction within word choices will test the skills of every individual taking the test. Being familiar with these instructions will help you save time on the day of testing. Remember, your focus is to score as many correct answers as possible. Using the following strategies will help you save time, thereby providing you with the opportunity to answer more questions correctly.

Context-Based Questions

The SAT Sentence Completion section can be broken down into two basic subsets: questions using vocabulary in context and questions that are logic-based. Although knowing the definition of the words in the answer choices gives you a better chance of selecting the correct answer, knowing how the words are used in the context of the sentence will help with in-context questions. This subset includes both one-blank and two-blank questions.

---

1. Male and female loons tend to act _____, actively helping each other forage for food to feed their young.

    A. aggressively
    B. surreptitiously
    C. cooperatively
    D. defensively
    E. erratically

The correct choice is **C.**

Explanation: The sentence question is actually asking how loons behave. The missing word is further defined after the comma and suggests that loons are seen "actively helping each other forage for food to feed their young." Only one word among the choices describes this behavior: *cooperatively.*

---

2. My grandmother, who never spent a dime and rarely talked, was considered both _____ and _____.

  A. miserly. . . taciturn
  B. frugal. . . effusive
  C. stingy. . . garrulous
  D. thrifty. . . raucous
  E. munificent. . . reticent

Same Meaning

The correct choice is **A.**

Explanation: Quite simply, you are to find the two words that describe my grandmother. One of the words must mean that she did not spend money willingly, and the other must mean that she did not talk much. The correct answer is "miserly. . . taciturn." Miserly means like a miser or extremely stingy, and taciturn means shy or unwilling to engage in conversation. Note that Choices A through D might meet the first blank criteria of not spending money easily, but only Choices A and E meet the criteria for being silent. As answer Choice A is the only choice meeting the demands of both context-based definitions, it is the correct answer.

Logic-Based Questions

Logic-based questions require you to know the meanings of the words, how the words are used in context, and understand the logical flow of the sentence. This subset also includes both one-blank and two-blank questions.

---

1. After witnessing a number of territorial skirmishes, Dr. Jarmen had to change his earlier opinion that these particular breeds of chipmunk were always _____ animals.

  A. curious
  B. harsh
  C. quarreling
  D. peaceful
  E. warring

The correct choice is **D.**

Explanation: Following the logical flow of the sentence will help alleviate incorrect answer choices. First, the introductory word "After" informs the reader that the information at the beginning of the sentence is going to impact what comes later in the thought or logical process. The word "change" informs the reader that there is a different thought or reaction than that previously described in the sentence. Events described in the beginning of the sentence are seen as the catalyst for the change, whatever it might be. Finally, the logic of the flow of ideas tells the reader what is changing, ". . . his earlier opinion that these particular breeds of chipmunk were always _____ animals." The word that best fits the blank necessarily should convey a meaning of revision after seeing the animals fighting. Answer Choice D, peaceful, is the only plausible selection.

2. Although teasers for the film were absolutely _____, the film itself was well presented, well timed, and represented a rather _____ work.

    A. scintillating. . . blasé
    B. tasteless. . . amateur
    C. risqué. . . bawdy
    D. breathtaking. . . familiar
    E. crude. . . polished

The correct choice is **E.**

Explanation: The introductory word "Although" in the first clause informs the reader that the tone in the second clause will be dichotomous to the first. This means that we are looking for basic antonyms in our correct choice. Answer Choices A, D, and E all qualify for a difference in tone. Additionally, however, the second word must complement the tone of well presented and well timed. In this case, looking at the second word choice actually leaves us with the only correct choice, E.

Practical Strategies

Having covered the basic format of the Sentence Completion section, we need to look at some practical strategies to use during the actual test. It is important to practice these strategies before the test to see which work best for you. Although all of the strategies are proven to help increment scores, some may work better for you personally.

- Begin by reading the entire sentence saying "blank" for the blank(s). This accomplishes a couple of things. First, it gives you a feel for the flow of the language used. Second, it helps you mentally diagnose any clue words including those setting up a transition, negative comparison, tone, introductory phrase, or positive reaffirmation.
- Generally speaking, standard definitions of words are used in the Sentence Completion section of the SAT. You needn't spend time looking for alternative definitions or nonstandard definitions.
- Try to insert words that make the sentence meaningful for you before looking at the answer choices. If you find a synonym for the word you chose, it is probably the correct choice.
- Introductory and transitional words are extremely important and clue the reader to the logic of the sentence. These words tell you what the relationship between two parts of the sentence will be. They may be complementary or indicate a contradiction. These are sometimes called signal words because they signal the relationship of the sentence parts to the reader. A listing of some introductory or transitional words or phrases follows:

Generic Transitions	*Inclusion*	*Resultants*	*Other*
Albeit	Additionally	Accordingly	Abnormal
although	also	because	anomalous
but	and	consequently for	illogical
despite	as	hence	incongruous
even though	besides	in order to	ironic
except	furthermore	therefore	never
however	in addition	thus	no
in contrast	in other words		not
in spite of	likened to		odd
instead	likewise		paradoxical

(continued)

Generic Transitions	Inclusion	Resultants	Other
nevertheless	moreover		surprising
nonetheless	therefore		unexpected
on the contrary			
on the other hand			
rather than			
regardless			
still			
yet			

- Read all sentences and answer choices carefully. This is especially true toward the end of the Sentence Completion section as the degree of difficulty increases as you go further into the section. Keeping up with the twists and turns of the direction and flow of the sentence will help you focus on the correct answer choice. Many errors are made because the reader failed to keep up with a transition and selected an answer that would have been correct if the sentence didn't change direction and ask for the negative rather than the positive or vice versa.

- This is not your classroom vocabulary review. You will encounter words you have never heard of before. Don't panic. Use the skills covered in this book and reduce some of the incorrect choices to improve your percentage of correct answers. Use context clues within the sentence to help understand alien words. Remember to use your prefix and suffix definitions to help align meaning. Think of parts of the root word you may understand in a different word. Finally, let your ears lend you a helping hand. Read the sentence with the remaining word choices to help determine which sounds correct. As a final check, reread the sentence with the answer choice filled in to satisfy yourself that it makes sense.

- When dealing with two blank questions, try to eliminate some answer choices based on just one blank at a time.

  - Sometimes, it is best to start with the second blank. To decide which blank to start with, read the question and select the blank that seems easier for you. If they both seem about the same, look at the answer choices to determine which set of words in the answer choices contain the most synonyms and start with the alternative set. This will help you alleviate incorrect answer choices rapidly.

  - After you have alleviated as many answer choices as possible with the first selected blank, repeat the process with the alternative set of choices and eliminate any that do not match for that blank.

  - If only one set of choices is left, this is the correct answer. If more than one set is left, go on to the next steps.

  - Now, combine both answer choices together and reread the sentence using both words in place of the blanks to determine which one makes the most sense and fulfills the requirement of being the best fit.

  - Finally, listen. Read with your ear and make the best selection.

- Keep in mind that the instructions for all the Sentence Completion questions ask that you choose the best answer. In order to make sure that you fulfill this requirement, you must read all the answer choices, not just until you find one that fits. Here is where your ability to comprehend the tone and texture of the sentence comes into play. This is really where having read extensively will help you more than any other preparation you attempt.

Let's take a look at a sample question that on the surface seems like a simple vocabulary question.

---

1. A decision based upon limited facts must be called _____.

    A. harsh
    B. deliberate
    C. sensible
    D. premature
    E. fair

The correct choice is **D.**

Explanation: If we practiced our strategies in order, we first read the sentence and substituted the word "blank" where the blank occurs. Then we predicted plausible words that would complement the meaning, flow, and logic of the sentence. Some prediction words might have been "rash" or "short-sighted" or "ill-informed." As we review the answer choices, we notice that none of our prediction words are present, so we go ahead and read the sentence attempting to eliminate answer choices that don't make sense. Since answer Choices B, "deliberate" and C, "sensible" suggest that the decision would have been made on an informed and educated basis, they can be eliminated immediately. We need to look a little closer at the remaining choices. Certainly, the word "harsh" could apply if we were taking about retaliation, potentially causing injury to someone before we knew all the facts. As the sentence does not lend itself to a judgment leaning toward harshness any more than leniency, we can eliminate Choice A. Likewise, the sentence does not lend itself to any degree of fairness, particularly in light of the decision being made with limited information. Answer Choice E, "premature" can, therefore, be eliminated as well. This leaves answer Choice D. Although "premature" was not one of our predictions, "rash," short-sighted," and "ill-informed" all have similar connotations as "premature."

Before we get into Sentence Completion skill sets, let's recap some of the highlights presented thus far:

- Familiarize yourself with all instructions prior to test day.
- Answer easy questions first, addressing the more difficult ones as time permits. Remember, sentence completion questions are arranged from easiest to hardest, so allocate your time accordingly.
- Begin by reading each sentence substituting the word "blank" for the actual blank(s) to help give you a feel for the overall flow of the sentence.
- Focus on the standard definitions as you know them to be for the words in the sentence and the answer choices. Although secondary or alternative meanings may be encountered in later sections, the Sentence Completion section usually relies on primary meanings.
- Use you prior knowledge and skills to determine meanings. Recognize like root words, prefixes, and suffixes to assist with word definitions. Utilize any context clues possible to help. Finally, allow your ear to help when necessary.
- Be extremely cognizant of key introductory and transitional words. These determine how different parts of the sentence relate to one another. They may set up a reaffirmation, a contrast, or a change in tone. And remember to be especially mindful of negatives that reverse answer choices.
- While reading through the sentence, think about the logic therein and predict plausible word substitutes that complement the logical flow of the sentence in meaning and tone. As you review answer choices, look for those predictions or words that connote similar meanings.
- When dealing with two-blank questions, determine which set to attack first. Remember, if you can eliminate one word of a two-word answer choice, the entire choice can be eliminated.
- Read through all answer choices before making a final selection. Remember, the SAT reviewers want the 'best' answer choice, not the first plausible choice.
- Reconfirm your selection by reading the entire sentence with your answer choice in place of the blank.
- Finally, eliminate as many choices as practical, read to let your ear assist in your judgment, and make an educated guess if necessary.

Sentence Completion Skill Set One

Note: Unlike the actual SAT, these questions are not arranged from easiest to hardest.

Each sentence below has one or two blanks, each blank indicating that something has been omitted. Beneath the sentence are five words or sets of words labeled A through E. Choose the word or set of words that, when inserted in the sentence, *best* fits the meaning of the sentence as a whole.

1. Football players, generally known for their elevated testosterone levels, would see crying as _____ unmanly rather than a humanistic trait _____ by either sex.

    A. sickeningly. . . thwarted
    B. inherently. . . experienced
    C. inexplicably. . . enjoyed
    D. intentionally. . . fostered
    E. plausibly. . . envisioned

2. Despite the fact that Frank Lloyd Wright communities are almost _____, they leave behind a _____ legacy of architecture and furniture design.

    A. obsolete. . . transitory
    B. dormant. . . modest
    C. extinct. . . vital
    D. self-sufficient. . . prodigious
    E. isolated. . . robust

3. The majority of the villagers in this seemingly forgotten land, are _____ vegetarians; that is, they only eat meat during a holy celebration, or whenever they can afford it, which, because of the ludicrously high prices, is practically never.

    A. sometimes
    B. clandestine
    C. staunch
    D. adamant
    E. reluctant

4. The _____ lecture hall could seat the entire graduating class including guests; some said it was it was even _____.

    A. burgeoning. . . elaborate
    B. bodacious. . . monumental
    C. elaborate. . . haughty
    D. commodious. . . enormous
    E. capacious. . . miniscule

5. The secretary _____ agreed to _____ the president's decision, knowing that the information was less than factual and against her basic beliefs regarding deceptive sales practices.

    A. grudgingly. . . abide by
    B. willingly. . . support
    C. secretively. . . acknowledge
    D. maliciously. . . sway
    E. furtively. . . foster

6. Either the fishing at Redington Beach is _____, or I went there on an off day.

    A. plentiful
    B. overrated
    C. caustic
    D. sporadic
    E. invigorating

7. His _____ remarks really detracted from the overall speech; he should not have so readily strayed from his subject.

    A. repugnant
    B. digressive
    C. redundant
    D. innocuous
    E. enigmatic

8. He acted with great _____, as if he were a diplomat without regard for crimination.

    A. emotion
    B. restraint
    C. concern
    D. statesmanship
    E. disdain

9. As I was describing my encounter with the alien, he had the most _____ stare, as if he didn't believe a word I was saying.

    A. amazing
    B. dumbfounded
    C. incredulous
    D. blank
    E. obdurate

10. The _____ of horns heard while gridlocked at the traffic jam was as discordant as an untamed orchestral performance.

    A. blaring
    B. harmonic
    C. sequencing
    D. cacophony
    E. syncopated

Answers and Explanations for Skill Set One

1. The correct choice is **B**.

   Explanation: Although Choice A, "sickeningly" may work in the first blank, to prevent an occurrence, or thwart, an action does not fit the second. Choice C, "inexplicably," might also fit the first blank, but crying is not typically something the testosterone-laden player would enjoy. Choices D and E, "intentionally" and "plausibly" don't fit the first blank and may be eliminated. This leaves Choice B, "inherently," or essentially or intrinsically unmanly rather than a trait "experienced" by either sex.

2. The correct choice is **C**.

   Explanation: The word "Despite" is the clue word in this sentence. It indicates that there is a contrast between the two parts of the sentence. The pair of words should necessarily be dichotomous or nearly opposites. As Choice C is the only pair with such a relationship, it should be the obvious answer.

3. The correct choice is **E**.

   Explanation: The phrase that is the clue here is "that is." This phrase tells you that there is an explanation coming to reason what has been previously stated. In this case, we know that the majority of the villagers are vegetarians and that what is about to follow will help explain or give reason for that fact. We are then told that the primary reason they are vegetarians is that meat is very high priced, and they are poor so they can afford to eat meat only infrequently. Choice A suggests that they chose at will whether to be abstaining from meat as "sometimes" indicates a selection process controlled by the selector rather than conditions outside their control. Choices C and D, "staunch" and "adamant" indicate a choice of determination to be vegetarian. We are told, however, that they eat meat when they can afford to buy it or for ceremonial purposes. Choice B, "clandestine" indicates a secretive vegetarianism and since we know they eat meat during holy celebrations, this choice cannot be true. This leaves choice E, "reluctant," as they eat meat during holy celebrations or "whenever" they can afford it.

4. The correct choice is **D**.

   Explanation: The clue given in this sentence is that the lecture hall is dealing with the volume of people it can contain. Further, the second blank must indicate a degree of increase of the first blank and be synonymous with it. Choice E is an antonym and, therefore, excluded. Although Choice B seems plausible, "bodacious" means something notable. Although "monumental" would seem to represent a degree of increase from notable, this is not the "best" selection to describe the size of the hall. Choices A and C both represent a degree of design or architecture rather than size and may be disqualified. Choice D, "commodious" and "enormous," indicate suitable capacity and the ability to hold a large quantity.

5. The correct choice is **A**.

   Explanation: Choices B and E include "foster" and "support," which cannot apply as the clue regarding a conflict between the decision and the secretary's basic beliefs are incongruent. Choice C is effectively impossible as one cannot secretively acknowledge. Choice D suggests the secretary would do something malicious, which is at odds with her character and morals indicated in the sentence. Choice A satisfies the condition of how she would go along with the decision, "grudgingly."

6. The correct choice is **B**.

   Explanation: As catching a lot of fish is generally the purpose of going fishing, the sentence would indicate that this was not the case on the day in question. Therefore, we are looking for a word choice that indicates some explanation for not catching fish. Answer Choice B, "overrated," would indicate that while the expectation was that this location would be good fishing, something was amiss.

7. The correct choice is **B**.

   Explanation: The clue here is in the phrase that states he should not have strayed from the subject of his speech. The best word is Choice B, "digressive."

8. The correct choice is **E**.

Explanation: The clue phrase here is, ". . .as if he were a diplomat without regard for crimination." This indicates that the actions needed to best fit the blank represent a disregard for the laws or rules of proper behavior. In this regard, Choice E, "disdain," best represents the actions akin to a disregard for laws or rules.

9. The correct choice is **C**.

Explanation: We are looking for a word that would indicate disbelief. We also know that we are looking for an adjective. Don't let a word like obdurate throw you. Although the listener might indeed be stubborn in his willingness to believe the story being told, the sentence clues still call for disbelief. Therefore, Choice C, "incredulous," or skeptical and showing disbelief is correct.

10. The correct choice is **D**.

Explanation: The clue phrase, ". . .was as discordant as. . ." indicates we are looking for a synonym to discordant. As Choice B, "harmonic," indicates pleasing tones musically aligned, it must be eliminated. Choices A, C, and E, "blaring," "sequencing," and "syncopated" or volume and timing have nothing to do with discordance and should likewise all be eliminated. Only answer Choice D, "cacophony," indicates discordant, displeasing sounds.

Sentence Completion Skill Set Two

Each sentence below has one or two blanks, each blank indicating that something has been omitted. Beneath the sentence are five words or sets of words labeled A through E. Choose the word or set of words that, when inserted in the sentence, *best* fits the meaning of the sentence as a whole.

1. Her _____ demeanor was understandable given the loss of her brother; indeed, most of us were rather _____.

   A. lachyromose. . . dolorous
   B. reprehensible. . . enigmatic
   C. subtle. . . raucous
   D. determined. . . committed
   E. displaced. . . focused

2. It was a rather _____ mystery, full of twists and turns and surprises and _____ most difficult to predict.

   A. tawdry. . .foreshadowing
   B. knotty. . .nuances
   C. subtle. . .characters
   D. obvious. . .reversals
   E. easily understood. . .clever redirections

3. He is the _____ of evil; he lies, cheats, steals, murders, and boasts of his anti-societal behavior.

   A. antithesis
   B. plaintiff
   C. epitome
   D. harbinger
   E. picture

4. It is commonly believed that statesman Frederick Douglass _____ patterned his autobiography after the _____ of the former slave Olaudah Equiano.

   A. effectively. . . notations
   B. knowingly. . . diary
   C. accidentally. . . writings
   D. intentionally. . . narrative
   E. expectantly. . . accomplishments

5. Legislative leaders found it desirable to _____ prohibition, partially in order to recover revenue from taxation on spirits.

   A. enforce
   B. abrogate
   C. stave
   D. modify
   E. obdurate

6. It is incomprehensible that the tax codes should be such a _____ instead of a straightforward bracket based on gross earnings, notwithstanding deductions.

   A. farce
   B. joke
   C. labyrinth
   D. calamity
   E. malfeasance

7. The editorial, in obvious opposition to the article appearing in yesterday's newspaper, was well-written, well-documented, factual, and nonconfrontational, the only intent of which seemed to be to _____ the article.

   A. repudiate
   B. contradict
   C. correct
   D. lend credence
   E. show support

8. It is within the _____ years that wisdom evidences itself, when those long in tooth, grayed in hair, and physically feeble demonstrate knowledge that is only paid for with the price of age.

   A. latent
   B. dormant
   C. transcended
   D. tenacious
   E. crepuscular

9. Now is not the time for _____ decisions, but _____ in our cause for freedom.

    A. difficult. . . acquiescence

    B. peaceful. . . tenacity

    C. austere. . . commitment

    D. tentative. . . resolution

    E. weak. . . discourse

10. In order to _____ ratings, the incumbent directed party loyalists to flood the media with _____ about recent developments in job creation.

    A. bolster. . . accolades

    B. improve. . . talk

    C. explain. . . data

    D. nullify. . . falsehoods

    E. mollify. . . rumors

Answers and Explanations for Skill Set Two

1. The correct choice is **A**.

Explanation: The sentence indicates that all persons felt basically the same way as the sister suffering the loss of her brother. We must look for a synonym in order to fit both blanks. Answer Choice E, "displaced. . . focused" reflect almost opposite states and should be immediately eliminated. Although Choice D seems plausible as "determined. . . committed" appear to be synonymous, they do not best fit the mood or tone of the sentence. Answer Choice B, "reprehensible. . . enigmatic" can be eliminated because if her demeanor was in fact "reprehensible," then it would not be understandable. Answer Choice C is another antonym leaving Choice A, "lachrymose. . . dolorous" indicating a tearful demeanor and most of us being sorrowful.

2. The correct choice is **B**.

Explanation: We are looking for the second blank to offer some continuation of a writing style that complements "twists and turns and surprises." Given this element, the first blank must indicate the type of mystery wherein the style would be found. As "foreshadowing" allows the reader to predict future events, Choice A could be discounted. Choice C, "characters," does not match the second blank looking for a continuation of styles and should be eliminated. Choices D and E, "reversals" and "clever redirections" look plausible, and we must look at the first blank to further determine viability. An "obvious" mystery or an "easily understood" mystery do not attend to twists, turns, and surprises and can be stricken. This leaves Choice B, "knotty. . . nuances." Knotty means complex or difficult to solve and, indeed, this matches the styles having twists, turns, and surprises. The complement to these styles is "nuances" or subtleties that are difficult to predict.

3. The correct choice is **C**.

Explanation: As the examples represent what is believed to be the societal reflection of evil, then we are looking for a word that suggests he represents that classical example. Answer Choice C, "epitome" correctly indicates that he is the representative example of evil, given his actions.

4. The correct choice is **D**.

Explanation: If, in fact, Douglass did pattern his autobiography after something, it would likely be another form of literature lending itself to this endeavor. Choices A, B, and E, "notations," "diary," and "accomplishments" do not lend themselves readily to be patterned as an autobiography. Choices C and D, "writings" and "narrative" appear plausible so we must look at the first blank to finalize our choice. As Choice C is most unlikely in that Douglass would "accidentally" pattern his autobiography after another leaving choice D, "intentionally. . . narrative."

5. The correct choice is **B**.

Explanation: Answer Choice A, "enforce" would only serve to keep revenues from being collected. Choice C, "stave" would only serve to alter prohibition or put it off, which does not match as this was a recovery of revenue that could happen only if the revenue was lost by prohibition already having been enacted. Choice D, "modify" would serve only to change but not necessarily recoup revenues. Choice E, "obdurate" is to confuse intentionally and that would not return the revenues. This leaves Choice B, "abrogate" or repeal prohibition, which would allow the sale and collection of revenue from that sale of spirits.

6. The correct choice is **C**.

Explanation: Although many believe the tax codes are a farce or joke, there seems to be nothing funny about filing taxes and figuring out the rules. Likewise, the tax code may be believed by many to be malfeasance on the part of those who wrote the code, but we are looking for a word that better aligns with incomprehensible in the structure of the code. Although many believe the code to be disastrous, it has nothing to do with nature. This leaves Choice C, "labyrinth," which best describes the complexities that could be better understood with a simple bracket flat tax.

7. The correct choice is **A**.

Explanation: The partial phrase, ". . . in obvious opposition to the article," alleviates Choices D and E automatically. Choices B and C certainly seem plausible but remember that the SAT reviewers want the "best" answer. As the writer of the editorial in opposition provided facts and was well documented, the writer was clearly trying to reject as unfounded the original article, ergo Choice A.

8. The correct choice is **E.**

Explanation: Here is where the College Board is looking for you to be able to determine the tone and flow of a sentence. This cannot be accomplished by surface reading and is likely not to be within the grasp of someone who is not well read. Remember, the best preparation is to read and read a lot. Read different authors, different genres, written at different periods to best understand how the tone, pace, and flow of a sentence will assist you in determining the best answer choice. Choices A and B, "latent" and "dormant," indicate inaction while the sentence clearly states that the there is an evidencing of this knowledge occurring. Choice C, "transcended," has the wrong tense as these years have passed and those with wisdom cannot be currently evidencing knowledge if the years are past. Choice D, "tenacious," is clearly the wrong tone for the sentence. We aren't talking about the leathery skin of the elderly, but rather the time before the setting sun of life wherein those who have experienced life to the fullest may share knowledge that is yet a mystery to younger generations. Choice E, "crepuscular" retains the mood of an evening, or the sun setting on a long life.

9. The correct choice is **D.**

Explanation: The key word clue here is "but," which announces a change in direction. We need to look for opposites to match this pair of blanks. Although Choice A meets the criteria, they appear to be opposite of what would be expected in the cause of freedom. Choice B, "peaceful," does not lend itself to decisions. Choice C does not offer enough opposition in terms. Choice E, "weak. . . discourse," individually fit within each clause but does not complement both clauses in the sentence. Choice D, "tentative. . . resolution" is the only pair offering both sufficient opposition and complement to both clauses.

10. The correct choice is **A.**

Explanation: Now is the time for a little common knowledge. Any time a politician and ratings are involved, you simply need to understand that an incumbent wants the best ratings possible. This means that when something good does happen, it is the responsibility of those with vested interests to make sure that the most positive spin possible gets into the media. In this regard, only Choices A and B, "bolster" and "improve," speak to desired ratings. We need to look at the second blank to complete the best selection. Between "accolades" and "talk," clearly the term "accolades" puts a more positive spin on the accomplishments. Therefore, Choice A is correct.

Sentence Completion Skill Set Three

Each sentence below has one or two blanks, each blank indicating that something has been omitted. Beneath the sentence are five words or sets of words labeled A through E. Choose the word or set of words that, when inserted in the sentence, *best* fits the meaning of the sentence as a whole.

1. Unfortunately, she was left with only a false hope of recovery, purely _____.

    A. derisive
    B. divisive
    C. delirious
    D. delusive
    E. derivational

2. To help counter a claim by some that the doctor was a _____, he was forced to _____ his rather impressive list of documented accomplishments.

    A. specialist. . . disclose
    B. charlatan. . . cite
    C. generalist. . . specify
    D. lark. . . mitigate
    E. masque. . . castigate

3. The seemingly common plague of invading a country steeped in centuries of traditions is finding oneself in a veritable _____ concerning what to do when the major fighting is over and pockets of resistance continue for years.

    A. nightmare
    B. circus
    C. challenge
    D. quagmire
    E. gridlock

4. Jeff would make a good student council leader if he weren't such an absolute confirmed pleasure seeker, party animal, and absolutely _____ in his endeavors.

    A. conservative
    B. workaholic
    C. consecrated
    D. committed
    E. hedonistic

5. Until Reagan and Gorbachev, the relationship between the USA and USSR had been rather _____.

    A. tenuous
    B. terse
    C. trite
    D. obscured
    E. poised

6. Given that she came to the mediation with such an _____ attitude, it is no wonder there was little movement toward any harmonious agreement; I mean, she was absolutely _____.

    A. exemplary. . .disciplined
    B. insolated. . .fixated
    C. immovable. . .outspoken
    D. open. . .maleable
    E. obdurate. . .incorrigible

7. In his attempt to appear to have superior intellect, the professor would intentionally obfuscate until he had a change of heart and admitted that his attitude was unprofessional and _____.

    A. colloquial
    B. illogical
    C. condescending
    D. immoral
    E. fortuitous

8. The president made the _____ statement that no immigrant who entered the country illegally would be allowed to stay, not even those who served in the military or contributed to the overall economic development of their community.

    A. conflagrant
    B. opinionated
    C. equivocal
    D. impertinent
    E. categorical

9. There is a growing belief among psychologists that the _____ shown the first-time offender tends to do little but _____ many youth to begin a pattern of breaking the law.

A. clemency. . . encourage
B. loathing. . . foster
C. nurturing. . . thwart
D. penalties. . . excite
E. harshness. . . predispose

10. Bill Gates possesses the ability to recognize business opportunities, and it is clearly this _____ that affords him the opportunity to also be known for his benevolence.

A. composure
B. craftiness
C. creativity
D. perspicacity
E. misanthropy

Answers and Explanations for Skill Set Three

1. The correct choice is **D.**

Explanation: This question is a fairly straightforward vocabulary question. It is simply asking that you select the word choice most closely synonymous with "false." Choice A, "derisive," means expressing ridicule or scorn, which does not match false. Choice B, "divisive," means creating disunity or division and can be eliminated. Choice C, "delirious," means marked with a mental disturbance characterized by some dysfunction in speech or physical behavior that, again, does not match with false. Choice E, "derivational," refers to word formations and can be discarded. This leaves Choice D, "delusive," which means something that is falsely believed as in "false hope."

2. The correct choice is **B.**

Explanation: The clue phrase here is, "To help counter a claim. . ." This lets us know that we are looking for something to counter what has been said about the doctor. First, we are looking for something that would tend to be a negative comment if we were going to counter the claim. Choices A and C, "specialist" and "generalist," respectively, do not convey something we would think might need to be negated. Choice E, "masque," might suggest he were hiding something but is not a direct claim. Choice D, "lark," might suggest he is not completely competent, but the second word choice, "specify," does not best match. Choice B, "charlatan" and "cite," best completes the sentence in that the doctor cited his documented, therefore provable, accomplishment to counter the claim he was a "charlatan," or a fake, phony, or quack.

3. The correct choice is **D.**

Explanation: To know that "veritable" means authentic or real helps tremendously in determining the correct choice. Since we know that Choices A and B, "nightmare" and "circus," are not viable, they may be discarded. Answer Choice C, "challenge," does not convey the strength or tone of the sentence in that it is too weak. Although Choice E, "gridlock," conveys a certain stagnation, it does not convey the dilemma of choice as well as the correct Choice D, "quagmire," which is to get bogged down, exactly the case conveyed in the sentence.

4. The correct choice is **E.**

Explanation: We are simply looking for something to complement the attributes of someone who is a "pleasure seeker" and "party animal." Someone who is "conservative," "workaholic," "consecrated," and "committed" is not likely to represent those attributes. But, someone who is "hedonistic" is contently seeking pleasure and possesses attributes within the same textual framework as those stated.

5. The correct choice is **A.**

Explanation: This question represents the subtleties for which SAT is known. The question is asking you to select from a selection of words that might make sense when used for the blank, but SAT asks you to make the subtle distinctions in tone, flavor, and connotation. The only obvious selection that can be omitted is Choice C, "trite," which is a term to describe overused words—words that do not excite or engage the reader through overuse. Although the relationship between the two superpowers was strained, Choice B, "terse," indicates concise or to the point. Answer Choice D, "obscured," certainly could describe the privacy of internal decisions but hardly the relationship when the two leaders met on specific agendas. Choice E, "poised," means calm and collected, which certainly would not describe the relationship until possibly these two leaders began a dialogue. This leaves only Choice A, "tenuous," which means flimsy, or not solid, which is an accurate reflection of the relationship until these two leaders met on various occasions and solidified relationships.

6. The correct choice is **E.**

Explanation: We're obviously looking for negatives here. Additionally, we know that the purpose of mediation is for attendees to modify positions or stances to allow for agreement on or settlement of issues. These clues help to decide the proper selection. If indeed, "she" would have come to the mediation with an "exemplary" attitude, there could have been agreement, so Choice A is incorrect. Also, Choice D, "open," indicates a good chance of agreement and can be discarded. Choice B, "insolated," would indicate difficulty in gaining agreement but not because of any obstinacy on her part. Choice C, "flagrant. . . outspoken," does not preclude any movement toward agreement but rather expresses her demeanor during the mediation. Choice E, "obdurate. . . incorrigible," indicates that she would not give into persuasion and was hardened in her opinion, thus precluding any movement toward harmonious agreement.

7. The correct choice is **C.**

Explanation: Although it is generally "illogical" for a professor to intentionally confuse or hide the meaning of his presentations, Choice B does not fit best with a change of heart. As we are looking for a negative to complement "unprofessional," Choice D, "immoral," does not complement "unprofessional" as there is little to suggest this was a moral issue. All other choices except C, "condescending," are positive and do not complement the term "unprofessional."

8. The correct choice is **E.**

Explanation: The clues in this sentence are more obscure than some. Given the president's fairly all-encompassing authority, Choice E, "categorical," is the best match for the sentence. Although his decision may indeed be opinion driven, the all-encompassing nature of the statement given the categories of no exclusions is of more weight.

9. The correct choice is **A.**

Explanation: SAT, unlike many state examinations, feels perfectly justified in including some aspects of prior knowledge within the scope of their questions. This question exemplifies this as the fact that there is a tendency to grant clemency to first-time offenders will assist in the correct choice. Knowing the recidivism rate or rate of young offenders returning to previous criminal behavior will add to the ease of selection. Clearly, Choice A, "clemency. . . encourage" best describes the growing belief among psychologists conveyed in the sentence.

10. The correct choice is **D.**

Explanation: We need to find only a synonym for the ability to "recognize business opportunity" to find the correct answer. Although Choices A, B, and C, "composure," "craftiness," and "creativity," are all possible attributes of Bill Gates, they are not synonymous with recognizing business opportunity. Choice E, "misanthropy," indicates a hatred or mistrust of humankind, and although that is felt by some to be an attribute to business success, again, it is not synonymous. Choice D, "perspicacity," means acuteness of perception or discernment and is the best fit for completing this sentence.

Sentence Completion Skill Set Four

Each sentence below has one or two blanks, each blank indicating that something has been omitted. Beneath the sentence are five words or sets of words labeled A through E. Choose the word or set of words that, when inserted in the sentence, *best* fits the meaning of the sentence as a whole.

1. Some have suggested that because Hemingway wrote with such _____ of words, he was like a poet writing prose.

   A. sensitivity
   B. economy
   C. grandeur
   D. relationship
   E. forbearance

2. The _____ was that this seemingly shy, otherwise completely reserved young girl was quite _____ when removed from the presence of adults.

   A. oddity. . . reclusive
   B. secret. . . intimidated
   C. paradox. . . gregarious
   D. reversal. . . eclectic
   E. confusion. . . unnerving

3. During the 1960s, many retirees moved to Arizona to enjoy the _____ climate promised to those suffering from many forms of breathing complications.

   A. relaxed
   B. commodious
   C. repressed
   D. placated
   E. salubrious

4. Given the overall significance of the issue, it was amazing to see the members acting with such _____, particularly given their seemingly polarized positions.

   A. placidity
   B. dispatch
   C. benevolence
   D. tenacity
   E. objectivity

5. Knowing he could be shot for his deception, Doc Holiday _____ placed the ace in his vest while the other players toasted the dance hall crooner.

   A. furtively
   B. blatantly
   C. eagerly
   D. brazenly
   E. overtly

6. Her teacher was heartened by the fact that she _____ her commitment to _____ her grades by arranging to stay after hours for tutoring.

   A. showed. . . stabilizing
   B. expressed. . . enhancing
   C. evinced. . . improving
   D. suggested. . . maintaining
   E. exhausted. . . augment

7. The _____ effects of smoking have cost untold sums, both personal and societal, notwithstanding the Surgeon General's _____ warning on each package for years.

   A. deleterious. . . blatant
   B. negative. . . modest
   C. unhealthy. . . understated
   D. addictive. . . poignant
   E. causal. . . printed

8. Notwithstanding his otherwise considered allegiance to his constituency, the commissioner did not _____ his posture on the issue, even after he was _____ by the press.

   A. alter. . . questioned
   B. abandon. . . chided
   C. modify. . . covered
   D. relinquish. . . quoted
   E. nullify. . . persuaded

9. We never argued in my family; instead, it was always a discussion in which words became weapons and the subtleties of irony and _____ were best employed.

    A.   discourse

    B.   humility

    C.   candor

    D.   innuendo

    E.   farce

10. The loss of life occurring when the Titanic sunk was shocking to most because engineers had depicted that her hull was _____.

    A.   indefatigable

    B.   preeminent

    C.   viscous

    D.   amorphous

    E.   impenetrable

Answers and Explanations for Skill Set Four

1. The correct choice is **B**.

   Explanation: This question is asking you to recall how a poet performs his craft. Words are carefully chosen to speak volumes even though their count may be few. In other words, they use "economy" of words to say a lot. In this way, Hemingway, who uses fewer words to express much emotion, is like a poet.

2. The correct choice is **C**.

   Explanation: Here is a situation in which it is best to employ looking at the second blank first. One way to decide to use this tool is that all the first choices in the pairs are plausible. They do not represent a significant diversity in tone or direction. We can begin by looking for clue words such as "seemingly shy," which indicate that the second blank would need a word that describes someone who is not shy. Choice C, "gregarious," satisfies this need. When we plug in the first blank with Choice C, "paradox," we see that this is the obvious choice.

3. The correct choice is **E**.

   Explanation: Simply put, we are looking for a word that suggests a climate that would help those suffering from breathing complications. Although Choice A, "relaxed," might help allay some of the environmental stimulants to breathing complications, Choice E, "salubrious," means conducive or favorable to health or well-being.

4. The correct choice is **E**.

   Explanation: We are told that the members have very different positions on a very significant issue. The tone of the sentence suggests this would cause a possible stalemate, rather than listening and potential compromise. Choice E, "objectivity," would be an "amazing" thing to see given the polarized views held by the members.

5. The correct choice is **A**.

   Explanation: Certainly, Choices B and D, "blatantly" and "brazenly," describe the act itself, but not how. The only selection describing how, is Choice A, "furtively," which means characterized by stealth.

6. The correct choice is **C**.

   Explanation: Sequencing is a good clue to determining which choice will best fit this question. As a rule, we know that teachers want their students to improve their grades so we need to look for such a word for the second blank given that her teacher will be "heartened" by this act. Choices A and D, "stabilizing" and "maintaining," don't meet this condition. For the first blank, Choices A, B, D, and E, showing, expressing, suggesting, and exhausting, do nothing to further a commitment. This leaves Choice C, "evinced. . . improving," which satisfies both conditions.

7. The correct choice is **A**.

   Explanation: We are looking for something negative for the first blank and something that describes the warning on each package for the second. Beginning with the second blank, Choices B and C, "modest" and "understated," do not match the health warnings thereby eliminating them as possibilities. Although Choice E, "printed," is an otherwise workable choice, it is too obvious. Also, the first word, "causal," does not match with "effects" further eliminating E as a choice. Choices A and D, "blatant" and "poignant," are both possible choices so we need to look at the first word in each choice. Choice D, "addictive," is certainly associated with smoking, but the addiction itself is not the reason for relational costs. Rather, Choice A, "deleterious," which means to have a harmful or injurious effect, best fits the first blank.

8. The correct choice is **B**.

   Explanation: Choice E is the only real choice that can be immediately dismissed as the choices contradict each other. All other choices are, to varying degrees, viable selections. Here is where the subtleties of language come into play. Choices A and C, "questioned" and "covered," do not suggest sufficient pressure brought by the press to convince anyone to either "alter" or "modify" a posture. This leaves Choices B and D, "chided" and "quoted," respectively. Again, commissioners get "quoted" by the press all the time, and this would not convey adequate pressure to "relinquish" a posture.

9. The correct choice is **D.**

Explanation: We're looking for a complement to irony that is also a subtlety. Choice A, "discourse," is simply to discuss and would be redundant. Choice B, "humility," is a characteristic, not a verbal weapon. Choice C, "candor," is not subtle at all as it entails directness. Choice E, "farce," is obvious in nature, almost a blatant humor with directed positioning. Choice D, "innuendo," is an indirect or subtle, usually derogatory, implication in expression.

10. The correct choice is **E.**

Explanation: Choice A, "indefatigable," means tireless, an attribute generally not given to metal. Choice B, "preeminent," certainly would qualify as a descriptor, but would have little to do with the destructibility of the hull. Choice C, "viscous," means sticky, and Choice D, "amorphous," means lacking shape or form. Choice E, "impenetrable," means impossible to penetrate or enter, which was the quality engineers had given to the Titanic's hull.

Sentence Completion Skill Set Five

Each sentence below has one or two blanks, each blank indicating that something has been omitted. Beneath the sentence are five words or sets of words labeled A through E. Choose the word or set of words that, when inserted in the sentence, *best* fits the meaning of the sentence as a whole.

1. It would seem _____ that if aspirin can help prevent a second heart attack from occurring, it should also be able to _____ the first occurrence.

   A. natural. . . enjoin
   B. logical. . . allay
   C. fanciful. . . foment
   D. reasonable. . . augment
   E. rational. . . alienate

2. The _____ youth who stopped the tank in Tiananmen Square gave rise to an _____ movement that has awakened the leaders of China in a way that the West had not been able to do in centuries.

   A. innocent. . . immediate
   B. calloused. . . awkward
   C. belligerent. . . awesome
   D. rebellious. . . infinitesimal
   E. recalcitrant. . . irrepressible

3. The distinction between editing and _____ has to do largely with what was modified, how it was changed, and even, at times, whether is was done with the prior knowledge and _____ of the author.

   A. critiquing. . . bias
   B. censorship. . . permission
   C. expurgating. . . disapproval
   D. decimation. . . disavowal
   E. correcting. . . recognition

4. As the airplane sped toward Earth during the daredevil air acrobatics show, the crowd grew more _____ with each passing moment.

   A. weary
   B. confounded
   C. disconcerted
   D. apprehensive
   E. distraught

5. The daunting task of crossing the desert with limited resources is a testimonial to the _____ of the immigrants entering the country from the southern border illegally.

   A. tenacity
   B. desire
   C. resilience
   D. lunacy
   E. waywardness

6. Given the conditions as presented in the Garden of Eden, it is most difficult for us to imagine anything _____ could be looming.

   A. halcyon
   B. untoward
   C. seemly
   D. conciliatory
   E. aggrandized

7. I might well vouchsafe for the Senator's honesty as I have always found him _____ and a protector of the truth.

   A. volatile
   B. plausible
   C. flagrant
   D. illusory
   E. veracious

8. After he registered as a sex offender, as required by law, his neighbors began to _____ him, avoiding him at all costs, whereas before his registry, he was included in many neighborhood activities.

   A. harass
   B. ridicule
   C. chide
   D. desecrate
   E. ostracize

9. In an effort to secure more members, health club representatives "warn" prospective members that their specialized and tailored fitness programs are _____, and that after you start, you may be unable to stop because you actually become dependent on the euphoric feeling you get when each session is complete.

    A. addictive

    B. economical

    C. bargains

    D. exhausting

    E. deprecating

10. It was commonly known that if some movement was not made, some concession or expression of good will not be forthcoming by either the district or the teacher's union, that the differences would be _____ and become so polarizing as to render them irreconcilable.

    A. imprudent

    B. exacerbated

    C. fathomless

    D. imponderable

    E. unimaginable

Answers and Explanations for Skill Set Five

1. The correct choice is **B.**

   Explanation: By using the tool of looking at the second blank first, we see that only Choice B, "allay," would be truly parallel with preventing a second occurrence. Choice E, "alienate," is a good distractor but connotes turning away through emotions rather than derivation.

2. The correct choice is **E.**

   Explanation: In looking for the characteristic of an individual who would interfere with such an event, Choices D and E, "rebellious" and "recalcitrant," are the only two that qualify. Both resist control or authority, unlike Choice C, "belligerent," which has more to do with hostility or aggression. Only Choice E, "irrepressible" best describes the movement that followed rather than Choice D, "infinitesimal."

3. The correct choice is **B.**

   Explanation: All five selections seem to be plausible when looking at the first word selections. Given the clue word "distinction," we know we are looking for a word that is at odds with editing so Choice E, "correcting," would be the weakest selection based on the first word blank. Looking at the remaining four second word choices, our clue phrase is, "done with the prior knowledge and . . . ." The only viable selection is Choice B, "permission," as all other choices have a negative connotation and do not work with the positive clue phrase.

4. The correct choice is **D.**

   Explanation: Choice A, "weary," suggests the crowd grew tired of watching the plane nearly crash. Choice B, "confounded," suggests that they were confused by the action, even though attending an acrobatics air show. Choice C, "disconcerted," suggests they were just plain disinterested. And Choice E, "distraught," suggests they were emotionally sorrowed before the conclusion of the event. Choice D, "apprehension," which means they were uneasy, anxious, or troubled by fears is the best choice.

5. The correct choice is **C.**

   Explanation: Choices D and E, "lunacy" and "waywardness," do not describe the character of the individuals who have chosen to undertake this daunting task. Choices A and B, "tenacity" and "desire," describe strong characteristics largely required of someone who would undertake this task, but only Choice C, "resilience," describes the characteristic and stamina for such a task.

6. The correct choice is **B.**

   Explanation: Activating prior knowledge about the serenity of this seeming paradise, there is simply no other selection than Choice B, "untoward," which means improper, unseemly, or perverse.

7. The correct choice is **D.**

   Explanation: Choice B, "plausible," might seem a likely choice but connotes only a degree of believability versus the strength of conviction required to best fit this sentence. Choice D, "veracious," which means honest and truthful, is the best fit. Be careful not to confuse this word with "voracious," which means ravenous.

8. The correct choice is **E.**

   Explanation: The clues in this sentence lie in the actions taken by the neighbors which actually define the word that best fits into the blank. They avoid him and modify their behavior as he is no longer included in any of the neighborhood activities. Although Choices A, B, and C, "harass," "ridicule," and "chide," are all possibly actions taken by neighbors, these actions do not complement the avoidance of him by neighbors. Choice D, "desecrate," suggests the violation of something sacred that is nonapplicable in this scenario. Choice E, "ostracize," means to exclude from a group, precisely the action taken by the neighbors.

9. The correct choice is **A.**

Explanation: Although the sentence leads the reader through the maze of business and sales tactics, the gist of the sentence is that, ". . . you actually become dependent. . . ." Now, we are simply looking for a synonym for a word fitting this phrase. Someone who is addicted is dependent upon so Choice A, "addictive," best fits.

10. The correct choice is **B.**

Explanation: In dissecting the sentence, we understand that the differences between the two parties would get worse. We need simply to select the best word to express getting worse. Choice B, "exacerbated," means to increase the severity or bitterness; aggravate, which is exactly the condition reflected in the scenario presented.

Sentence Completion Skill Set Six

Each sentence below has one or two blanks, each blank indicating that something has been omitted. Beneath the sentence are five words or sets of words labeled A through E. Choose the word or set of words that, when inserted in the sentence, *best* fits the meaning of the sentence as a whole.

1. Having inside information as to when auditors were scheduled prevented the bank teller's _____ involving large sums of missing money from being discovered, until the year she was absent due to illness.

   A. scrutiny
   B. illegitimacy
   C. embezzlement
   D. plan
   E. scheme

2. His preference of reading a book in the privacy of his own room instead of attending the fraternity party with his friends, indicated he was _____ by nature.

   A. egotistical
   B. hedonistic
   C. territorial
   D. introverted
   E. acquiescent

3. Sometimes the negative criticism of a loved one becomes the more _____ as they are the most hurtful to hear.

   A. disparaging
   B. disingenuous
   C. disengaging
   D. distrustful
   E. disdainful

4. He had an _____ passion for sports; so much so that it severely altered his social life in that no one who was not an avid sports fan could hold an otherwise meaningful conversation with him.

   A. unassailable
   B. inordinate
   C. inclined
   D. understandable
   E. eerie

5. My senior prom was an absolute _____; the ballroom was too small, the band did not show up, and the food was cold, not to mention the fact that someone tripped and spilled punch all over the formal my date was wearing.

   A. delight
   B. phenomena
   C. gesticulation
   D. joust
   E. debacle

6. The grand old hotel room was adorned with quite elaborately carved furniture of the Baroque period and with its irreverent flowing lines was breathtakingly _____.

   A. linear
   B. articulate
   C. ornate
   D. carnival
   E. polished

7. Although he had a _____ as to which movie he wanted to attend, he showed great _____ to her by courteously suggesting they view the selection she preferred.

   A. notion. . . adornment
   B. guess. . . love
   C. preference. . . deference
   D. clue. . . disrespect
   E. choice. . . insolence

8. You can be fairly sure that disaster is _____ when the engine on your single-engine plane catches on fire.

   A. prominent
   B. unlikely
   C. averted
   D. imminent
   E. futuristic

9. Accolades given for his first novel for its _____ and freshness were not forthcoming for his second work widely criticized for its predictability and unimaginativeness, even stagnancy.

   A. originality
   B. monotones
   C. redundancy
   D. repetition
   E. acridness

10. His writing lacked spontaneity in that it was too structured, restricted by archaic convention, and generally was described by critics as too _____.

    A. lurid
    B. harmonious
    C. parsimonious
    D. formulaic
    E. digressive

Answers and Explanations for Skill Set Six

1. The correct choice is **C.**

Explanation: Choices D and E, "plan" and "scheme," are weak choices as auditors finding money missing evidences the act has already taken place. Choice C, "embezzlement," means to take something for one's own use in violation of trust.

2. The correct choice is **D.**

Explanation: Choice A, "egotistical," suggests he thought too much of himself to join the others, but there is nothing in the sentence to suggest this is true. Choice B, "hedonistic," suggests he sought pleasures of the senses and staying in his room reading would not fulfill this desire. Choice C, "territorial," suggests that he didn't want anyone else in his room, and again, there is nothing in the sentence to support this position. Choice E, "acquiescent," suggests that he gave in and did what others wanted him to do, which is clearly not the case. This leaves Choice D, "introverted," which means to turn inward or concentrate one's efforts on oneself.

3. The correct choice is **A.**

Explanation: Choice A, "disparaging," means to reduce in esteem or rank, which best fits the sentence, as negative criticism from someone held in high regard can be the most devastating. Choice B, "disingenuous," means insincere or calculating, hardly attributes of comments from a loved one. Choice D, "distrustful," is again, not worthy of trust and is not the attribute of one who cares. Choice E, "disdainful," means scornful or contemptuous and clearly are not attributes of someone who is a loved one offering guidance, albeit from a negative perspective.

4. The correct choice is **B.**

Explanation: The clue here is that this passion was effectively debilitating in that it had an effect on his life that was restrictive. Choice A, "unassailable," means that it could not be challenged. Choices C and D, "inclined" and "understandable," do not show or connote anything wrong with the degree of his passion and can be excluded. Choice E, "eerie," may be true in that it seems strange to most, but again, this does not reflect the negativity of the passion. Choice B, "inordinate," means exceeding reasonable limits or excessive, clearly representing the degree of the passion leading to the social demise stated.

5. The correct choice is **E.**

Explanation: There is a better than even chance we are looking for a word that means something less than grand and glorious given the incidents that are reported. Choice D, "joust" means a combat between two mounted knights, and although I'm sure each incident reflected might have seemed so, this answer does not best fit. Choice E, "debacle," means a total, often ludicrous failure; to be sure, the prom described.

6. The correct choice is **C.**

Explanation: Choice A, "linear," does not represent the flowing lines but rather contradicts the flow. Choice B, "articulate," refers to speech rather than design. Choice D, "carnival" represents merriment but at a festive gathering not lending itself to description of furniture. Choice E, "polished," refers simply to the condition of the furniture. Choice C, "ornate," means flashy, showy, or floral in style and matches the description of the carving style describing the furniture in the sentence.

7. The correct choice is **C.**

Explanation: Choice A, "adornment" for the last word refers more to a decoration to beautify and does not fit. Choice B, "guess," is simply impractical as it would not be a guess if he had any idea as to which movie he wanted to attend. Choices D and E, "disrespect" and "insolence," respectively, for the last words don't reflect a courteous act to her at all. Choice C, "preference. . . deference," shows that although he had a personal choice, he submitted or courteously yielded to her opinion as to which movie to select.

8. The correct choice is **D.**

Explanation: Choice **A,** "prominent," certainly describes the obvious nature of the occurrence—that is the engine burning—but does not describe the impending disaster. Choices B and C, "unlikely" and "averted," indicate that there is no real disaster or that it has been avoided, which is not reflected in the sentence. Choice E, "futuristic," suggests something that will happen when we understand that the event or cause has already taken place. Choice D, "imminent," means about to occur, which fits well given the only source of staying aloft is on fire.

9. The correct choice is **A.**

Explanation: We are looking for a complement to "freshness" that would describe a novel. Choice B, "monotones," suggests something flat, not fresh. Choices C and D, "redundancy" and "repetition," are also counter to fresh, and the prefix "re" is a real clue. Choice E, "acridness," means caustic in language or tone and would not fit with something fresh so may be discarded. Choice A, "originality," complements "freshness."

10. The correct choice is **D.**

Explanation: We're looking for a word that describes a restrictive structure. Choice A, "lurid," means marked by sensationalism and has really nothing to do with structure. Choice D, "formulaic," means based on an established model or approach, which best completes the sentence meaning. None of the other choices addresses writing style and should not be considered.

Sentence Completion Skill Set Seven

Each sentence below has one or two blanks, each blank indicating that something has been omitted. Beneath the sentence are five words or sets of words labeled A through E. Choose the word or set of words that, when inserted in the sentence, *best* fits the meaning of the sentence as a whole.

1. Rumors abound that immigrant workers, fearing loss of agricultural jobs, _____ newly developed harvesting machinery such that yields were actually _____ when this new technology was employed.

   A. learned. . . increased
   B. sabotaged. . . diminished
   C. thwarted. . . embellished
   D. adopted. . . climbing
   E. repaired. . . marginalized

2. A theory fostered in the recently published work about Elvis Presley involved the suggestion that he gave away cars, property, and valuables, expecting that his _____would endear him to and ensure the _____ of his fans.

   A. largesse. . . fidelity
   B. grace. . . neediness
   C. hypocrisy. . . following
   D. frugality. . . allegiance
   E. demureness. . . wantonness

3. Unfortunately, often, misleading graphs and charts _____ the real story and lead readers to accept otherwise _____arguments.

   A. alter. . . good
   B. modify. . . valid
   C. slant. . . virtuous
   D. represent. . . wrongful
   E. distort. . . spurious

4. The elusive and extraordinarily timid Leprechaun is thought by the Irish to be so _____of humans that it is indeed good fortune to ever see one, much less capture one for reward.

   A. insidious
   B. suppressed
   C. wary
   D. sought
   E. fractious

5. The term best describing the approach teachers take to develop lesson plans today would be _____ because they rely upon material from such a variety of sources, ideologies, disciplines, and methodologies.

   A. eclectic
   B. sporadic
   C. idyllic
   D. invidious
   E. dogmatic

6. The country of Switzerland is long known for their _____, preferring not to engage in matters of conflict between countries regardless of their predilection one way or the other.

   A. sincerity
   B. impotency
   C. military
   D. neutrality
   E. conservation

7. Scientists struggled to find what was _____ about the microbe, what made it so special and different from the others in order for it to be impervious to the virus.

   A. complex
   B. simple
   C. unique
   D. universal
   E. isolated

8. Studying abroad for several years to hone linguistic skills, she was the very epitome of the _____ American from the wide open spaces of Montana where she spent her entire childhood.

   A. rude
   B. expatriate
   C. provincial
   D. conservative
   E. royalist

9. As I looked around the sparsely adorned cabin, I noticed more religious artifacts than tools generally needed for survival _____ the _____ role faith played in their lives.

    A. evidencing. . . miniscule
    B. alleviating. . . necessary
    C. suggesting. . . limited
    D. demonstrating. . . crucial
    E. obviating. . . magnanimity

10. The genius of the _____ for the stage production of *One Flew Over the Coo Coos Nest* was that the floor was tilted on a 30-degree angle, making it extraordinarily difficult for stage movement by the actors, but gave tremendous insight and representation to the imbalances represented both physically and mentally.

    A. plot
    B. mood
    C. direction
    D. setting
    E. presentation

Answers and Explanations for Skill Set Seven

1. The correct choice is **B.**

   Explanation: Given that workers were fearful of losing jobs as a result of newly developed harvesting technology, it is highly unlikely that they would do anything to assist in this effort. Choices A, D, and E, "learned," "adopted," and "repaired," would help in this effort and thereby can be eliminated based on the first words in these pairings. Choice C, "embellished," can be eliminated as this means to make seem better than reality by adding fictitious details, again not something that would help the plight of the migrant worker. Choice B, "sabotaged. . . diminished," fit both blanks as rumors that migrant workers "sabotaged" or hindered the action or cause of the machinery that would replace them such that yields were "diminished" or lessened makes perfect sense.

2. The correct choice is **A.**

   Explanation: We need two matches for this question. The first is a word that defines the action of giving away cars, property, and valuables. Choice B, "grace," would be a stretch but given that it can be defined as a disposition to be generous, we need to look at the second word of Choice B, "neediness." Ensuring the "neediness" of his fans through any act would be self-serving and at odds with the virtue of "grace." Choice A, "largesse," means liberally bestowing gifts particularly in a lofty manner. The second word in Choice A, "fidelity," means faithfulness to obligations or duties, which is what the theory suggests is his motivation for his giving.

3. The correct choice is **E.**

   Explanation: If a graph or chart is misleading, it cannot be a good thing because they change the facts. So, we look for a negative in the first word groups, or at least one that indicates change. Choices A, B, C, and E, "alter," "modify," "slant," and "distort," all qualify so we need to immediately look at the second word choices to match the required condition of that blank. Since the graphs are misleading to the real story, this apparently leads readers to accept information that is bad or wrong. In this condition, Choices D and E, "wrongful" and "spurious," are the only qualifiers. As we have already dismissed Choice D, Choice E is the correct selection.

4. The correct choice is **C.**

   Explanation: Choice A, "insidious," means beguiling or harmful, which does not match the blank. Choice E, "fractious," means inclined to make trouble or unruly and does not match. Choice C, "wary," means on guard, watchful, or cautious, which is exactly how Leprechauns feel about humans making it very difficult for them to be caught, even if seen.

5. The correct choice is **A.**

   Explanation: The clue word is "because" and the actions that follow. Teachers get material from a variety of sources to develop lesson plans. Choice B, "sporadic," means having no pattern, but the pattern described in the sentence is the pattern of multiple source selection. Choice C, "idyllic," means simple and carefree, which is most certainly not how teachers develop lessons in this sentence. Choice D, "invidious," means rousing ill will or animosity, but the only ill will created is thrust upon the teacher because they have to search all these sources to develop lessons. Choice E, "dogmatic," suggests an almost dictatorial approach, which is incorrect. Choice A, "eclectic," means employing individual elements from a variety of sources, which is exactly how the sentence says teachers develop their plans today.

6. The correct choice is **D.**

   Explanation: We are basically told of a country not wishing to enjoin any conflict regardless of how they might feel about the situation. We are looking for a word that means staying out of or abstaining from. Choice D, neutrality means staying neutral or non-engaged, especially in matters of war.

7. The correct choice is **C.**

   Explanation: Alright, we need a word that means special and different. Choices A and B, "complex" and "simple," are merely opposite ends of the spectrum of difficulty and have many partners in that arena. Choices D and E, "universal" and "isolated," represent both ends of the degree of association from everyone to no one. Only Choice C, "unique," which means being the only one of its kind, qualifies for special and different.

8. The correct choice is **B.**

Explanation: We are clued to two facts: she is studying abroad, and she is an American who grew up in Montana. Now we need to find out what she is the epitome of. We need a word to describe someone with the two conditions given. Choice A, "rude," certainly describes how many foreigners think of Americans, but this has little to do with the two conditions given. Choice C, "provincial," or being limited in perspective certainly would not describe this traveling student. Choice D, "conservative," does not begin to identify this explorer. Choice E, "royalist," or someone active in monarchy is not likely for someone spending their childhood in Montana. Choice B, "expatriate," means to remove oneself from one's native land, which is exactly the condition presented herein.

9. The correct choice is **D.**

Explanation: Since the proof of the importance of religion is a given within the sentence, we need to find words that express that fact. The adjective describing the faith must, therefore, be a positive. Choices A, C, and E, "miniscule," "limited," and "magnanimity," don't make this threshold. Choice B, "alleviating," doesn't fit the first blank and can be eliminated. Choice D, "demonstrating. . . crucial," best fits the conditions for this sentence.

10. The correct choice is **D.**

Explanation: Our answer will be found following the clue word "was." Condensed, the sentence would read more like: "The genius of the _____ was. . ." What comes next will lead us to the correct choice. As the floor was tilted, and the flooring is a part of the set, Choice D, "setting" is correct.

Sentence Completion Skill Set Eight

Each sentence below has one or two blanks, each blank indicating that something has been omitted. Beneath the sentence are five words or sets of words labeled A through E. Choose the word or set of words that, when inserted in the sentence, *best* fits the meaning of the sentence as a whole.

1. Hot Springs, Arkansas, is well known because of the _____ effects of the thermally heated springs with a mixture of sulfur and saline providing tourists soothing relief from various ailments.

   A. farcical
   B. gravitational
   C. rigid
   D. therapeutic
   E. succulent

2. The Drill Instructor took all forms of _____ to be ridiculous psychobabble and felt that any of his troops attempting same were loathsome _____.

   A. compliments. . . sycophants
   B. lethargy. . . miscreants
   C. adulation. . . rebels
   D. grovel. . . tyrants
   E. stroking. . . loons

3. Were it not for the fact that we are a _____ society, schools of law would likely have many more openings.

   A. reckless
   B. obese
   C. reprehensible
   D. litigious
   E. free-speech

4. Although he was receiving pressure from his publisher, the real reason he _____ devoted himself to the completion of the book was because he was a diligent scholar.

   A. unwittingly
   B. assiduously
   C. sporadically
   D. universally
   E. hesitatingly

5. Prior to the 1940s, it would have been _____ to see a black couple picnicking with a white couple in a public park.

   A. synchronous
   B. caustic
   C. acrimonious
   D. deleterious
   E. anachronistic

6. Scientific facts are represented as truths and widely published as such until such time as new data is developed, which assuredly will necessitate the _____ of the heretofore known truth.

   A. assertion
   B. validation
   C. revision
   D. concurrency
   E. fortification

7. His overall character including his demeanor, submissive manner, self-deprivation, and quiet nature made it most _____ he would be _____ as Chief Executive Officer of this Fortune 100 company.

   A. suspect. . . overlooked
   B. certain. . . chosen
   C. unlikely. . . selected
   D. natural. . . recognized
   E. believable. . . elected

8. Banning television cameras from courtrooms is seen as a challenge to the First Amendment and as _____ the public access to the legislative process.

   A. denying
   B. guaranteeing
   C. fostering
   D. affording
   E. decreasing

9. Although the positive news that the cancer was caught in time to treat it with radiation therapy is often a momentary time for celebration, that temporary _____ is quickly _____ with the understanding that the treatments may take months.

   A. buoyancy. . . augmented

   B. gladness. . . elevated

   C. sorrow. . . alleviated

   D. euphoria. . . moderated

   E. distress. . . raised

10. Notwithstanding increased police patrols in beach access parking lots, tourists reported car burglaries were still _____.

   A. sensational

   B. commonplace

   C. occasional

   D. belied

   E. sporadic

Answers and Explanations for Skill Set Eight

1. The correct choice is **D.**

Explanation: Choice E, "succulent," means highly interesting or enjoyable but has little to do with relieving ailments. In order to find the best fit, we need to select the word that deals with some sort of ailments. Choice D, "therapeutic," means having or exhibiting healing powers and is the best fit for this sentence.

2. The correct choice is **A.**

Explanation: The clue here is the subject, namely, the Drill Instructor who is thought to generally be a surly individual. Choices A, and C, "compliments" and "adulation," mean about the same thing and likely would be something a drill instructor would not embrace. The second blank needs to reflect the result of the Drill Instructor having such feelings about either. Choice C, "rebels," would not appropriately describe someone who spoke positively to someone about their actions. Choice A, "sycophants," means a self-server who attempts to win favor by flattering influential people. . . and they don't come much more influential than the Drill Instructor.

3. The correct choice is **D.**

Explanation: We need to make the connection between the type of society and the need for lawyers. Although Choice A, "reckless," works for automobiles and personal injury lawyers, but this is too limited in scope. Similarly, Choice B, "obese," might lead to some class-action suits involving fast-food restaurants, this too is limited. And although Choice C, "reprehensible," means deserving rebuke or censure might be true, it does not generally lead to a need to hire an attorney. Choice D, "litigious," means tending to engage in lawsuits and is the best fit for this sentence.

4. The correct choice is **B.**

Explanation: Choice A, "unwittingly," suggests he didn't know he was completing the book which, of course, can't be true. Choice C, "sporadically," which means occurring at irregular intervals hardly qualifies as devotion. Choice D, "universally," while all encompassing, is not directed or focused toward a singular cause such as the completion of a book. Choice E, "hesitatingly," would fit if the only catalyst were pressure from the publisher, but the real reason, we are told, is that he is a diligent scholar. Choice B, "assiduously," means unceasing and persistent, proper descriptors rationalizing his singularly focused purpose.

5. The correct choice is **E.**

Explanation: Choice A, "synchronous," means occurring at the same time, which is nonsensical given the historical perspective of the statement. Choice B, "caustic," means corrosive or dissolving, which might have been appropriate for a social commentary on the times but not best fitting this statement. Choice C, "acrimonious," means bitter in tone or rancorous and has nothing to do with the actual incident. Choice D, "deleterious," means having a harmful effect which again, might describe a social commentary, but does not complement this sentence. Choice E, "anachronistic," means the representation of something happening in other than chronological order, best fitting this sentence.

6. The correct choice is **C.**

Explanation: Choice A, "assertion," would only serve to restate the formerly known truth, not any changes due to new knowledge. Choice B, "validation," would likewise only serve to confirm the former truth, thus ignoring the new contradicting data. Choice D, "concurrency," means happening at the same time and is impossible. Choice E, "fortification," means to fortify or make stronger, which cannot be the case with data that causes modification to previously believed truths. Choice C, "revision," means a rewriting or alteration, which is exactly what new data does to previously known data and former truths.

7. The correct choice is **C.**

Explanation: The characteristics described are generally not those most sought in a CEO position. This makes the first word choice necessarily at odds with the second word choice. It would either be negative followed by a positive or positive followed by a negative. We'll look for this pattern in the choices. Only Choice C, "unlikely. . . selected," has this unique opposition and, in fact, is the correct choice.

8. The correct choice is **A.**

Explanation: Choices B, C, and D, "guaranteeing," "fostering," and "affording," go against the logical reasoning of the sentence. Banning cannot create a positive access. Choice E, "decreasing," is effectively an understatement or litotes as banning is considerably more than "decreasing." Choice A, "denying," is an effect of the cause "banning."

9. The correct choice is **D.**

Explanation: The first clue is that the first blank refers back to the word "celebration." We know that the first word must be positive. Choices A, B, and D, "buoyancy," "gladness," and "euphoria," are all possibilities. The second clue is that we know the first positive is "temporary" leading us to a negative second blank. This only leaves Choice D, "euphoria. . . moderated," which is the only answer choice that matches both blanks.

10. The correct choice is **B.**

Explanation: "Notwithstanding" suggests the adjective describing or modifying the car burglaries was not pleasant. Answer Choice B, "commonplace," is the correct adjective to modify or describe car burglaries.

Sentence Completion Skill Set Nine

Each sentence below has one or two blanks, each blank indicating that something has been omitted. Beneath the sentence are five words or sets of words labeled A through E. Choose the word or set of words that, when inserted in the sentence, *best* fits the meaning of the sentence as a whole.

1. The movie was billed as being full of great action scenes guaranteed to keep the audience riveted to the edge of their seats, when in fact, after the first 20 minutes and three car chases, it grows _____ and never regains the _____ of the opening scenes for the rest of the movie.

   A. repetitive. . . slothfulness
   B. beguiling. . . calm
   C. routine. . . lethargy
   D. exciting. . . placidity
   E. redundant. . . verve

2. No one can claim that any of the speakers at the club were _____, and in actuality, because no one ever spoke more than ten sentences comprised of less than five words each, speeches were actually _____.

   A. verbose. . . vague
   B. misdirected. . . timed
   C. ambiguous. . . raucous
   D. experts. . . elongated
   E. dramatists. . . rambling

3. A goodly portion of the cuisine in the Far East contains significant amounts of stimulating spices not generally given to the American palate, qualifying them to be known as _____.

   A. palatable
   B. tasty
   C. piquant
   D. bland
   E. torrid

4. Justice Thomas may be the most _____ justice appointed in the last 20 years given the polls that showed as many whole-heartedly supporting him as unequivocally opposing him.

   A. professional
   B. controversial
   C. popular
   D. uniting
   E. notorious

5. Certainly Sir Gwain was a _____ foe whose thunderous presence on the battlefield caused the hearts of many a would-be foe to quiver like jelly.

   A. methodical
   B. mythical
   C. farcical
   D. rancorous
   E. timorous

6. The fact that most elevators today have battery back-up systems to safely deliver passengers to the next level in the event of a power failure, this does not alleviate the _____ fears of small, enclosed, confined places.

   A. kleptomaniac
   B. hypochondriac
   C. agoraphobic
   D. claustrophobic
   E. achluophobia

7. During World War II, it was not uncommon for one to _____, taking on the entire persona of the alternate individual, in order to pass through checkpoints.

   A. intimate
   B. altercate
   C. alternate
   D. consecrate
   E. subrogate

8. It seems that hardly a generation goes by but that the youth are caught in the _____ of war exposing young, fertile minds to the ravages, chaos, and turbulence of conflict.

   A. throngs
   B. distance
   C. paragons
   D. pendants
   E. maelstrom

9. Given the seemingly countless number of linguistic variations found in America, in order to reflect the _____ of those variations, writers often employ a mixture of dialects.

 A. intonation
 B. heterogeneity
 C. homogeneity
 D. exclusivity
 E. profundity

10. The con man's _____ is usually a person who is greedy, believes he can beat the system, and can't resist the swindler's trap.

 A. challenge
 B. nemesis
 C. prey
 D. legend
 E. quarry

Answers and Explanations for Skill Set Nine

1. The correct choice is **E**.

   Explanation: The change in tone and direction come following the phrase, "when in fact." Up to this point, the movie was a great action adventure. Given that there were three car chases in the first 20 minutes, a certain amount of repetition or redundancy is obvious. As there is nothing to counter them being exciting, "slothfulness" would not be what was to be regained, as this was not existent to this point. Choice E, "redundant. . . verve," satisfies the repetition of the car chases and the vitality or liveliness that was never regained.

2. The correct choice is **A**.

   Explanation: One clue is the phrase, "and in actuality." This tells us that there will be a difference between the first and second blanks. Further, since the description in actuality is the brevity of the speech, the opposite is what we need to find for the first blank. Choice A, "verbose" means using or containing a great and usually excessive number of words, which certainly qualifies as different than those with so few words. The second blank will be the synonym for few words or brevity, which is "vague."

3. The correct choice is **C**.

   Explanation: We are simply looking for a word that describes spicy food, which is not generally appreciated by Americans. Choices A and B, "palatable" and "tasty," clearly do not fit as they are positive experiences. Choice D, "bland," does not fit the condition of containing "stimulating spices." Choice E, "torrid," refers more to the heat of the sun or heat of passion and the spices discussed do not restrict them to being hot. Choice C, "piquant," means having an agreeably pungent taste albeit that which is agreeable to a local may not be as agreeable to an American palate.

4. The correct choice is **B**.

   Explanation: We are told that opinions are evenly split regarding positive and negative opinions of the Justice. Choice B, "controversial," means a dispute, generally public in nature, between two sides holding opposing views which exactingly matches the conditions set in the sentence.

5. The correct choice is **D**.

   Explanation: Choices B, C, and E, "mythical," "farcical," and "timorous," are not adjectives defining a foe who causes hearts to quake on the battlefield. Choice A, "methodical," while a quality desired in battle, again, it does not cause a heart to quiver. Choice D, "rancorous," means bitter, long-lasting resentment or ill will establishing Sir Gwain as the type foe to make hearts quiver.

6. The correct choice is **D**.

   Explanation: Although all choices deal with specific phobias and fears, Choice D, "claustrophobic," is the one dealing with the fear of confinement to small places.

7. The correct choice is **E**.

   Explanation: We need a word that means someone changing for another, even to the extent of "becoming" the other person. Choice E, "subrogate," means to substitute one person for another, a tactic used to smuggle people through security during World War II.

8. The correct choice is **E**.

   Explanation: Choice A, "throngs," means a large group of things versus the conditions of "ravages, chaos, and turbulence of conflict." Choice C, "paragon," means a model of excellence, which doesn't fit. Choice E, "maelstrom," means a violent or turbulent situation such as the ravages and chaos of conflict.

9. The correct choice is **B**.

   Explanation: Choice A, "intonation," refers to speech inflexion. Choice E, "profundity," means something profound or abstruse. Choice B, "heterogeneity," means completely different or incongruous, which is the best fit for this sentence. In order to reflect the completely different linguistic variations, writers employ a mixture of dialects in their writing.

10. The correct choice is **C.**

Explanation: Choice A, "challenge," is not the target who is greedy and wants to challenge the swindler himself. Choice B, "nemesis," does not work as again, this is the target of the swindler. Choice C, "prey," is the one who is victimized or made a profit from, which fits the conditions best.

Sentence Completion Skill Set Ten

Each sentence below has one or two blanks, each blank indicating that something has been omitted. Beneath the sentence are five words or sets of words labeled A through E. Choose the word or set of words that, when inserted in the sentence, *best* fits the meaning of the sentence as a whole.

1. Many find the writings of Mark Twain obscure and dense such that upon first reading, particularly his essays, one finds its _____ hard to penetrate.

   A. floridity
   B. opacity
   C. rigidity
   D. alliteration
   E. assonance

2. The Mount St. Helens eruption _____ thousands of tons of volcanic ash and debris, helping to restore to the soil nutrients _____ years ago by excessive mining and farming for decades.

   A. destroyed. . . marginalized
   B. returned. . . fertilized
   C. cleared. . . traded
   D. deposited. . . depleted
   E. eroded. . . windblown

3. Facing the onslaught of the massive German Army, smaller countries had little option but to adopt a _____ approach to Hitler.

   A. precarious
   B. hasty
   C. reconstituted
   D. conciliatory
   E. dependent

4. Because he was abused as a child, abandoned as a teenager, and wrongfully charged and convicted for crimes he didn't commit as an adult, it was perfectly understandable that he became _____, shunning human contact.

   A. an anomaly
   B. a misanthrope
   C. a miser
   D. an eyesore
   E. a nonentity

5. To our absolute amazement and astonishment, the entire commencement audience rose cheering to their feet at the conclusion of our Salutatorian's speech because until this event, in all the times we had heard him speak, he was merely _____ in his delivery.

   A. pedestrian
   B. lofty
   C. enthralling
   D. auspicious
   E. accomplished

6. She was unmistakably pleased by the accolades received during her book review; like most people, she enjoyed being _____.

   A. chided
   B. childlike
   C. vindicated
   D. resolute
   E. praised

7. Chewing tobacco was long thought to be a safe _____ to cigarette smoking because users don't inhale, but users are still subject to _____ various diseases inherent with this habit.

   A. answer. . . avoiding
   B. alternative. . . contracting
   C. rebuttal. . . emphysema
   D. transition. . . taxing
   E. rejoinder. . . acquiring

8. The comedian put on a scathingly brilliant _____ rendition of the president addressing Congress who were costumed as hogs representative of pork bellies.

   A. farcical
   B. serious
   C. genuine
   D. sardonic
   E. satirical

9. Portraying love or a relationship as foolish, risky, nonsensical, and worthless exposes him for what he really is, a _____.

    A. recluse

    B. philanthropist

    C. ingrate

    D. misogynist

    E. spinster

10. In order to resolve the issue of immigration, all parties need a discussion based on solid facts, not baseless fears; realities, not _____.

    A. concepts

    B. postulations

    C. retribution

    D. regimentation

    E. myths

Answers and Explanations for Skill Set Ten

1. The correct choice is **B.**

   Explanation: Choice A, "floridity," simply means covered in flowers and has nothing to do with the language or style of writing. Choice C, "rigidity," means stiffness in a literal sense and likewise has nothing to do with the language or style of writing. Choices D and E, "alliteration" and "assonance," are literary devices but do not complement difficulty in comprehension. Choice B, "opacity," means obscure or impenetrable which best fits the sentence.

2. The correct choice is **D.**

   Explanation: One of the clue words is "restore," which means whatever action happened previously helped to restore nutrients. If restoration was needed, some action negatively impacted the soil. Given the need for the volcanic ash, it could not be displaced or destroyed so the only two choices are Choice B, "returned" and Choice D, "deposited." The second blank needs to explain how the soil was affected by excessive mining and farming and Choice D, "depleted," explains that event satisfying both components of the sentence.

3. The correct choice is **D.**

   Explanation: Given the limited options available to any smaller country, the best choice would naturally be to attempt to appease or acquiesce. The word that most closely matches this conditions is Choice D, "conciliatory" which means to appease or make or attempt to make compatible.

4. The correct choice is **B.**

   Explanation: The phrase, "shunning human contact" is the one that defines the missing word. Choice A, "anomaly," means one that is peculiar or abnormal, but not necessarily avoiding contact. Choice C, "miser," means one who lives meagerly in order to hoard money. Choice D, "eyesore," means ugly or offensive but not disassociated. Choice E, "nonentity," means a person regarded as being of no importance but does not have anything to do with his social contacts. Choice B, "misanthrope," means one who hates or mistrusts humankind making this the best selection to rationalize why he is shunning human contact.

5. The correct choice is **A.**

   Explanation: We are looking for a word that actually is not particularly complimentary of the speaker as it has to be on the other end of the spectrum of all the accolades presented. The only really viable selection is Choice A, "pedestrian," which means undistinguished or ordinary.

6. The correct choice is **E.**

   Explanation: We need only find the synonym to "accolades" to make the correct selection for this sentence. Choice A, "chided" means scolded or reprimanded; hardly accolades. Choice B, "childlike," may be an accurate statement, but it does not fit the match for accolades. Choice C, "vindicated," suggests she had been wrongly accused in some matter, which is not disclosed in this context. Choice D, "resolute," means firm or determined as in unwavering, which does not match our synonym to accolades. Choice E, "praised," means expression of approval as in receiving accolades.

7. The correct choice is **B.**

   Explanation: We're looking for some kind of offset or switch from one product to another initially. Since one might be an "alternative" or a way to "transition," Choices B and D may be considered. For the second blank, we're looking for some word to suggest that those who chew can still get diseases and only Choice B, "contracting," matches this requirement.

8. The correct choice is **A.**

   Explanation: The ridiculousness of the presentation coupled with the fact that it was performed by a comedian suggests this was neither "serious," "genuine," "sardonic," nor "satirical." This leaves Choice A, "farcical," which means resembling a farce or ludicrous best matching the sentence requirements.

9. The correct choice is **D.**

Explanation: The sentence describes the traits of the individual, and we need to find only the word that matches that description. Choice A, "recluse," is someone who does not socialize, and even though it appears his social life is a mess, he must socialize to portray this as truth. Choice C, "ingrate," means someone who is ungrateful, but this is not what is being described to us in the sentence. Choice E, "spinster," means a single woman beyond normal age for marriage so this doesn't work. Choice D, "misogynist," means one who hates women, and this certainly appears to describe our wretched soul in the sentence.

10. The correct choice is **E.**

Explanation: The clue given in this sentence is the parallel between "solid facts" and "baseless fears," and "realities" and the blank offset. We need to find the opposite to "realities" with the same parallel as "baseless fears" is to "solid facts." Choice E, "myths," is the parallel contrast to "realities" and best fits this sentence.

PART II

READING
COMPREHENSION

The reading comprehension sections of the SAT further test vocabulary skills. Although the Sentence Completion section focuses primarily on vocabulary, knowing the structure of sentences greatly assists in the correct recognition of plausible definitions. This same tool should be used in the reading comprehension sections. Understanding the structure of sentences will assist with vocabulary questions that ask for the meaning of a word or phrase in the passage. Common types of questions found in the reading sections also include the following:

- Identifying main idea, main point, author's purpose, or an alternate title for the passage
- Recognizing the tone of the passage or identifying the style
- Comprehending information directly stated in the passage
- Answering relational questions about the author's opinions or ideas, even if not directly stated
- Recognizing the structural methodology employed to develop the passage, for example, sequencing
- Extending limited information given by the author to a logical conclusion using inference

Several strategies for success in this section will follow, but first, let's take a look at what you will see on test day. The College Board tells us that instructions for the Short Reading Comprehension section of the SAT will be something like the following:

The passages below are followed by questions based on their content; questions following a pair of related passages may also be based on the relationship between the paired passages. Answer the questions on the basis of what is <u>stated</u> or *implied* in the passages and in any introductory material that may be provided.

Before looking at a sample set of questions, let's make sure that we understand the instructions. It is only natural to skip over initial instructions in order to get to the meat of the subject. This approach is foolhardy when it comes to the SAT. The very first sentence is of critical importance. You are being told that the questions are based purely on the actual content of the passages. In other words, you need not have prior knowledge of any particular subject prior to taking the test. To be sure, knowing that O'Henry generally writes surprise endings would be greatly beneficial in answering a developmental question, but that knowledge would not be necessary to answer any question asked on the test. That information alone should help put your mind at ease. Generally, informational introductions are not given in the Short Reading Comprehension section but are normally found in the Long Reading Comprehension section.

Let's look at the next instruction. SAT tells us that questions following a paired passage may be based on the relationship between the passages. These paired passages will share a common issue or theme. One of the passages supports, opposes, or complements the other's point of view or position. Questions related to the paired passages will ask you to identify the similarity or difference regarding a particular point.

Now for the meat of the instructions, which many will mistakenly consider to be the first *real* instruction. The SAT instructions tell you to answer the questions following the passage(s) based upon what is "stated" or "implied" in the passages "and" in any introductory material that may be provided. We need to look at this instruction by breaking it into its two main components. First, we are told to answer the questions based on what is "stated." This is simply an instruction to look for the answer within the text and apply that information to select the best answer choice. If the answer cannot be based upon what is actually "stated" in the text, it must necessarily be based upon what is "implied" in the text. Remember, inferences are only logical extensions of the data actually stated in the text. This inference is what is "implied," and the correct answer choice will be that logical extension of facts or data actually stated in the text of the passage.

Finally, we are told to base our answer choices on information given in the introduction to the passage, if any. It is a natural tendency to give short shrift to introductory information. This may be a critical error in judgment when it comes to the SAT. In fact, the information given in the introductory material may be the most beneficial information leading you to the best answer choices, particularly as it relates to tone or implication questions.

Now you know what to expect on test day regarding instructions for the reading passage sections and appreciate how to gain the most direction from them. It's time to dissect the passages and develop some strategies to get the highest possible score.

The Short Reading Comprehension passages will average between 100–150 words and the Long Reading Comprehension passages will average between 150 – 800 words. Topics covered will range from the humanities, social studies, natural sciences, and literary fiction. You may expect the greater dimension to be in the informational text area. Like most of the state high-stakes tests now presented as a result of the No Child Left Behind legislation, most text is informational rather than literary. This is based on independent research that shows that approximately 70 percent of text read post graduation will relate to information, generally related to career. Since colleges and universities prepare you for post-graduate endeavors, it only makes sense that informational text will be focused upon to get you the proper training and preparation. As a result, test makers are writing questions based upon articles of more informational orientation.

Although the question types will be the same on both the short and long reading passages, the number of questions following each passage will vary. For the Short Reading Comprehension section, there will be only two or three questions for each passage. The number of questions found in the Long Reading Comprehension section will vary greatly depending upon the passage.

Passages will vary in style and tone and include basic narrative, persuasive, expository, and argumentative text. They also will include a variety of literary elements and devices from which questions will be derived. Questions will follow each passage in the reading comprehension sections or, in the case of a comparative piece, a pair of related passages.

It is important to note that the questions that follow each reading passage are not arranged in order of difficulty. This was true only in the Sentence Completion section. In other words, do not shut down when you come to a difficult reading comprehension question. You may find the next question to be surprisingly less challenging. It is important to note that, as a rule, questions follow the passage development. In other words, initial questions about the text will come from the beginning of the passage. Generally speaking, questions will flow with the development of the passage. Obviously, questions relating to theme, tone, purpose, and so on may be asked toward the end of the questions, albeit the answer is developed throughout the passage.

Finding the Right Approach

A number of approaches can be taken for both reading comprehension sections of the SAT. Since we all have our individual learning styles, we all develop our own best approaches to assessments. It would not be prudent for anyone to tell you the best way for you to approach any given assessment (particularly one as complex as the SAT), without having monitored your particular traits and assessment practices. What is appropriate is to present you with a variety of methodologies that have proven to be very successful with measured results. By individually applying these methodologies in the skill sets that follow, you can determine the best approach for your particular style.

Some authorities will tell you to read the passage actively, after reading the questions. Some will tell you to only skim the passage and then look up the answers to the questions. Some will tell you that reading the entire passage is a waste of time. We'll discuss these approaches in depth, and try to include some of the positives and negatives with each methodology to help you select an approach that best fits your individual style.

Reading the passage actively after reading the questions is one of the popular approaches heralded by some. With this approach, you read the questions only (not the answers) and then actively read the passage. By not reading the answer choices, you do not read material that is not accurate and will only have to be read again prior to making your final selection. As you read the questions, underline key words that will trigger you brain as you read the passage. By reading the questions only, you front-load your brain in terms of what to look for as you read. Prior to reading the passage, read any informational materials that might be presented, including the title if given. This approach will activate any prior knowledge you may have about this particular time period, event, or author. (Although prior knowledge is not required to do well on the SAT, it can help your comfort level, which will trend better results. And, as a word of caution, if an answer choice is not given in the passage, or text-based, it is not the best answer choice.) Active reading involves something referred to in pedagogy as **monitoring understanding** or **check yourself** relating to comprehension. One way to ensure checking comprehension is to very selectively underline key words or phrases in the passage. Note the word selectively as used in this instruction. Underlining too much information is like not noting any key information. After reading each paragraph, make a one- or two-word margin note indicating what the paragraph was about. This is especially helpful when reading longer passages. Some suggest this step is not necessary on short reading passages because of the brevity of the passages. Your individual style will determine whether this is a good practice for you to employ. Others believe that since SAT generally refers you to the sentence number being questioned, this step is unnecessary. Still, when dealing with questions of a more general nature such as tone or theme, margin notes are a helpful recap without rereading the text.

Another approach is to quickly skim the passage for a general overview of the content presented. Next, read the questions and mark key words or phrases to help you understand exactly what the question is asking. Finally, go back to the text and look up the answers to the questions. Simply put, some questions on the SAT do not lend themselves to correct answers by skimming the text. Also, if you have not developed this skill in advance, it should not be employed beginning on the day of the SAT. The positive argument for this approach is that, if previously honed, skimming can save you valuable time and provide you the opportunity to expend additional time where needed. It is true that SAT does not test your complete and total mastery of the entire text; however, some questions will force you to read at least some portion of the text in-depth in order to correctly answer the question.

An approach, generally more appropriate in the Long Reading Comprehension section, albeit useable in the Short Reading Comprehension section, is to read and mark a couple of questions and then read or skim the passage until those questions are answered. Next, read another couple of questions and find the answers to them in the text. Follow this approach until all questions are answered.

All three of these approaches, and any partial combination of any of them, have proven successful to thousands of test-takers in the past. You need only determine which works best for you. You may find that the best methodology for the Short Reading Comprehension section needs to be modified to best suit the Long Reading Comprehension section. Again, try these approaches during the skill sets that follow to determine your individual approach.

Question Specifics

Now it is time to look at even more specifics of the questions and ensure that you understand how the SAT asks them, including some of the givens that test-takers are presumed to understand. Here is a listing and some notations regarding question types, assumptions, and hints to know just what the SAT is asking:

Literal Information Questions

Many questions will ask you to lift information that is literally right in the text. Since much of the reading you will do in college is for the purpose of your obtaining information independently from reading, SAT is going to help determine your ability in this area, and therefore, your probability of success in college.

Remember that the order of questions generally follows the order of the passage. Find sufficient information in the text to correctly answer the question. Verify that your prediction is correct and make the appropriate selection. Keep in mind that the best answer will be supported by the text, not from your prior knowledge. Also, just because an answer is right does not make it the best answer.

In matching the information in the text to the question, remember that assessment questions are often reworded, reverse-worded, or inverted from the answer information in the passage. Additionally, keep in mind that test-makers will sometimes ask questions in the negative, even when the information in the text is stated in the positive.

Verify your answer selection. After you read the question and predict the correct answer, verify your prediction with information from the text. Remember, every correct answer selection in a literal information question can be validated in the text, regardless of juxtapositioning of the information.

Watch for key words in the question itself. Key words such as *except, not,* and *only* specifically direct the reader and often completely alter the correct choice.

One of the standard aids for test-takers is the ability to mark up their test booklets. Take advantage of this not only to better understand the passage and question, but to eliminate obvious wrong answer choices. Since time is one of the most precious commodities of the SAT, preserve as much as you can with this simple tool. This will keep you from rereading incorrect choices as you get down to the two most probable correct choices.

Vocabulary Questions

In context-based reading passages, vocabulary becomes an important tool and, consequently, good material for testing. It is not necessary for you to know the meaning of each word or all of the possible multiple meanings for any given word in order to answer vocabulary questions correctly. It is important that you know how to decipher or decode the meaning of a word based on surrounding text. Sometimes, the tone of the passage will give clues as to which meaning of a particular word the author intends for effect. An example would be the word "bright." In the sentence, "John was obviously a bright student," the context tells us that smart would be a better choice for the definition of "bright" than radiant or luminous simply based upon how it is used in that sentence.

Keep in mind that in the English language, one word can have many meanings, and answer choices will include many proper meanings but only one best fitting the context in which it was used.

When asked a vocabulary question, never answer it based upon your prior knowledge alone. Always go back and read the referenced word in context to ensure the proper meaning. Many test-takers lose valuable points by relying upon what they know to be true or accurate, but, unfortunately, it is not the best choice based upon context.

Reasoning Questions

Beyond the Literal Questions and Vocabulary Questions lie the Reasoning Questions. This is the area of greatest concern and trepidation to most test-takers. Ironically, this is the area in which the author gives you the most available information to enable you to answer questions correctly. These questions do ask you to go beyond what is directly stated in the passage and into the realm of inference, overall theme, main idea, meaning of the passage, relevance to a position, purpose, attitude, or tone of the writer. Generally speaking, these questions are the ones that will cause you to want to read more actively in order to follow the logic in the passage and recognize points of strength or weakness in the author's position.

These questions will ask you to identify the main idea of a passage or determine the author's purpose for writing the piece.

Reasoning questions will ask you to understand narrow ideas or relationships in a passage concerning seemingly dichotomous informational flows.

Questions of this type will ask you not simply for the meaning of a given word, phrase, or section but how it contributes to the overall purpose or how the author used that specific language to accomplish his purpose or possibly to contribute to the tone of the passage.

These questions may ask you to determine the strength of argument based upon given facts, assumptions, or inferences to which the reader is led.

Keep in mind that statements used by authors generally fall into three categories:

- Fact: these are statements generally known to be universal truths such as, "There are 100 centimeters in a meter."
- Assumption: these are statements of supposition or proposition the author uses as assumptions of truth as they are presented. They call for a judgment to be made by the reader as to validity. Regardless of what you may empirically know to be truth, you must assess whether the author is purporting these assumptions to be truth and answer related questions based on that presentation, not what you may know to be otherwise.
- Inference: is the result of thinking through what the author has presented. It is a conclusion reached following close reflection, reasoning, and thought based on what has been presented in the passage.

Remember that you will experience at least one paired reading paragraph that will have a common theme or subject. The second passage will support, oppose, or otherwise relate to the first passage. When questions ask you to compare the two passages, it does not necessarily mean that all of the answer choices will have included the necessary information *from* both passages. When comparing two passages, eliminate any choices that are not presented in both passages. Then you just have to choose among the remaining choices.

Let's recap some of the key elements before we get into some short reading skill sets:

- As answers come from the passage, make sure that the passage supports your answer. This is true with all types of questions, even those asking you to make an inference since that inference must be supported with details from the passage.

- Consider the word choice in each question and passage. Test-makers choose their words for very specific reasons. Each word is individually selected by the maker to serve a very specific purpose. Just be cognizant of the tone each word conveys and the specific way it contributes to the overall purpose for existence.

- It is important to remember that an answer can be both correct and wrong. The answer that makes the best choice is not necessarily the first choice that makes a true statement. Be sure to confirm your selection by verifying that the passage supports your selection. Sometimes, that support will be stated in terms that are only synonymous with the terms of the question. There may also be times when the question and passage support are stated in opposites; one in the positive and one in the negative.

- Eliminating obvious incorrect choices and marking through them in the test booklet helps save time and reduce possible choices, making it easier to find the passage support to make your final correct answer selection.

- It is better to focus on one passage at a time instead of jumping from passage to passage. Try to answer all questions in one passage before moving to the next passage. Remember, there is no correct or mandated order for you to follow. It is recommended that you address passages that you feel more comfortable with first. This approach will help you understand the flow of the questions and get the most answers possible in the shortest amount of time.

Short Reading Comprehension Skill Set One

Note: Skill sets may contain more questions than the actual SAT to show the potential range of questioning.

The passages below are followed by questions based on their content; questions following a pair of related passages may also be based on the relationship between the paired passages. Answer the questions on the basis of what is *stated* or *implied* in the passages and in any introductory material that may be provided.

Questions 1–4 are based on the following passage.

But in the main, I feel like a brown bag of miscellany propped against a wall. Against a wall in company with other bags, white, red, and yellow. Pour out the contents, and there is discovered a jumble of small things: priceless lengths of string, a key to a door long since crumbled away, a rusty knife-blade, old shoes saved for a road that never was and never will be, a nail bent under the weight of things too heavy for any nail, a dried flower or two still
(5) a little fragrant. In your hand is the brown bag. On the ground before you is the jumble it held—so much like the jumble in the bags, could they be emptied, that all might be dumped in a single heap and the bags refilled without altering the content of any greatly. A bit of colored glass more or less would not matter. Perhaps that is how the Great Stuffer of Bags filled them in the first place—who knows?

1. The primary purpose of the passage is to

    A. describe the contents of bags.

    B. suggest people are not predisposed to prejudice.

    C. recommend all people share wealth with others.

    D. purport that all people have some value.

    E. identify that even with age, memories are valued.

2. What statement best describes the author's meaning of the phrase "a nail bent under the weight of things too heavy for any nail?" (line 4)

    A. Life presents hardships that will test the mettle of any individual.

    B. There are times in life when a curved object is a better tool than a straight one.

    C. Planning will help the individual have the correct equipment for the job at hand.

    D. People tend to keep items that are no longer useful.

    E. The nail is simply another article to place in the bag.

3. "Great Stuffer of Bags" is an example of what literary device?

    A. onomatopoeia

    B. personification

    C. allusion

    D. assonance

    E. alliteration

4. The entire passage qualifies as which of the following devices?

    A. allegory

    B. extended metaphor

    C. epic

    D. litotes

    E. hyperbole

Questions 5–7 are based on the following passage.

It seemed to me, as I kept remembering all this, that those times and those summers had been infinitely precious and worth saving. There had been jollity and peace and goodness. The arriving (at the beginning of August) had been so big a business in itself; at the railway station the farm wagon drawn up, the first smell of the pine-laden air, the first glimpse of the smiling farmer, and the great importance of the trunks and your father's enormous authority
(5)　in such matters, and the feel of the wagon under you for the long ten-mile haul, and at the top of the last long hill catching the first view of the lake after eleven months of not seeing this cherished body of water. The shouts and cries of the other campers when they saw you, and the trunks to be unpacked, to give up their rich burden. (Arriving was less exciting nowadays, when you sneaked up in your car and parked it under a tree near the damp and took out the bags and in five minutes it was all over, no fuss, no loud wonderful fuss about trunks.)

5. The device used by the author in this passage is called

  A. foreshadowing.
  B. deja vu.
  C. flashback.
  D. flash forward.
  E. recollection.

6. In the passage, the author emphasizes which aspect of the childhood memory?

  A. the anticipation
  B. the aromas
  C. enjoying friends
  D. wagon rides
  E. the arrival

7. The overall tone of the passage is

  A. melancholy.
  B. sad.
  C. angry.
  D. sedate.
  E. soothing.

Questions 8–10 are based on the following passage.

I fretted the other night at the hotel at the stranger who broke into my chamber after midnight, claiming to share it. But after his lamp had smoked the chamber full and I had turned round to the wall in despair, the man blew out his lamp, knelt down at his bedside, and made in low whisper a long earnest prayer. Then was the relation entirely
(4)　changed between us. I fretted no more, but respected and liked him.

8. In line 1, "fretted" most nearly means

  A. wondered.
  B. considered.
  C. vaguely recognized.
  D. worried.
  E. panicked.

9. The probable purpose of the author using the phrase, "lamp had smoked the chamber full" is to

  A. establish a period of time.
  B. show a low grade fuel was used.
  C. establish the faultiness of the lamp.
  D. indicate the lamp was turned up too high.
  E. utilize figurative language.

10. What can the reader infer about the speaker based on the passage?

  A. He is a brave man.
  B. He is used to sharing his room with strangers.
  C. He easily overcomes fear.
  D. He is a religious man.
  E. He is easily put off.

Answers and Explanations for Skill Set One

1. The correct choice is **B**.

   Explanation: The idea of prejudice is introduced with the various colors of bags. The relation to a bag being the body or vessel of the human being is that the author feels like a brown bag filled with various articles that we are told are important, regardless of their seeming lack of monetary value. Since the contents of the bags are dumped in a commingled mass without much variance except for different colored glass, the author reasons that they could each easily be refilled without altering the content of any greatly but moderating the amount of colored glass or preference (seen as prejudice) to any other color. In fact, "the Great Stuffer of Bags," as suggested by the author (a metaphor for the creator of bags) may have filled them this way to begin with. . . not predisposed to prejudice for any color. Answer B is correct.

2. The correct choice is **A**.

   Explanation: Since the author establishes the contents of the bags as personal historical experiences, those items that make up the moral character or fiber of the individual, it is reasonable to ascribe relational meaning to those objects. In the case of the bent nail, we are told that the bending was a result of it being asked to bear something too heavy. In this regard, the bent nail alludes to hardships in life creating grief or anxiety greater than the frailty of man was meant to bear. In this regard, Choice A best fits the meaning.

3. The correct choice is **C**.

   Explanation: The "Great Stuffer of Bags" relates to the creator of bags who allows or places contents within the bags. In this instance, the "Great Stuffer of Bags" relates to God and is, therefore, an allusion. It would behoove those taking any standardized test to refresh their memories as to the meaning of literary devices as this will enhance their understanding of literary passages.

4. The correct choice is **B**.

   Explanation: The author establishes the metaphor of a bag representing an individual in the opening line of the passage. As this relationship is carried throughout the passage, it qualifies as an extended metaphor. Choice B is correct.

5. The correct choice is **C**.

   Explanation: Although Choice E, "recollection," is clearly what the author is doing, the literary device used by the author to recall is Choice C, "flashback."

6. The correct choice is **E**.

   Explanation: In this particular passage, the author goes to great lengths to share the excitement of the entire arrival process after being absent for eleven months. Although individual aspects experienced in the process are presented with much figurative language, thusly making each action of seeming great importance in and of itself, the overall focus is placed on Choice E, the "arrival."

7. The correct choice is **E**.

   Explanation: Clearly, the ending of this passage reflects a sad or melancholy tone, but the "overall tone" of the passage is very uplifting. The memories are fond ones, and as the author states, "It seemed to me, as I kept remembering all this, that those times and those summers had been infinitely precious and worth saving." As he goes on to relate the experiences from his childhood memory, they are fondly remembered, causing a calming, soothing experience. Answer Choice E is the best choice.

8. The correct choice is **D**.

   Explanation: Although the original tenet certainly had the right to wonder why someone would be joining him in his room, the stranger was not challenged so the reader can only infer that this was a somewhat common practice when and where this incident took place. There is no evidence of any panic on the part of the author, but until the stranger's prayer was overheard, the author fretted, which is another way of saying "worried" about the stranger. Choice D is correct.

9. The correct choice is **A.**

Explanation: Instead of saying that a certain amount of time had passed, the author chose to indicate the amount of time passed by an event. Had candles been used, the measure of diminishment could have been used. As a lamp was used, the time indicator was the time it took for the chimney or chamber of the lamp to become fully smoked or charred. This blackening of the chamber establishes a period of time passed, making Choice A correct.

10. The correct choice is **D.**

Explanation: The easing of nerves, the ceasing of any fretting took place following the specific of the stranger/intruder kneeling and praying a sincere, earnest prayer. Note that this was not some ritualistic prayer said before bedtime, some mere offering, or gesture, or accommodation to appease his audience. First, the author would have to have been able to determine the difference between a mere gesture and a prayer offered in earnest. Second, this would only have had a calming impact on the author if he believed that anyone who prayed in this manner would be of a general good nature and not cause harm to others. In order for him to understand and accept this as fact, the reader can infer that the author was a religious man himself, making Choice D correct.

Short Reading Comprehension Skill Set Two

The passages below are followed by questions based on their content; questions following a pair of related passages may also be based on the relationship between the paired passages. Answer the questions on the basis of what is *stated* or *implied* in the passages and in any introductory material that may be provided.

Questions 1–4 are based on the following passage.

Love is necessary to righting the estate of woman in this world. Otherwise nature itself seems to be in conspiracy against her dignity and welfare; for the cultivated, high-thoughted, beauty-loving, saintly woman finds herself unconsciously desired for her sex, and even enhancing the appetite of her savage pursuers by these fine ornaments she has piously laid on herself. She finds with indignation that she is herself a snare, and was made such. I do not (5) wonder at her occasional protest, violent protest, against nature, in fleeing to nunneries, and taking black veils. Love rights all this deep wrong.

1. The author's attitude toward women can best be described as one of

   A. admiration.
   B. suspicion.
   C. incredulity.
   D. condescension.
   E. understanding.

2. Sans love, what does the author purport to be the state of woman in this world?

   A. in a piteous state with little alternative but to be sought for her pleasures
   B. held in lofty esteem adorned much by nature with a raw beauty
   C. a bobble to be greatly appreciated and gifted beyond compare
   D. a conduit of pleasure greatly sought particularly as a result of her own adornment
   E. a soul without indignation and a snare of such prowess as to catch any suitor

3. According to the passage, plausible remedies to ward off being sought only for pleasure include

   A. marrying to gain a rightly estate as warranted by nature.
   B. aligning herself with the cultivated, dignified, and well-thought-of man.
   C. removing herself to a place where men are unwelcome.
   D. adorning herself with ornaments piously laid on herself.
   E. making a pact with nature to lessen the adornments and ornaments given by her.

4. The phrase, "savage pursuers," in line 3 refers to

   A. men who would provide love and stability.
   B. jealous women who desire to be more beautiful.
   C. potential suitors who would provide wealth and happiness.
   D. men who don't easily give up once they discover the woman they love.
   E. men who would not provide love and strip her of dignity.

Questions 5–10 are based on the following passage.

To set down such choice experiences that my own writings may inspire me and at last I may make wholes of parts. Certainly it is a distinct profession to rescue from oblivion and to fix the sentiments and thoughts which visit all men more or less generally, that the contemplation of the unfinished picture may suggest its harmonious completion. Associate reverently and as much as you can with your loftiest thoughts. Each thought that is welcomed and
(5)   recorded is a nest egg, by the side of which more will be laid. Thoughts accidentally thrown together become a frame in which more may be developed and exhibited. Perhaps this is the main value of a habit of writing, of keeping a journal—that so we remember our best hours and stimulate ourselves. My thoughts are my company. They have a certain individuality and separate existence, aye, personality. Having by chance recorded a few disconnected thoughts and then brought them into juxtaposition, they suggest a whole new field in which it was possible to labor
(10)   and to think. Thought begat thought.

5. The purpose of this passage is

   A. to provide a rationale for the thought process.

   B. to establish a reason for thinking and the self-service thinking provides.

   C. to evidence that thinking is a reward unto itself.

   D. to herald the writing of thoughts.

   E. to instruct on how to capture thoughts on paper.

6. During the course of the passage, the author

   A. provides a rationale for his writing as stimulating thought.

   B. suggests that all men should keep a journal to aide them in thinking.

   C. admonishes thinkers to write in order to become inspired.

   D. praises random thoughts as a beginning of writing.

   E. informs that the only way to develop thought is to think.

7. In line (2), to what does the author wish to "rescue from oblivion?"

   A. the experiences of sitting and relaxing to think about historical thoughts

   B. the opportunity to write thoughts which may finalize the completion of thought

   C. the time to labor at thinking about life and planning future movements

   D. the time to remember lofty accomplishments and think upon improving them

   E. the reasoning of time as it passes and to remember to complete unfinished plans

8. The term "nest egg" in line (5), is a metaphor for

   A. a surprise heretofore not discovered.

   B. a thought that will manifest itself as yet another thought.

   C. a journal entry to be treasured and joined with other entries.

   D. a reserved treasure one can rely upon as needed.

   E. a memory that will stimulate thought and solicit a recording in a journal.

9. The author suggests that the main reason to journal is

   A. to enable us to recall our finest moments and cause us to rejuvenate.

   B. so we can remember the untoward sides of humanity and reverse course.

   C. because in no other way can the measure of a man be determined following life.

   D. that journaling is the pastime that renews thoughts to modify behavior.

   E. it is necessary for man to understand his reason for being.

10. Line (10), "Thought begat thought" means

   A. that when someone doesn't think for a long time, thought will be stimulated to rescue itself.

   B. that a thought has the power to reason and by so doing, has the ability to procreate abilities.

   C. that reasoning as a component of thought must be the primary focus for forward development of the mind.

   D. that the process of thinking initiates other thoughts, which in return will foster still other thoughts.

   E. that the practice of thinking will lead to stimulation that will lead to journal writing and harmony.

Answers and Explanations for Skill Set Two

1. The correct choice is **D.**

   Explanation: Although the author does not blame women for their position entirely, he suggests that they further the injustices of nature by adorning themselves with "fine adornments she has piously laid on." He further suggests that, though perfectly understandable, she does consider protesting her position by running away, "fleeing to nunneries" where she can avoid being viewed as a sex object. The author suggests the only real way out, other than fleeing, is to find love. The entire piece is written with a condescending tone making Choice D correct.

2. The correct choice is **A.**

   Explanation: Although Choice D seems correct, it is not the best answer. In fact, the answer suggests that woman is found to be in this situation "particularly as a result of her own adornment" when this is but an augmentation to that which the author suggests was actually done by nature. Choice A is a better selection as it follows the author's tone by placing her in a "piteous" state with little alternative unless she finds love.

3. The correct choice is **C.**

   Explanation: Choice A involves "marrying," which would certainly remove woman from the situation, presumably, of being sought for pleasure, but it does not conform to the author's position that "love" must be an ingredient. According to the passage, there are only two plausible ways of warding off "being sought for pleasure," and they are finding "love," which was not an answer choice, or removal of herself to places where men are unwelcome such as a nunnery; therefore, Choice C is best.

4. The correct choice is **E.**

   Explanation: Choice A is incorrect because the man who would provide "love" is what the author suggests is needed, and this disqualifies the man from being "savage." Choice C is incorrect because a man who would provide "happiness" would qualify as providing "love" eliminating him from savagery. Choice D seems plausible, but if they were actually pursuing a woman they had fallen in love with, they would not qualify as savage or those only pursuing for personal gratification. Choice E fully matches the conditions of the term "savage pursuers" in that they would "not" provide love and, gleaning from the woman what they wanted, would "strip her of dignity," making it the best selection.

5. The correct choice is **D.**

   Explanation: The entire passage is devoted to the writing or journaling of thoughts in order to "Associate reverently and as much as you can with your loftiest thoughts," making Choice D the best answer.

6. The correct choice is **A.**

   Explanation: Choice B seems correct, but a close reading of the passage will reveal that the journal is the extension of thinking and serves as a catalyst to foster more thinking upon reflection of the thoughts previously written. Choice A best sums the passage in that the author, in writing, thinks first, records, and then reflects, which will serve to begat more thought.

7. The correct choice is **B.**

   Explanation: Choice B is the best selection, but this answer must be worked from the actual line given through the passage to make it complete. The actual "rescue" is the saving of the "distinct profession." That "distinct profession" is the experience of "my own writings," which "may inspire me, and at last I may make wholes of parts." This "profession" of writing allows the author to finalize or complete thoughts to make connections and sense of them overall.

8. The correct choice is **D.**

   Explanation: The term "nest egg" refers to the egg, generally chicken, that has yet to be gathered from the hen house. As such, it is an asset for future use. Any asset reserved for future use, like a savings account, is commonly referred to as a "nest egg." In this case, the author considers each thought that is recorded as an asset reserved or kept for future use.

9. The correct choice is **A.**

Explanation: The author states that perhaps the main value is "so that we remember our best hours and stimulate ourselves," making Choice A the best selection.

10. The correct choice is **D.**

Explanation: This is only another way of asking a vocabulary question in context. The sentence in line (10) reads, "Thought begat thought." This simply suggests that thinking about something makes or stimulates additional thoughts as questions or interests arise as a result of thinking about the original subject. This is much akin to looking up a word in the dictionary only to find you want to look up another word, possibly one that was used to define the first word. Choice D best reflects this paradigm.

Short Reading Comprehension Skill Set Three

The passages below are followed by questions based on their content; questions following a pair of related passages may also be based on the relationship between the paired passages. Answer the questions on the basis of what is *stated* or *implied* in the passages and in any introductory material that may be provided.

Questions 1–3 are based on the following passage.

It was four o'clock when he landed on the rocks, which the rays of an intensely scorching sun had rendered so hot that I could scarcely place my foot upon them. How the people without shoes bore it I cannot imagine. Never shall I forget the extraordinary spectacle that met our sight the moment we passed the low range of bushes, which formed a screen in front of the river. A crowd of many hundred Irish emigrants had been landed during the present
(5)   and former day and all this motley crew—men, women, and children, who were not confined by sickness to the sheds (which greatly resembled cattle-pens)—were employed in washing clothes or spreading them out on the rocks and bushes to dry.

1. The reader may infer all of the following from the passage except:

   A.   the narrator was wearing shoes.

   B.   there was a goodly number of sick among the emigrants.

   C.   the memory of the sight of the emigrants will fade over time.

   D.   the narrator had been hidden from view of the emigrants by natural boundaries.

   E.   it was summertime or on a latitude close to the equator.

2. Which is the best description of the word "motley" as used in line (5)?

   A.   a diverse mix of emigrants

   B.   a group who was in need of bathing

   C.   a group with dirty clothes

   D.   a mix of rich and poor settlers

   E.   a group including all sexes and ages

3. The use of the term "spectacle" in line (3) suggests the narrator was

   A.   expecting to see an eclectic mix of emigrants at the river.

   B.   surprised to see so many people who had landed within two days.

   C.   understandably elated to find others who were seeking to establish homes.

   D.   shocked to see the scene presented with so many emigrants and what they were doing.

   E.   thrilled at the final joining up with the remainder of the emigrant settlers.

Questions 4–8 are based on the following passage.

I think I knew General Washington intimately and thoroughly; and were I called on to delineate his character, it should be in terms like these.

His mind was great and powerful, without being of the very first order; his penetration strong, though not so acute as that of a Newton, Bacon, or Locke; and as far as he saw, no judgment was ever sounder. It was slow in
(5)   operation, being little aided by invention or imagination, but sure in conclusion. Hence the common remark of his officers, of the advantage he derived from councils of war, where hearing all suggestions, he selected whatever was best; and certainly no general ever planned his battles more judiciously.

4. Why does the author write the first two lines (1–2) before writing about Washington?

   A. as simply an introduction to establish his topic
   B. to serve as a notification that he is about to expose Washington
   C. to prepare the reader for the limitations he found in Washington
   D. to suggest that he was able to observe Washington in various surroundings
   E. to qualify himself as one who is knowledgeable enough to fully present the subject

5. Which of the following best describes the treatment of Washington in this passage?

   A. presented only those aspects of Washington that are deemed positive
   B. reflected primarily on the negative sides of Washington
   C. presented only enough positive attributes to suggest his leadership was questionable
   D. presented both the positives and the flat sides of Washington
   E. reflected upon the personality of Washington as opposed to his accomplishments

6. What may we infer about the author as it relates to the assessment of Washington's mind?

   A. He knew enough of the top minds of his day and could relate them to Washington.
   B. He was informed from sufficient sources as to make a relative comparison to those with first order minds.
   C. He believed he had the ability to properly assess the abilities of Washington's mind and could appropriately compare it to those he could recognize as having a mind of the very first order.
   D. A mind of the very first order was indeed a rarity and that only he and a very few others, certainly not Washington, possessed such a mind.
   E. Washington must have had a good mind to be selected for the positions he was assigned but not a good enough mind as to get any better positions; such as a mind of greater order would.

7. What does the author mean by the term "penetration" as used in line (3)?

   A. power to read minds
   B. ability to enter or pass through objects
   C. genius to engage those who are of a first order mind
   D. ability to assess and figure out difficult tasks
   E. power to reason with the assistance of leaders of the day

8. What may be inferred about Washington's judgment based on the passage?

   A. He was quick to decide and held to his decision.
   B. He was slow and methodical, but committed.
   C. He required the assistance of others and then quickly decided.
   D. He ignored input from the greatest minds of the day when deciding.
   E. He rushed to judgment before considering the consequences.

Questions 9–10 are based on the following passage.

Ohio State was a land grant university and, therefore, two years of military drill was compulsory. We drilled with old Springfield rifles and studied the tactics of the Civil War, even though the World War was going on at the time. At 11 o'clock each morning thousands of freshmen and sophomores used to deploy over the campus, moodily creep-
(5) ing up on the chemistry building. It was good training for the kind of warfare that was waged at Shiloh, but it had no connection with what was going on in Europe. Some people used to think there was German money behind it, but they didn't dare say so, or they would have been thrown in jail as German spies. It was a period of muddy thought and marked, I believe, the decline of higher education in the Middle West.

9. The passage is a good example of what type of writing?

   A. humor

   B. satire

   C. sardonic

   D. situational irony

   E. historical fiction

10. Based on the knowledge that chemical agents were used in the World War depicted in the passage, what event qualifies as ironic?

   A. Daily military drills involved creeping up on the chemistry building.

   B. The training was representative of the tactics used at Shiloh.

   C. German money was believed to be behind dated training methodologies.

   D. Ohio State was a land grant university wherein chemical development took place.

   E. A goodly number of chemistry majors attended Ohio State at the time of the World War.

Answers and Explanations for Skill Set Three

1. The correct choice is **C**.

    Explanation: All of the answer choices are supported in the passage except that "the memory of the sight of the emigrants will fade over time" because the passage reads, "Never shall I forget the extraordinary spectacle that met our sight the moment. . .". Therefore, Choice C is correct.

2. The correct choice is **E**.

    Explanation: The term "motley" literally means "of diverse colors or elements," which describes the mix of ages and genders encountered, or Choice E.

3. The correct choice is **D**.

    Explanation: "An impressive public display" is one definition of "spectacle." Only Choices B and D, "surprise" and "shocked," respectively, lend themselves to qualifying as "impressive." The sheer numbers alone would not necessarily qualify as a spectacle, but coupled with their activities this makes Choice D the best selection.

4. The correct choice is **E**.

    Explanation: Although Choice A seems an obvious choice, it is too limited in scope. Certainly, it serves the function of a simple introduction, but goes much further. Choice D is also plausible, but the simple observance of someone does not qualify one to make the personal and detailed reflections presented in the passage. The author is clearly presenting his qualifications about the subject matter. In this case, General Washington is the subject, and the author is informing the reader how intimately and thoroughly he knew the General in order to qualify his following remarks. Therefore, Choice E is correct.

5. The correct choice is **D**.

    Explanation: The author was careful to present a positive point or characteristic and a qualification to that praise throughout the passage. In this regard, he further establishes his credibility for his remarks and positions himself as a qualified, impersonal assessor. Choice D is correct.

6. The correct choice is **C**.

    Explanation: Here, the speaker presents himself as an authoritarian, without any qualification. He qualified himself regarding the focus of the passage, General Washington; the speaker infers he is not only qualified to assess the mind of Washington, but to have the mental faculty to be able to qualify a mind "of the very first order." Choice C supports this position.

7. The correct choice is **D**.

    Explanation: Although choice B satisfies the definition of "penetration," it does not best describe the definition as it was used in this passage. Remember, an answer choice may be true, but not be the best choice. In this case, "penetration" is meant to be able to "see into" or observe all aspects and reason based on the variations and perhaps in spite of missing components. The author likens this particular quality to those of Newton, Bacon, and Locke making Choice D correct.

8. The correct choice is **B**.

    Explanation: The passage informs the reader that Washington's judgment was, ". . .slow in operation. . .but sure in conclusion." Choice B satisfies this assessment.

9. The correct choice is **B**.

    Explanation: Satire is the only correct style for this passage. Throughout, the author ridicules with humor the training forced upon students as being archaic for the current situation. As this is done without malice and involves the making of a point more than simply humorous writing, Choice B is correct.

10. The correct choice is **A**.

    Explanation: Since various chemical gasses were used in the World War being written about in this passage, the fact that students would have to creep up on the chemistry building creates an ironic situation within this satiric literary work making Choice A correct.

Short Reading Comprehension Skill Set Four

The passages below are followed by questions based on their content; questions following a pair of related passages may also be based on the relationship between the paired passages. Answer the questions on the basis of what is *stated* or *implied* in the passages and in any introductory material that may be provided.

Questions 1–2 are based on the following passage.

The stories he told to amuse his children of adventures in the Alps—but accidents only happened, he would explain, if you were so foolish as to disobey your guides—or of those long walks, after one of which, from Cambridge to London on a hot day, "I drank, I am sorry to say, rather more than was good for me," were told very briefly, but with a curious power to impress the scene. The things that he did not say were always there in the background. So, (5) too, though he seldom told anecdotes, and his memory for facts was bad, when he described a person—and he had known many people, both famous and obscure—he would convey exactly what he thought of him in two or three words. And what he thought might be the opposite of what other people thought. He had a way of upsetting established reputations and disregarding conventional values that could be disconcerting, and sometimes perhaps wounding, although no one was more respectful of any feeling that seemed to him genuine. But when, suddenly opening (10) his bright blue eyes and rousing himself from what had seemed complete abstraction, he gave his opinion, it was difficult to disregard it. It was a habit, especially when deafness made him unaware that this opinion could be heard, that had its inconveniences.

1. All of the following character attributes may be made of the story subject except

    A. sincerity.

    B. timidity.

    C. forgetfulness.

    D. brevity.

    E. respectful.

2. What is meant by "inconveniences" in line (12)?

    A. He often did not wait his turn to speak when involved with group discussions.

    B. He spoke loudly after his becoming deaf.

    C. His deafness caused him experience a slurred speech.

    D. Due to his affliction, he forgot what he said could be heard by others.

    E. He stopped caring what others thought after he became deaf.

Questions 3–6 are based on the following passage.

If a man were to accost the first homely featured or plain-dressed young woman of his acquaintance, and tell her bluntly, that she was not handsome or rich enough for him, and he could not marry her, he would deserve to be kicked for his ill manners; yet not less is implied in the fact, that having access and opportunity of putting the question to her, he has never yet thought fit to do it. The young woman understands this as clearly as if it were put into
(5) words; but no reasonable young woman would think of making this the ground of a quarrel. Just as little right have a married couple to tell me by speeches, and looks that are scarce less plain than speeches, that I am not the happy man—the lady's choice. It is enough that I know I am not: I do not want this perpetual reminding.

3. How does the author choose to inform the reader that he does not wish to be reminded of his situation?

   A. by presenting an analogous situation with role reversals

   B. by simply stating that he does not want to be reminded of what he already knows

   C. by showing how easy it is for people to just say what they are thinking

   D. by inferring that all unmarried people are homely and poor and can expect no suitors

   E. by referencing looks and money as the only personal attributes necessary for happiness

4. What does the author mean in the phrase, "and looks that are scarce less plain than speeches," line (6)?

   A. People should say what is on their mind rather than just convey it in looks.

   B. It is impolite to not say what you are trying to convey with looks.

   C. You don't need to say anything if your looks are clearly understood.

   D. Looks may convey almost the exact meaning as words.

   E. Words are the best way to fully communicate because looks can be misunderstood.

5. What is the overall theme of this passage?

   A. The verbalization of certain acts or omissions may be considered more rude than those same acts or omissions thereof.

   B. It is rude for people to convey to the author by simple looks that they know he is not a happily married man and probably won't be for some time, if ever.

   C. It is better to say what is on your mind in order to reduce the risk of someone misunderstanding a look or a gesture.

   D. Looks can hurt just as much as words but words are better.

   E. It is rude not to propose if you are involved with someone for a period of time.

6. What does the author mean with the phrase, "putting the question to her," as used in line (3–4)?

   A. asking her whether he is handsome

   B. asking her whether she has money

   C. asking her to accept him the way he is

   D. asking her to marry him

   E. asking her for another date

Questions 7–10 are based on the following passage.

Of the wall [of China] it is very easy to assign the motives. It secured a wealthy and timorous nation from the incursions of the Barbarians, whose unskillfulness in arts made it easier for them to supply their wants by rapine than by industry, and who from time to time poured in upon the habitations of peaceful commerce, as vultures descend upon domestic fowl. Their celerity and fierceness made the wall necessary, and their ignorance made it efficacious.

(4)

7. What is the author inferring by comparing Barbarians pouring in upon the habitations of peaceful commerce as vultures descending upon domestic fowl?

   A.   Like the domestic fowl, only minimal skills at survival were needed as they are fed from their owners like citizens were fed by their government.
   B.   Barbarians were not really given the credit they deserved as they were able to cull out a living by pillaging.
   C.   Universally, good triumphs over evil given opportunity and condition for countermeasures.
   D.   Like the domestic fowl, civilized cultures lost their necessity for defense among themselves, and as a result, lost the skill to defend against intruders.
   E.   While fowl are all the same like humans, there are some good, and some bad.

8. In line (1), what is meant by the word "timorous" as used in this context?

   A.   harmonious
   B.   civilized
   C.   cultured
   D.   revered
   E.   fearful

9. In line (2), what is meant by the word "rapine" as used in this context?

   A.   accosting
   B.   exculpating
   C.   rampaging
   D.   acquiescing
   E.   plundering

10. In line (4), what is meant by the word "celerity" as used in this context?

   A.   prowess
   B.   efficiency
   C.   thoroughness
   D.   speed
   E.   agility

Answers and Explanations for Skill Set Four

1. The correct choice is **B.**

Explanation: The entire passage indicates that the subject character possessed all of the attributes except for timidity. On the contrary, he was very outspoken and at times, even embarrassingly so. Choice B is correct.

2. The correct choice is **D.**

Explanation: The author states that he gave his opinion freely as a habit, albeit sometimes injurious. His affliction of deafness only made the situation worse, causing "inconveniences" as his opinions were exposed even if he didn't realize anyone could hear him, making Choice D correct.

3. The correct choice is **A.**

Explanation: The author opens with a situational role reversal and proceeds to show how inappropriate the behavior presented would appear to any rational individual. He furthers that situation by offering the same posture on omitted speech that is simply reinforced through behavior. By establishing the argument using an analogous situation to his own, he is presenting his own argument for similar treatment as the initial victim, making Choice A correct.

4. The correct choice is **D.**

Explanation: The author clearly indicates that looks can communicate and often serve that purpose. However, there is the position in the statement that looks are "less plain" even if only scarcely less understood, making Choice D correct.

5. The correct choice is **A.**

Explanation: Choice A summarizes the passage in that verbalization of acts or omitted acts may be more rude than the acts or omissions themselves. This is correct as the author considers it ill mannered to ever vocalize the true meanings of certain acts, even if that vocalization is hidden within disparaging looks.

6. The correct choice is **D.**

Explanation: The reference is made to the purported acts of a man telling a woman why he could not marry her and thereby explaining why he had not, nor would not, ask her to marry him, making Choice D correct.

7. The correct choice is **D.**

Explanation: In using the simile of vultures descending upon domestic fowl, an inference is made to the domesticated Chinese whose lifestyle of peaceful commerce makes them easy prey for the Barbarians who only survive, as do the vultures, on the spoils of others. As the Barbarians exist off of the labors and stores of others, so do the vultures live from the labors and stores, or spoils, of others' acts. Choice D shows this parallel.

8. The correct choice is **E.**

Explanation: By using context clues such as the motives or reasons why the Chinese built the wall, the correct definition for timorous may be found. If the Chinese are suffering repeated incursions from the Barbarians, certainly they want to protect themselves from such attacks. As Barbarians are known for their destructive nature and disregard for human life, fear should be a primary consideration for the building of the wall, making Choice E more clearly recognized as correct.

9. The correct choice is **E.**

Explanation: Since the author used the phrase, "by rapine than by industry," we can see that there is an understood "rather" that informs us that a contrast in terms is being presented. The contrasting term is "industry," which is a positive, so we must look for a negative in the answer choices, and a term that is an antonym if possible. The best term in opposition to "industry" would be "plundering," which is to rob rather than produce oneself, making Choice E correct.

10. The correct choice is **D.**

Explanation: As the joining "and" is used in the phrase, "celerity and fierceness," we are looking for a complement to fierceness. All choices save D indicate a measure of intelligence or mastery. Using context clues gleaned from the last sentence, we know that the Barbarians were ignorant, indicating that all choices other than D, "speed," would be incorrect.

Short Reading Comprehension Skill Set Five

The passages below are followed by questions based on their content; questions following a pair of related passages may also be based on the relationship between the paired passages. Answer the questions on the basis of what is *stated* or *implied* in the passages and in any introductory material that may be provided.

Questions 1–5 are based on the following passage.

This aversion to noise I should explain as follows: If you cut up a large diamond into little bits, it will entirely lose the value it had as a whole; and an army divided up into small bodies of soldiers, loses all its strength. So a great intellect sinks to the level of an ordinary one; as soon as it is interrupted and disturbed, its attention distracted and drawn from the matter in hand; for its superiority depends upon its power of concentration—of bringing all its
(5)   strength to bear upon one theme, in the same way as a concave mirror collects into one point all the rays of light that strike upon it. Noisy interruption is a hindrance to concentration. That is why distinguished minds have always shown such an extreme dislike to disturbance in any form, as something that breaks in upon and distracts their thoughts. Above all have they been averse to that violent interruption that comes from noise. Ordinary people are not much put out by anything of the sort. The most sensible and intelligent of all nations in Europe lays down the
(10)   rule, Never Interrupt! as the eleventh commandment. Noise is the most impertinent of all forms of interruption. It is not only an interruption, but also a disruption of thought. Of course, where there is nothing to interrupt, noise will not be so particularly painful. Occasionally, it happens that some slight but constant noise continues to bother and distract me for a time before I become distinctly conscious of it. All I feel is a steady increase in the labor of thinking—just as though I were trying to walk with a weight on my foot. At last I find out what it is.

1. The main idea of the passage is

   A. noise destroys concentration of those with great minds.
   B. those who lack concentration and dominion over noise are not great thinkers.
   C. non-discernable noise does not affect the thinker like discernable noise.
   D. less intelligent people don't have the mental strength to bear noise.
   E. noise levels are directly proportional to the thought process and production.

2. According to the passage, superiority of a "great intellect" is dependent upon which of the following?

   A. an uninterrupted period of time to reflect
   B. silence
   C. an environment conducive to nondistracted attention
   D. power of concentration
   E. observational abilities

3. Which of the following terms best describes the author's feeling regarding noise?

   A. reservation
   B. inconvenience
   C. ordination
   D. subliminal
   E. disdain

4. According to the passage, people that are not disturbed much by noise are considered

   A. inordinate.
   B. moderate.
   C. focused.
   D. superior.
   E. ordinary.

5. What can we infer that the author feels about people not greatly hindered by noise?

   A. They are of the most superior intellects as they possess the ability to ignore noise and not give in to the interruption to thought normal people would.
   B. They do not possess a great intellect albeit they are able to cope with interruption from noise.
   C. They could gain a greater intellect if noise bothered them and broke their concentration.
   D. They have developed a defense mechanism that allows them to not take offense at noise or when they are otherwise interrupted.
   E. They are not given to reaction from what ordinary people would let bother them such as noise.

Questions 6–10 are based on the following passage.

The plan which I adopted, and the one by which I was most successful, was that of making friends of all the little white boys whom I met in the street. As many of these as I could, I converted into teachers. With their kindly aid, obtained at different times and in different places, I finally succeeded in learning to read. When I was sent on errands, I always took my book with me, and by going one part of my errand quickly, I found time to get a lesson
(5) before my return. I used also to carry bread with me, enough of which was always in the house, and to which I was always welcome for I was much better off in this regard than many of the poor white children in our neighborhood. This bread I used to bestow upon the hungry little urchins, who, in turn, would give me treat more valuable bread of knowledge. I am strongly tempted to give the names of two or three of those little boys, as testimonial of gratitude and affection I bear them; but prudence forbids; not that it would injure me, but it might embarrass them; for
(10) it is almost an unpardonable offence to teach slaves to read in this Christian country. It is enough to say of the dear little fellows, that they live on Philpot Street, very near Durgin and Bailey's shipyard. I used to talk this matter of slavery over with them. I would sometimes say to them, I wished I could be as free as they would be when they got to be men. "You will be free as soon as you are twenty-one, but I am a slave for life! Have not I as good a right to be free as you have?" These words used to trouble them; they would express for me the liveliest sympathy, and con-
(15) sole me with the hope that something would occur by which I might be free.

6. What device did the author use to befriend the boys in the street?

   A. discussed the impropriety of slavery and implored them to help him escape

   B. befriended them by offering them money to teach him to read

   C. praised their superior intelligence so they would like him and teach him to read

   D. gave them food so they would be friends with him so he could ask them for help

   E. wooed them into a sense of ease before asking them for anything

7. What about the statement in lines (9–10), "for it is almost an unpardonable offence to teach slaves to read in this Christian country" qualifies as irony?

   A. Given the belief of Christians that you should treat others as you want to be treated, not to teach someone to read knowing that they wanted to learn to read would not qualify as Christian behavior.

   B. A slave wanted to know how to read and was willing to pay for lessons with bread when the white, free boys of the neighborhood knew how to read but didn't have enough bread to eat.

   C. The notion that any act would be "unpardonable" in a forgiving Christian society or country.

   D. The mention of any names of those who taught the author to read would likely get them in trouble or embarrass them because they didn't have as much food as the slave.

   E. Slaves could learn to read and were willing to pay handsomely to learn.

8. How does the author give credit to those who helped him learn to read?

   A. by talking to them about how he wished he could be free like them

   B. by not exposing their names as those who helped him learn to read would be frowned upon by the Christian country and they might be prosecuted for their actions

   C. by stating that he would like to list their names but as that might not be good for them, recognize them by indicating where they who helped had lived so they would know of his thanks

   D. by writing that the 'bread' he gave them was much less valuable than the 'bread of knowledge' they gave him

   E. by referring to them as "teachers"

9. What can the reader infer from the passage about the willingness of the white boys in helping the author learn to read?

   A. Without bread, friendships would have naturally developed leading some of the white boys to help the author learn to read.

   B. Knowledge of the white boys that a slave who could read would have a greater chance of being freed than one who could not read motivated them to help.

   C. Without some reason beyond friendship, the likelihood of them helping would be greatly reduced because teaching a slave to read was not accepted behavior.

   D. Knowing that the author could not read was security for the white boys continuing to get free bread as the author would not know whether what they were teaching was correct or not.

   E. Based on the passage, Christians were not supposed to help slaves learn to read so the white boys were not Christians.

10. Given the facts presented during the time in which the story in the passage takes place, which term best describes the setting?

   A. understandable

   B. unlikely

   C. usual

   D. normal

   E. likely

Answers and Explanations for Skill Set Five

1. The correct choice is **A.**

   Explanation: The passage establishes that "a great intellect sinks to the level of an ordinary one, as soon as it is interrupted and disturbed, its attention distracted and drawn of from the matter in hand." The passage relates interruptions or disturbances as noise. Finally, noise destroys concentration that the author attributes to a superior or great mind, making Choice A correct.

2. The correct choice is **D.**

   Explanation: The passage states, when referring to "great intellect," "its superiority depends upon its power of concentration," making Choice D correct.

3. The correct choice is **E.**

   Explanation: This is a reverse type vocabulary question wherein the best answer selection depends upon an initial understanding of the passage and then a selection of a word that correctly describes that interpretation. So passionate is this author about noise and its power or concentration, Choice E, "disdain" is the only plausible answer.

4. The correct choice is **E.**

   Explanation: Referring to noise, the passage states, "Ordinary people are not much put out by anything of the sort," making Choice E correct.

5. The correct choice is **B.**

   Explanation: Again, the passage states, "Ordinary people are not much put out by anything of the sort" when referring to noise. As ordinary people cannot possess superior intellect, Choice B is correct.

6. The correct choice is **D.**

   Explanation: The passage states, "I used also to carry bread with me, enough of which was always in the house, and to which I was always welcome for I was much better off in this regard than many of the poor white children in our neighborhood. This bread I used to bestow upon the hungry little urchins, who, in turn, would give me treat more valuable bread of knowledge." By feeding them, he would befriend them and make as many teachers as practical, making Choice D correct.

7. The correct choice is **A.**

   Explanation: The irony is that a country in which Christian beliefs are extolled, slavery exists, but is furthered by not following one of the basic tenets of faith wherein a believer is to do or perform acts to another as you would like done to you. Given a role reversal, certainly the Christian would want to learn to read, making for the irony and seeming contradiction of philosophy to deed. Answer Choice A supports this irony.

8. The correct choice is **C.**

   Explanation: The author goes about as far as possible without exposing actual names. It can be inferred that the author does this in order to recognize those who helped him without wanting them to suffer misfortunes for the act nor suffer any potential embarrassment from the knowledge that they accepted bread from a slave, making Choice C correct.

9. The correct choice is **C.**

   Explanation: As risk generally requires some reward, the reward of bread offset the risk involved with befriending a slave particularly given required lessons in reading. It is, therefore, unlikely that without this incentive, the likelihood of the white boys' participation would have been greatly diminished, making Choice C correct.

10. The correct choice is **B.**

   Explanation: As we are told that slavery still exists during this time, it is "unlikely," Choice B, that there would be whites and slaves living in the same neighborhood. The setting seems incongruent with the time established for this passage.

Short Reading Comprehension Skill Set Six

The passages below are followed by questions based on their content; questions following a pair of related passages may also be based on the relationship between the paired passages. Answer the questions on the basis of what is *stated* or *implied* in the passages and in any introductory material that may be provided.

Questions 1–5 are based on the following passage.

The second preliminary point which I wish to make is the unimportance—indeed the evil—of barren knowledge. The importance of knowledge lies in its use, in our active mastery of it—that is to say, it lies in wisdom. It is a convention to speak of mere knowledge, apart from wisdom, as of itself imparting a peculiar dignity to its possessor. I do not share in this reverence for knowledge as such. It all depends on who has the knowledge and what
(5) he does with it. That knowledge which adds greatness to character is knowledge so handled as to transform every phase of immediate experience. It is in respect to the activity of knowledge that an over-vigorous discipline in education is so harmful. The habit of active thought, with freshness, can be generated only by adequate freedom. Undiscriminating discipline defeats its own object by dulling the mind. If you have much to do with the young as they emerge from school and from the university, you soon note the dulled minds of those whose education has
(10) consisted in the acquirement of inert knowledge. Also the deplorable tone of English society in respect to learning is a tribute to our educational failure. Furthermore, this over-haste to impart mere knowledge defeats itself. The human mind rejects knowledge imparted in this way. The craving for expansion, for activity, inherent in youth is disgusted by a dry imposition of disciplined knowledge. The discipline, when it comes, should satisfy a natural craving for the wisdom which adds value to bare experience.

1. The author's attitude toward knowledge without use can best be described as one of

    A. tolerance for the acquisition of knowledge for knowledge sake as it is in the seeking of knowledge that wisdom is developed.

    B. total disdain for not gaining as much knowledge as possible because without the acquisition of knowledge, wisdom in the use therein is not possible.

    C. absolute rejection based upon such beliefs that disciplined knowledge without a practical application, or use, is but a convention.

    D. disciplined knowledge is best gained through formal educational endeavors allowing for the practical application and use thereof.

    E. the discipline of gaining knowledge is paramount to the exercise of wisdom.

2. According to the author, "disciplined knowledge" provides for

    A. the active mastery of a given subject wherein one may employ wisdom

    B. freedoms to act with discriminating discernment.

    C. a satisfying of a natural craving for knowledge without limitation.

    D. an educational hierarchy wherein the discipline can manifest itself in wisdom.

    E. a dulling of the mind if not properly directed.

3. According to the author, the difference between "inert" and "active" as it relates to knowledge is best described as

    A. knowledge for knowledge sake versus knowledge put to use in any given discipline.

    B. knowledge learned for future versus knowledge needed to use today.

    C. stored knowledge in specific categories versus general knowledge applied uniformly.

    D. knowledge gained through school versus knowledge gained through life experiences.

    E. conversational knowledge versus written knowledge.

4. The general belief about our educational system as related by the author is

A. it is the primary area for development of use-oriented knowledge.

B. it is more of a problem when imparting knowledge for knowledge sake.

C. it teaches knowledge for ready activation and use in daily situations.

D. it provides a basis for continuing to expand a practical knowledge base.

E. it does not provide sufficient opportunities for gaining knowledge.

5. What is the best selection to convey the author's meaning in the sentence, "Undiscriminating discipline defeats its own object by dulling the mind," line (8)?

A. The discipline of gaining knowledge creates an opportunity to keep the mind sharp through the addition of even more knowledge.

B. Knowledge gained through any avenues other than those gained in a disciplined environment such as a university serve no purpose and will negatively affect the mind.

C. The objective of discipline is lost when discipline and knowledge is sought randomly.

D. The discipline of securing knowledge without application fills the mind with useless facts, therefore dulling it.

E. Without discipline, the obtaining of the object of knowledge is barren.

Questions 6–10 are based on the following passage.

On the other side, heat and vivacity in age is an excellent composition for business. Young men are fitter to invent than to judge, fitter for execution than for counsel, and fitter for new projects than for settled business. For the experience of age, in things that fall within the compass of it, directeth them, but in new things abuseth them. The errors of young men are the ruin of business; but the errors of aged men amount but to this, that more might have been done, or
(5)   sooner. Young men, in the conduct and manage of actions, embrace more than they can hold; stir more than they can quiet; fly to the end, without consideration of the means and degrees; pursue some few principles which they have chanced upon absurdly; care not to innovate, which draws inconveniences; use extreme remedies at first; and, that which doubleth all errors, will not acknowledge or retract them; like an unready horse that will neither stop nor turn.

6. What does the author mean in line (1–2) when he writes, "Young men are fitter to invent than to judge, fitter for execution than for counsel, and fitter for new projects than for settled business"?

A. Young men are better thinkers, doers, and at established projects than older men.

B. Older men are better suited to assess, counsel, and new venture determination.

C. Young men are better thinkers and doers but older men launch new projects more effectively.

D. Older men are better at assessing and counseling but younger men are better with established business.

E. The young are better suited for those areas demanding less wisdom, less negotiation, and more physical exertion.

7. What does the author mean in line (2–3) when he writes, "For the experience of age, in things that fall within the compass of it, directeth them, but in new things abuseth them"?

A. Experience learned over time may be insightful when dealing with new areas as historical knowledge may be applied to these new areas.

B. New experiences may be an actual detriment when it comes to items involving new areas.

C. New experiences can refresh business direction rather than relying upon past lessons learned.

D. Experience learned over time may be usefully applied in areas where the experience was learned but becomes a hindrance when new areas are encountered.

E. Lessons from the past will direct forward steps as learned experiences are drawn from in order to direct the future.

8. As established in the passage, which comparative would best describe the assessment of young to older men in business?

   A. methodical versus hardened

   B. stately versus rambunctious

   C. diplomatic versus harried

   D. extreme versus irrational

   E. brash versus seasoned

9. What does the author mean with the phrase, "like an unready horse that will neither stop nor turn," line (8)?

   A. He is comparing a young man to a horse that is either too young or has not been adequately trained and therefore will not yield or follow instruction.

   B. He is praising the tenacity of the young man who does not stop even though he may be tired and he does not turn from his assigned duties.

   C. He is likening the young man to a horse that while is not yet ready to fully conduct business as a seasoned older man, he is listing some of the qualities that a young man possesses.

   D. He means that the young man is like a horse that is not yet ready to ride or work because he has not been prepared by the seasoned older man yet but once started will not let his trainer down.

   E. He is saying that the young man is not yet ready for instruction and should be assigned new projects where he can use his youth and vitality exclusively.

10. What is the main idea of the passage?

   A. There is a certain business savvy that can be accomplished only over time.

   B. There is more opportunity for business success when young men control.

   C. There is little need to keep older men beyond their current projects.

   D. Retention of older men preserves the newness of the business to older clients.

   E. New strategies and ventures are best implemented with the younger men in control.

Answers and Explanations for Skill Set Six

1. The correct choice is **C**.

   Explanation: Of knowledge, the author states, "It all depends on who has the knowledge and what he does with it." Without application—wisdom—knowledge is useless if acquired for the sake of acquisition. Answer Choice C is correct.

2. The correct choice is **E**.

   Explanation: The author exposes the error of seeking knowledge for knowledge sake. As "disciplined knowledge" is that which is related to the acquisition of knowledge through acquiring inert knowledge through our universities, the author states that you will note as you encounter this youth, "you soon note the dulled minds of those whose education has consisted in the acquirement of inert knowledge," making Choice E correct.

3. The correct choice is **A**.

   Explanation: The author explains that those whose education consisted in the acquirement of "inert" knowledge through discipline only serves to dull the mind wherein active knowledge ". . .adds greatness to character. . ." and, ". . .is so handled as to transform every phase of immediate experience." Choice A best explains this relationship.

4. The correct choice is **B**.

   Explanation: The author attributes the push toward the "undiscriminating discipline" or "inert knowledge" as "our educational failure" wherein universities are "over-vigorous" in imparting knowledge without the freedom to exercise or employ meaningfully that knowledge, making them more of the problem as identified in Choice B.

5. The correct choice is **D**.

   Explanation: Questions like this on SAT are really asking you to parse information and put it into different words that convey the same meaning. Since the author considers any knowledge other than that which is actively put to use as wasted because it fills the mind with nonapplicable knowledge, which dulls the mind, making Choice D appropriate.

6. The correct choice is **E**.

   Explanation: This is another question asking for interpretation. Following each step with the alternate word choices will lead to the correct choice. Analyzing Choice E, we see that since wisdom is an attribute given to judging, young men would need less wisdom. As counseling requires excellent negotiation skills, young men need less negotiation skills. Finally, as a settled business requires less strain and physical exertion than a new project, young men are better suited for this extra physical need. The combination of relationships and word comparisons makes Choice E best.

7. The correct choice is **D**.

   Explanation: Yet another interpretation question. Following the logical progression, "For the experience of age" or experience learned over time; "in things that fall within the compass of it directeth them" or may be usefully applied in areas where the experience was learned; "but in new things abuseth them" or but becomes a hindrance when new areas are encountered. This progression leads us to the best Choice D.

8. The correct choice is **E**.

   Explanation: Here, we look for a single word to summarize the author's perspective of a young man versus an older man as it relates to the business world related in the passage. Choice E, "brash verses seasoned," best reflects the author's view of each. As a reminder, young men, "fly to the end, without consideration of the means and degrees" versus older men whose, "heat and vivacity in age is an excellent composition for business."

9. The correct choice is **A.**

Explanation: Horses that have not been broken (generally because they are too young), have not yet learned to take instruction, and will not stop or return as directed. The parallel is to the young man in business who, not as yet fully instructed in the ways to conduct business, hasn't learned the guiding instruction from the seasoned older man. Choice A most closely reflects the author's view.

10. The correct choice is **A.**

Explanation: The author opens with a position of need for the older aged individual in business, and Choice A best reflects that position, which is continuously developed throughout the passage.

Short Reading Comprehension Skill Set Seven

The passages below are followed by questions based on their content; questions following a pair of related passages may also be based on the relationship between the paired passages. Answer the questions on the basis of what is *stated* or *implied* in the passages and in any introductory material that may be provided.

Questions 1–5 are based on the following passage.

Perhaps the quickest way to understand the elements of what a novelist is doing is not to read, but to write; to make your own experiment with the dangers and difficulties of words. Recall, then, some event that has left a distinct impression on you—how at the corner of the street, perhaps, you passed two people talking. A tree shook; an electric light danced; the tone of the talk was comic, but also tragic; a whole vision, an entire conception, seemed
(5)   contained in that moment.

But when you attempt to reconstruct it in words, you will find that it breaks into a thousand conflicting impressions. Some must be subdued; others emphasized; in the process you will lose, probably, all grasp upon the emotion itself. Then turn from your blurred and littered pages to the opening pages of some great novelist—Defoe, Jane Austen, Hardy. Now you will be better able to appreciate their mastery.

1. Which of the following best reflects the author's purpose for writing this passage?

   A. to instruct the reader how to write as a master

   B. to inform the reader that writing is a process requiring plot

   C. to suggest ways to better enjoy the reading material of the masters

   D. to help the reader better appreciate the toils involved in writing

   E. to assist a new writer in better understanding what a novelist goes through

2. Why would the author suggest writing would encounter, "dangers and difficulties of words," line (2)?

   A. As an experienced writer, she knows all too well, the dangers and difficulties encountered when trying to convey a specific vision, emotion, or experience.

   B. In order to dissuade people from taking up a profession in writing that would serve only to create more competition in an already maximized field.

   C. Choosing the wrong words can cause animosity and stir emotions leading to a dangerous situation.

   D. Partially due to a lack of understanding of how specific styles are developed with words and what trouble they can get the writer in.

   E. Often the specific choice of words an author uses can convey double meanings that can get the author into some trouble with publishers.

3. What does the author say, "breaks into a thousand conflicting impressions," lines (6 and 7)?

   A. the words you are attempting to reconstruct

   B. the event that you experienced

   C. the emotion you are trying to recapture and convey

   D. the entire setting as it is fractioned

   E. the overall intonation due to the complexity of the process

4. Why does the author call your pages, "blurred and littered," line (8)?

   A. because she understands that anyone going through this process will enjoy the experience to such a degree that they will litter the floor with page after page and will write until their vision blurs

   B. because she believes the task assigned is of such difficulty that pages will blur and corrections will fully litter the pages

   C. because she understands the inherent love of writing and can envision the work area of the novice writer just beginning to enjoy the experience

   D. because she believes it will take the novice writer sufficient time to complete the task at hand that they will have eaten at their desk littering everywhere

   E. because she understands that most beginning writers will not be a neat as experienced masters

5. Why doesn't the author suggest the reader simply read more masters to gain an appreciation of their art?

   A.   The author understands that reading would take such a long time before a partial understanding of the process could be understood and people would give up on learning.

   B.   The author realizes that in order to truly understand the process a good writer goes through requires being with him/her as they formulate a storyline.

   C.   The author knows that the passages written by masters are much too difficult for the reader to understand how it was developed.

   D.   The author wants the reader to know how easy it is to get confused when you try to write.

   E.   The author believes teaching the elements a great novelist employs is best done through experiencing the process as the author does.

Questions 6–10 are based on the following passage.

Being told I would be expected to talk here, I inquired what sort of a talk I ought to make. They said it should be something suitable to youth—something didactic, instructive, or something in the nature of good advice. Very well. I have a few things in my mind which I have often longed to say for the instruction of the young; for it is one's tender early years that such things will best take root and be most enduring and most valuable. First, then, I will say to
(5)   you, my young friends—and I say it beseechingly, urgingly—

Always obey your parents, when they are present. This is the best policy in the long run, because if you don't they will make you. Most parents think they know better than you do, and you can generally make more by humoring that superstition than you can by acting on your own better judgment.

6. As used in line (2), the term "didactic" most nearly means which of the following

   A.   intended to be inspirational

   B.   received as comical

   C.   seen as fatherly

   D.   teaching a moral lesson

   E.   sharing an informational experience

7. What device does the author decide to use to present his talk?

   A.   irony

   B.   humor

   C.   satire

   D.   inference

   E.   logic

8. Why does the author suggest that it is "superstition" that "parents think they know better than you do," line (7)?

   A. The author is preparing the audience for his presentation of modern day superstitions and he is hopeful this engagement will help keep their attention.

   B. The author understands the importance of keeping an audience actively listening and by acknowledging that the statement is ludicrous, he aligns his thoughts to those of the audience.

   C. The author is making light of the proposition that parents might know more than youth which helps captivate the audience allowing the speaker to make his actual points.

   D. The author appreciates that less than 10 percent of what is spoken is retained by the listener unless the listener is entertained.

   E. The author notices that the audience is very young and in order to make a lasting impression, revelations of this nature are imperative.

9. How does the author suggest the young might make more as it relates to the main instruction given in the speech?

   A. by obeying parents when they are present and reserving your own actions until you are not with them

   B. by agreeing that they know much more than you and provide superior advice

   C. by playing along and fostering the idea that parents know better than you

   D. by setting rules that you are no longer subject to their charge and act independently

   E. by acknowledging that you live in a dichotomous world with divergent aspirations

10. What likely would have been the audience response to the speaker's beseeching and urging?

   A. As the audience was young, it is likely they would have wondered what the words meant and listened attentively.

   B. Without further instruction, the audience response would have likely been one of completely ignoring the speaker, unless their parents were present.

   C. It is unlikely they would have listened to their neighbor and been attentive to the speaker.

   D. Given the pre-established notion that the speech would be instructive, it is likely the audience would have diverted their attention.

   E. As a result of the speaker sharing the background of how he came to speak to the group, they likely would have already determined what the speech would be about and began talking to neighbors.

Answers and Explanations for Skill Set Seven

1. The correct choice is **D.**

Explanation: Perhaps there is no better way to appreciate another person's craft than to try to replicate it. The author provides instruction for a reader to attempt to ply the writer's craft in order to better teach what has happened before the reader sees it on the page. Choice D specifically matches this point.

2. The correct choice is **A.**

Explanation: Choice A captures the rationale from the passage reflecting the difficulties in the craft of writing and capturing the specific mood, emotion, tone, clarity, and so on.

3. The correct choice is **B.**

Explanation: Here, we simply trace back the reference until we find the source. In this case, you are reconstructing in words everything you experienced in that moment: the event, in this case, at the corner of the street. Choice B is correct.

4. The correct choice is **B.**

Explanation: As a writer who has experienced the difficulties in relating an event, she is fully aware of the trials and tribulations awaiting the young writer. It is with this clarity of vision that she can see the future chaos and disarray certain to befall all novice writers, making Choice B correct.

5. The correct choice is **E.**

Explanation: The author basically informs us in the first sentence that she believes that, "Perhaps the quickest way to understand the elements of what a novelist is doing is not to read, but to write. . ." supporting Choice E.

6. The correct choice is **D.**

Explanation: Given the still serious nature of the passage at this point, a standard definition as used in context would be the correct choice as opposed to some double entendre. In this regard, Choice D, "teaching a moral lesson" is correct.

7. The correct choice is **B.**

Explanation: Although the author clearly demonstrates wit, wit is not among the possible selections. A closely related tactic is Choice B, "humor."

8. The correct choice is **C.**

Explanation: Choice C furthers the author's use of humor to keep the audience engaged while delivering his original message in such a fashion as to help keep them focused. By making light of the proposition that there is superstition involved, he furthers his own cause of delivering a meaningful message.

9. The correct choice is **C.**

Explanation: It is necessary to first determine what the main instruction is and then determine what the author suggests the reader might make more off of it. Choice C relates the idea in the passage of "humoring" the superstition concerning parents knowing better than their children.

10. The correct choice is **D.**

Explanation: Universal truths are generally not considered prior knowledge as it relates to SAT. In this case, the forgone conclusion that youth will readily divert their attention the moment their interest drifts is the given. Since the speaker already informed the audience the what and what for, it is likely their attention has already been diverted, making Choice D correct.

Short Reading Comprehension Skill Set Eight

The passages below are followed by questions based on their content; questions following a pair of related passages may also be based on the relationship between the paired passages. Answer the questions on the basis of what is *stated* or *implied* in the passages and in any introductory material that may be provided.

Questions 1–10 are based on the following passages.

Passage 1

We love, we dearly love our country, and it is due to your honorable bodies, as well as to us, to make known why we think the country is ours, and why we wish to remain in peace where we are.

The land on which we stand we have received as an inheritance from our fathers, who possessed it from time im-memorial, as a gift from our common Father in Heaven. We have already said, that, when the white man came to (5) the shore of America, our ancestors were found in peaceable possession of this very land. They bequeathed it to us as their children, and we have sacredly kept it, as containing the remains of our beloved men. This right of inheri-tance we have *never ceded,* nor ever *forfeited.* Permit us to ask, what better right can the people have to a country, than the right of *inheritance* and *immemorial peaceable possession?* We know it is said of late by the State of Georgia, and the Executive of the United States, that we have forfeited this right—but we think this is said gratu-(10) itously. At what time have we made the forfeit? What great crime have we committed, whereby we must forever be divested of our country and rights?

Passage 2

When centuries hence, (as it must, in my opinion, be centuries hence before the life of these States, or of Democracy, can be really written and illustrated) the leading historians and dramatists seek for some personage, some special event, incisive enough to mark with deepest cut, and mnemonize, this turbulent nineteenth century of (15) ours, (not only these States, but all over the political and social world)—something, perhaps, to close that gorgeous procession of European feudalism, with all its pomp and caste prejudices, (of whose long train we in America are yet so inextricably the heirs)—something to identify with terrible identification, by far the greatest revolutionary step in the history of the United States, (perhaps the greatest of the world, our century)—the absolute extirpation and erasure of slavery from the States—those historians will seek in vain for any point to serve more thoroughly (20) their purpose, than Abraham Lincoln's death.

1. Which of the following best describes the position of the author in Passage 1?

A. entreating
B. placating
C. placid
D. demonstrative
E. indifferent

2. What does the author mean in the phrase, "and it is due to your honorable bodies" Passage 1, line (1)?

A. because of your government
B. creates an obligation to discuss
C. is a question of ownership
D. qualifies a division of two sides
E. presents an individual perspective

3. The reference to "our common Father in Heaven" Passage 1 line (4) is used to

   A. declare the false claims of the authorities

   B. establish a common basis point of reference

   C. present a position of civilization instead of savagery

   D. confirm their belief in a supreme being

   E. disavow any rights predicated upon a universal being

4. What is the significance of the phrase, "sacredly kept it" Passage 1 line (6)?

   A. suggests the white man only had interest in the land for commerce

   B. creates a relationship to the earlier reference to "Father in Heaven"

   C. qualifies the relationship of nature to Indians

   D. alleviates the common belief that Indians were only savage creatures

   E. established the importance of the land as containing remains of ancestors

5. The purpose of Passage 2 is to

   A. establish the general understanding and need for slavery.

   B. expose the faults of Europe and the relationship to America.

   C. qualify the use of slavery as a stepping stone in the history of America.

   D. establish the errant ways of early America as it relates to enslaving men.

   E. compare the ills of Europe with the feudalist methods employed in early America.

6. What best describes the author's position on slavery in Passage 2?

   A. Slavery was an extension of European feudalism and necessary for the development of early America.

   B. America was developed in the pattern of European feudalism and slavery was simply a byproduct of that development.

   C. Slavery was a complete and total ill and the eradication of this practice sets America apart from European ideology.

   D. America tolerated slavery only as long as necessary for development and growth.

   E. From a historical perspective, slavery was a dark period, albeit justified predicated upon ancestry.

7. The author of Passage 2 suggests which event was responsible for the growth beyond feudalism in early America?

   A. the passage of time away from the control of European alliance

   B. the recognition that the feudalistic way of life was a historical blight

   C. the demarcation of abolishment of slavery historically tied to Lincoln's death

   D. the realization that Democracy could not be realized so long as slavery was existent

   E. the understanding that historical alliances with European feudalism could not prevail

8. Which of the following best describes the author's feeling about European feudalism in Passage 2?

   A. full of arrogance and segregation of classes

   B. matured as a society but unfit for early America

   C. hierarchical governance with appreciable maintenance of class separations

   D. dominantly appropriate for an established and mature society

   E. a natural procession beginning with feudalism and progressing to Democracy

9. How would the author of Passage 1 most likely align with the position of Passage 2?

   A. appreciation for the change of heart evidenced by a country to free slaves and an appreciation that their plight was sufficiently different to warrant dissimilar actions

   B. understanding that the times had changed and the hearts of men opened to the acceptance of the full development of a Democracy

   C. disdain that slaves should be freed then their people were still kept in a kind of slavery by being ostracized

   D. discontentment that the government would not see the red man at least equal to the black man as opposed to the red man being a savage and the black man being worthy of freedom

   E. disbelief that the governance who had the compassion to free slaves had the cruelty to take the land of their forefathers, the land of their birthright

10. Which of the following statements best represents the position of Passage 1 and Passage 2, respectively?

   A. Passage 1 is presenting a case for retaining land and Passage 2 is celebrating freed slaves being able to acquire land.

   B. Passage 1 seeks justification for the rights of ownership of someone else's land wherein Passage 2 questions the ownership rights of another individual.

   C. Passage 1 represents that man cannot be separated from his land and therefore taking one is to enslave the other where Passage 2 separates the freed slave and provides for him the opportunity to join with land.

   D. Passage 1 presents freedoms lost and Passage 2 presents freedoms won.

   E. Passage 1 presents questions for justification of the acts of the government and Passage 2 condemns the government for their acts albeit regarding separate issues.

Answers and Explanations for Skill Set Eight

1. The correct choice is **A**.

Explanation: Although Choice D, "demonstrative," would have been generally understood, the position of the author is best identified with Choice A, "entreating," as they were asking for help in understanding the actions of the government as it related to the taking of their heritage, their land.

2. The correct choice is **B**.

Explanation: The author is basically saying we owe it to you and to ourselves to tell you why we believe the land, this country, is rightly ours, making Choice B, "creates an obligation to discuss," correct.

3. The correct choice is **B**.

Explanation: Choices C and D, "present a position of civilization instead of savagery" and "confirm their belief in a supreme being," sound feasible. This would do little to further the position of rightful ownership as it creates no common ground or set of rules by which to engage. By establishing a common basis point of reference that gives very specific direction regarding proper behavior, that being a supreme being, the presenters of the argument act from a logical position of strength. If we share the same God, wouldn't He want what is best for both of us? Further, if we share the same God, we can't be the savage and deserve to be treated as equal men in the sight of our common God. Choice B is correct.

4. The correct choice is **E**.

Explanation: Burial grounds are sacred grounds in effectively all civilizations. By including the land as ancestral burial grounds of forefathers since the beginning of time, the land becomes sacred and hallowed. The understood argument is that if it is taken, those who take it desecrate the land and offend the common God. Choice E presents this position.

5. The correct choice is **D**.

Explanation: Passage 2 chastises the country for her actions collectively as it relates to condoning slavery and praises Lincoln's commitment and sacrifice in order to abolish same, making Choice D correct.

6. The correct choice is **C**.

Explanation: Criticism of early America following European feudalism was a common theme throughout the passage. This lead to the adoption of slavery and not until the final abolishment of this practice did America gain separation from the misguided practices of Europe, making Choice C correct.

7. The correct choice is **C**.

Explanation: Passage 2 states, ". . .the absolute extirpation and erasure of slavery from the States—those historians will seek in vain for any point to serve more thoroughly their purpose, that Abraham Lincoln's death" thus praising the and directly relating the abolishment of slavery to Lincoln, making Choice C correct.

8. The correct choice is **A**.

Explanation: The author has nothing positive or even neutral to say about this type governance, effectively alleviating all choices but A.

9. The correct choice is **E**.

Explanation: This is a question calling for speculation but based on facts as presented in the respective passages. On the one hand, the government is set on taking ownership of land tantamount to invasion and conquering whereas on the other hand, a government accepts that slavery is inappropriate and rights this wrong. Surely, the question of why one and not the other must arise as disbelief; therefore, Choice E.

10. The correct choice is **E**.

Explanation: Nowhere in Passage 2 does it present the ability or right of freed slaves to acquire land so Choice A is wrong. Passage 2 doesn't actually question the rights of ownership of another individual; it condemns the practice and praises the overturning of it, making Choice B incorrect. Like Choice A, Choice C indicates that Passage 2 provides for the freed slave to acquire land making it an incorrect choice. Choice D is too simplistic to be the best answer. Although it is accurate, Choice E more fully reflects the comparison between the two passages.

Short Reading Comprehension Skill Set Nine

The passages below are followed by questions based on their content; questions following a pair of related passages may also be based on the relationship between the paired passages. Answer the questions on the basis of what is *stated* or *implied* in the passages and in any introductory material that may be provided.

Questions 1–5 are based on the following passage.

> I shall now therefore humbly propose my own thoughts, which I hope will not be liable to the least objection.
>
> I have been assured by a very knowing American of my acquaintance in London, that a young healthy child well nursed is at a year old a most delicious, nourishing and wholesome food, whether stewed, roasted, baked or boiled; and I make no doubt that it will equally serve in a fricassee or a ragout.
>
> (5)   I do therefore humbly offer it to public consideration that of the hundred and twenty thousand children, already computed, twenty thousand may be reserved for breed, whereof only one fourth part to be males, which is more than we allow to sheep, black cattle, or swine; and my reason is that these children are seldom the fruits of marriage, a circumstance not much regarded by our savages, therefore one male will be sufficient to serve four females. That the remaining hundred thousand may at a year old be offered in sale to the persons of quality and fortune
>
> (10)   through the kingdom, always advising the mother to let them suck plentifully in the last month, so as to render them plump and fat for a good table. A child will make two dishes at an entertainment for friends; and when the family dines alone, the fore or hind quarter will make a reasonable dish, and seasoned with a little pepper or salt will be very good boiled on the fourth day, especially in winter.

1. This type of writing is known as

    A. an extended metaphor.

    B. irony.

    C. argumentative.

    D. informational.

    E. satire.

2. Why does the author begin with the line, "I shall now therefore humbly propose my own thoughts, which I hope will not be liable to the least objection" line (1)?

    A. Knowing what he is about to present, the author wishes to establish the tone of the passage immediately, knowing that there will be major objections to what he is about to present.

    B. Recognizing that the proposal holds merit, the author is reconfirming his belief that the proposition he is about to deliver will satisfy the needs of the community.

    C. Appreciating that there will be some small children in the audience, he is warning the adults that there should be no tolerance for any child crying out in objection to the proposal.

    D. He is about to present a rather controversial position on a serious issue and knows that because a portion of his justification is based on the word of an American, knows some will try to object.

    E. Given the sensitivity of new mothers, he anticipates that some will try to object to his position and he wants to control these objections until the elders can fully hear and appreciate the rationale for this plan.

3. Which of the following best reflects how the author presents his plan to the audience?

    A. in a humorous manner

    B. in a way as to get people rallied behind the plan

    C. in a matter-of-fact tone

    D. with reserved indignation

    E. with giddy excitement about the prospects of success

4. The presenter rationalizes the plan in all of the following except

    A. by noting that an American friend confirms the results.

    B. by providing actual numbers in support of the plan.

    C. by providing that older children could be sold at discount.

    D. by comparing actual numbers to what works for sheep, cattle and swing.

    E. by offering a diet plan go gain the fullest measure from the plan.

5. Which of the following best represents the author's view of society?

    A. accepting given the state of impoverishment

    B. lacking in morals primarily due to lack of education and apathy

    C. lethargic and unwilling to work or study to improve their lots in life

    D. currently in a state of moral degradation and whose practices are ruinous

    E. representational of governmental social programming

Questions 6–7 are based on the following passage.

Someone may say: there have been plenty of princes, very successful in warfare, who have had a reputation for generosity. But I answer: either the prince is spending his own money and that of his subjects, or he is spending someone else's. In the first case, he ought to be sparing; in the second case, he ought to spend money like water. Any prince at the head of his army, which lives on loot, extortion, and plunder, dispose of other people's property,
(5)   and is bound to be very generous; otherwise, his soldiers would desert him. You can always be a more generous giver when what you give is not yours or your subjects'; Cyrus, Caesar, and Alexander were generous in this way. Spending what belongs to other people does no harm to your reputation, rather it enhances it; only spending your own substance harms you. And there is nothing that wears out faster than generosity; even as you practice it, you lose the means of practicing it, and you become either poor and contemptible or (in the course of escaping poverty)
(10)   rapacious and hateful.

6. According to the passage, what information makes the first sentence, "Someone may say: there have been plenty of princes, very successful in warfare, who have had a reputation for generosity" lines (1–2) self-evident?

   A. The author tells us that one of the ways for a prince to be generous is to give away what personal wealth and that of his subjects.

   B. The author explains that generosity is easily achieved if you have sufficient means with which to be generous but if that reliance is upon what you or your subjects have instead of pillage, generosity will be short lived.

   C. The author informs that those giving away other's possessions are bound to be generous and since the prince presented in the first sentence is very successful, he must have plenty of other's possessions.

   D. The author takes the position that the important issue is to be considered as generous even if that is not the case.

   E. The author presents the position that in order for one to be generous, he must be a great warrior.

7. According to the article, what might cause desertion among soldiers?

   A. harsh living conditions without adequate food

   B. long periods of time away from family and home

   C. insufficient portion of bounty

   D. long periods of time without permanent shelter

   E. long stays in harsh elements and weather

Questions 8–10 are based on the following passage.

The history of mankind is a history of repeated injuries and usurpations on the part of many toward woman, having in direct object the establishment of an absolute tyranny over her. To prove this, let facts be submitted to a candid world.

He has never permitted her to exercise her inalienable right to the elective franchise.

He had compelled her to submit to laws, in the formation of which she had no voice.

(5)   He had withheld from her rights which are given the most ignorant and degraded men—both natives and foreigners.

Having deprived her of this first right of a citizen, the elective franchise, thereby leaving her without representation in the halls of legislation, he has oppressed her on all sides.

8. The primary purpose of the passage is to

   A. explain a situation.
   B. refute a common belief.
   C. propose a modification.
   D. predict an outcome or action.
   E. honor resilience of women.

9. As used in line (1), the word "usurpations" most nearly means

   A. to shackle with impunity.
   B. to force situations upon.
   C. to intimidate repeatedly.
   D. to confine in deed and thought.
   E. to restrict movement in membership.

10. The overall tone of the passage is

   A. critical.
   B. snide.
   C. curt.
   D. poignant.
   E. empathetic.

Answers and Explanations for Skill Set Nine

1. The correct choice is **E**.

Explanation: This is a clear case of satire, Choice E. There also is a goodly bit of irony, and if the connection been made relating the situation to some injustice, the writing might have been considered an extended metaphor.

2. The correct choice is **A**.

Explanation: As the presenter knows what he is about to deliver is satirical in nature, he wants to establish a tone of seriousness up front, and this opening is how he accomplished this objective, making Choice A correct.

3. The correct choice is **C**.

Explanation: Although Choice D sounds like a feasible choice, there is nothing indignant about his presentational style. Certainly, some will see that Choice A, "humorous," could fit but again, not in the way presented. Choice C, "in a matter-of-fact manner," is precisely the manner in which it is presented; in a pure businesslike, direct, make-sense type format.

4. The correct choice is **C**.

Explanation: The only selection that was not covered in the presentation was Choice C, the discounting of older children, presumably because their meat would be tougher.

5. The correct choice is **D**.

Explanation: Although several choices seem practical given the subject matter, only Choice D is actually supported in the passage. We are told that, "these children are seldom the fruits of marriage," indicating the moral degradation resulting from an overabundance of children to feed, thereby qualifying as ruinous practices in creating the problem.

6. The correct choice is **C**.

Explanation: If a prince is successful in warfare, as presented in the first sentence, then he will have ample stores from pillaging to afford to be generous, thereby being self-evident; Choice C.

7. The correct choice is **C**.

Explanation: The article states, "Any prince at the head of his army, which lives on loot, extortion, and plunder, dispose of other people's property, and is bound to be very generous; otherwise, his soldiers would desert him." This makes Choice C correct.

8. The correct choice is **A**.

Explanation: There is no call for action within the passage, no outward recommendation to change; only explaining an existing situation, making Choice A correct.

9. The correct choice is **B**.

Explanation: Although all answer choices are correct by extension, Choice B, "to force situations upon" most nearly defines "usurpations."

10. The correct choice is **A**.

Explanation: The author cannot be empathetic with the plight of a woman having never faced the circumstances from the female perspective, and although the facts themselves are poignant, the tone of the piece is "critical," making Choice A correct.

Short Reading Comprehension Skill Set Ten

The passages below are followed by questions based on their content; questions following a pair of related passages may also be based on the relationship between the paired passages. Answer the questions on the basis of what is *stated* or *implied* in the passages and in any introductory material that may be provided.

Questions 1–3 are based on the following passage.

Poetry begins in trivial metaphors, petty metaphors, "grace" metaphors, and goes on to the profoundest thinking that we have. Poetry provides the one permissible way of saying one thing and meaning another. People say, "Why don't you say what you mean?" We never do that, do we, being all of us too much poets. We like to talk in para-
(4) bles and in hints and in indirections—whether from diffidence or some other instinct.

1. What is the author's attitude toward the metaphor?

  A. It has become a customary tool.
  B. It is useful but overused.
  C. It allows the broadest range of thought.
  D. It stimulates writers to keep things simple.
  E. It offers an avenue of expression on only the simplest level.

2. Why does the author suggest we never say what we mean?

  A. because we do not want to hurt people's feelings by speaking too directly
  B. because we are a society based on principles that you should not hurt other's feelings
  C. because we are all poets and like to speak indirectly regardless of the catalyst
  D. because as poets, we speak in parables so no one else will understand
  E. because some of us are quiet and don't speak directly to others

3. What selection best describes the word "diffidence" line (4) as used in the passage?

  A. shyness
  B. consternation
  C. bewilderment
  D. reservations
  E. caution

Questions 4–5 are based on the following passage.

I went, therefore, to the shelf where the histories stand and took down one of the latest, professor Trevelyan's *History of England*. Once more I looked up Woman, found "position of," and turned to the pages indicated. "Wife-beating," I read, "was a recognized right of man, and was practiced without shame by high as well as low. . ." "Similarly," the historian goes on, "the daughter who refused to marry the gentleman of her parents' choice was
(5) liable to be locked up, beaten and flung about the room, without any shock being inflicted on public opinion. Marriage was not an affair of personal affection, but of family avarice, particularly in the 'chivalrous' upper classes. . . Betrothal often took place while one or both of the parties was in the cradle, and marriage when they were scarcely out of the nurses' charge." This was about 1470, soon after Chaucer's time. The next reference to the position of women is some two hundred years later, in the time of the Stuarts. "It was still the exception for women
(10) of the upper and middle class to choose their own husbands, and when the husband had been assigned, he was lord and master, so far at least as law and custom could make him."

4. What is the purpose of this passage?

A. to present models for adoption in today's society

B. to inform such as to ensure nonreturn to such practices

C. to educate on various ways women might expect to be treated

D. to suggest successful restrictions available for adoption

E. to empower women to take a stand for their rights today

5. What does the information about the timeline and observations tell the reader?

A. It doesn't take long for changes in society to take place.

B. Change comes slowly even for such atrocities.

C. Marriage is better left to parents who are more mature.

D. Society doesn't see a need for change in the treatment of women.

E. Women didn't want to get involved in legislation until the sixteenth century.

Questions 6–10 are based on the following passage.

Any one who has common sense will remember that the bewilderments of the eyes are of two kinds, and arise from two causes, either from coming out of the light or from going into the light, which is true of the mind's eye, quite as much as of the bodily eye; and he who remembers this when he sees anyone whose vision is perplexed and weak, will not be too ready to laugh; he will first ask whether that soul of man has come out to the brighter life, and
(5) is unable to see because unaccustomed to the dark, or having turned from darkness to the day is dazzled by excess of light. And he will count the one happy in his condition and state of being, and he will pity the other; or, if he have a mind to laugh at the soul which come from below into the light, there will be more reason in this than in the laugh which greets him who returns from above out of the light into the den.

That, he said, is a very just distinction.

6. What progression is presented in the passage as it relates to life?

A. There is a progression from eyes to mind's eyes to the soul.

B. There is a progression from light to darkness to excess of light.

C. There is a progression from darkness to light to excess of light.

D. There is a progression of the mind to the soul from eyes.

E. There is a progression in the mind's eye to the soul.

7. What moral value is the author attempting to establish?

A. a relationship between light and darkness of the mind's eye

B. a distinction in progression from darkness to light or a digression from light to darkness

C. an admonishment that one who comes from the darkness into the light has better reason to celebrate

D. that we should be aware of the direction of those around us and act accordingly

E. that all men should be aware of other's directions and try to help them to a clear mind's eye

8. Which selection best represents the light the mind's eye and soul could pass through metaphorically?

A. sunlight

B. moonlight

C. unfiltered light

D. artificial light

E. light of salvation

9. Which of the following does the author suggest will warrant more joy?

A. he who returns to the den from the light

B. he who stays in the light and out of the den

C. he who does not leave the den

D. he who comes into the light from the den

E. he who constantly moves from one to the other

10. This style of writing qualifies as

A. an epic.

B. an allegory.

C. a choral.

D. a parable.

E. a reflection.

Answers and Explanations for Skill Set Ten

1. The correct choice is **C.**

   Explanation: The author tells us that, "Poetry begins in trivial metaphors, petty metaphors, "grace" metaphors, and goes on to the profoundest thinking that we have," making answer Choice C correct.

2. The correct choice is **C.**

   Explanation: The author tells us when responding to the idea that we never say what we mean, "We never do that, do we, being all of us too much poets," making Choice C correct.

3. The correct choice is **D.**

   Explanation: All answer choices may be used to describe conditions, causing us not to speak directly, Choice D, "reservations," is the best selection.

4. The correct choice is **B.**

   Explanation: Although there is no specifically stated reason for the writing of this passage, we can infer that this kind of information is presented as an admonishment to not return to historical misdeeds, making Choice B the best selection.

5. The correct choice is **B.**

   Explanation: Because we are given information from one era and somewhat similar information from an era 200 years following the first, we can surmise that change comes slowly notwithstanding the egregious acts reported factually over time.

6. The correct choice is **A.**

   Explanation: The passage begins by presenting the eye of vision, progresses to the mind's eye, and finally to the soul making Choice A correct.

7. The correct choice is **B.**

   Explanation: Although Choice C, "an admonishment that one who comes from the darkness into the light has better reason to celebrate," seems like a good choice, there is less of a statement of moral value but rather a statement of fact about the progression made as a result of moral or immoral choices. Choice B, "a distinction if progression from darkness to light or a digression from light to darkness" best relates to a moral value.

8. The correct choice is **E.**

   Explanation: All selections other than E are physical lights leaving only Choice E, "light of salvation" to qualify as the metaphorical relationship.

9. The correct choice is **D.**

   Explanation: The passage reads, "if we have a mind to laugh at the soul which come from below into the light, there will be more reason in this than in the laugh which greets him who returns from above out of the light into the den," making Choice D correct.

10. The correct choice is **D.**

    Explanation: A parable tells a moral story, which makes Choice D the only correct choice.

Long Reading Comprehension Review Questions

Long Reading Comprehension Skill Set One

Note: Skill sets may contain more questions than the actual SAT to show the potential range of questioning.

The passages below are followed by questions based on their content; questions following a pair of related passages may also be based on the relationship between the paired passages. Answer the questions on the basis of what is *stated* or *implied* in the passages and in any introductory material that may be provided.

Questions 1–10 are based on the following passage.

The following passage is taken from an article relating two of Aristotle's four causes: the efficient cause and the final cause.

In every part of the universe we observe means adjusted with the nicest artifice to the ends which they are intended to produce; and I the mechanism of a plant, or animal body, admire how every thing is contrived for advancing the two great purposes of nature, the support of the individual, and propagation of the species. But in these, and in all such objects, we still distinguish the efficient from the final cause of their several motions and organiza-
(5)   tions. The digestion of the food, the circulation of the blood, and the secretion of the several juices which are drawn from it, are operations all of them necessary for the great purpose of animal life. Yet we never endeavour [sic] to account for them from those purposes as from their efficient causes, nor imagine that the blood circulates, or that the food digests of its own accord, and with a view or intention to the purposes of circulation or digestion. The wheels of the watch are all admirably adjusted to the end for which it was made, the pointing of the hour. All their various
(10)   motions conspire in the nicest manner to produce this effect. If they were endowed with a desire and intention to produce it, they could not do it better. Yet we never ascribe any such desire or intention to them, but to the watch-maker, and we know that they are put into motion by a spring, which intends the effect it produces as little as they do. But though, in accounting for the operations final cause, in accounting for those of the mind we are very apt to confound these two different things with one another. When by natural principles we recommend to us, we are very
(15)   apt to impute to that reason, as to their efficient cause, the sentiments and actions by which we advance those ends, and to imagine that to be the wisdom of man, which in reality is the wisdom of God. Upon a superficial view, this cause seems sufficient to produce the effects which are ascribed to it; the system of human nature seems to be more simple and agreeable when all its different operations are in this manner deduced from a single principle.

1. Which of the following best describes the word "means" line (1), as used in this passage?

   A. middle point
   B. material resources
   C. intention
   D. indications
   E. apparitions

2. Which of the following best describes the word "artifice" line (1), as used in this passage

   A. trick
   B. ingenuity
   C. object
   D. particle
   E. manipulation

3. According to the passage, what two natural purposes are supported by individual mechanisms?

   A. aging and reproduction
   B. physical maintenance and intellect
   C. the individual and furtherance of the species
   D. propagation and physical enhancement
   E. individual systems functions for age retardation

4. What selection best paraphrases the meaning of the sentence, "Yet we never endeavour [sic] to account for them from those purposes as from their efficient causes, nor imagine that the blood circulates, or that the food digests of its own accord, and with a view or intention to the purposes of circulation or digestion" lines (6–8)?

   A. We do not try to imagine the completion of the whole without considering the intricacies and completeness of each integral part thereof.
   B. It is not necessary to understand the concept that each component of a mechanism is complete and fully functional unto itself in order to understand the significance of that component.
   C. Interpretation of dissected components is one way to understand the total function of the entire being.
   D. Regarding the individual components necessary for the whole as a complete entity unto itself is not done.
   E. Each and every component, regardless of how infinitesimal, is critical to the overall functions and must be seen as complete for its own purpose.

5. Why does the author utilize an analogy of a watch in his presentation of the animal body?

   A. By using a watch as a comparative, the author represents each individual component of the watch as a relational offset to each bodily function enabling the overall comparative to the entire watch to the body.
   B. A watch functions with a measured set of mechanisms as does the body so a comparison to a watch represents the timing of all the functions necessary to sustain the body.
   C. Because a watch needs a driving mechanism such as a battery or a spring to keep it functioning, so does the body need fuel from food sources and therefore, the analogy is accurate.
   D. The author uses this analogy to show that a watch requires maintenance just as does the body in that if the watch is mistreated, it will not function – just like the body if it is mistreated.
   E. The author uses a watch as an analogy because a watch has a protective casing that keeps all the fragile inside workings from harm just as the exoskeleton of the body keeps all fragile organs protected.

6. Which of the following best interprets the sentence; "Yet we never ascribe any such desire or intention to them, but to the watchmaker, and we know that they are put into motion by a spring, which intends the effect it produces as little as they do" lines (11–13)?

   A. The watchmaker doesn't ascribe any special purpose to the spring other than to provide power.
   B. The spring of the watch has no greater individual purpose in telling time than any of the component wheels.
   C. The spring is what makes the watch tell time and function.
   D. The spring doesn't have any greater effect on the watch than the wheels in the watch.
   E. All the parts of the watch are like all the parts of the body in that there has to be something fueling it.

7. By inference, the author most directly compares God to

    A. the most infinitesimal component of life.

    B. the entire functions of a watch as all the components of life to propel time.

    C. the watchmaker who utilizes each component to accomplish the whole.

    D. digestion of food, circulation of the blood, and secretion of fluids.

    E. the entire universe of plants and animals.

8. Which of the following best interprets the sentence, "Upon a superficial view, this cause seems sufficient to produce the effects which are ascribed to it; the system of human nature seems to be more simple and agreeable when all its different operations are in this manner deduced from a single principle" lines (16–18)?

    A. At the top layer, human nature would agree that individual functions must be self-fulfilling as opposed to a complement for the whole.

    B. Human nature is really quite simple when one looks only at the integral components of life.

    C. Nature is not concerned with any specific mechanism but with only the top layer of existence.

    D. When complex mechanisms generate from a single source of intent, all component parts work in uniform harmony.

    E. Nature satisfies its own need for a synergistic relationship between plant and animal orders.

9. This passage serves mainly to

    A. provide an analysis of the workings of a watch.

    B. delineate the support mechanisms of the animal body.

    C. provide a discourse on the similarities of watchmakers to nature.

    D. assess the importance of having common goals and keeping the end in sight.

    E. present the idea that nature serves common goals due to singleness of design.

10. Which phrase might best reflect the meaning of this passage in a commercial environment?

    A. Apply yourself to the individual task assigned and consider how it can improve the overall output.

    B. Be content with your assigned tasks as long as they significantly contribute to overall successes.

    C. It's alright to question your role on the team as long as you gain recognition for your contributions.

    D. Be aware of opportunities as they open and prepare to move for advancement.

    E. Pay attention to the task at hand and the common goal will be met.

Answers and Explanations for Skill Set One

1. The correct choice is **B.**

   Explanation: The introduction to this writing establishes the scope of the observations that follow. Context clues that the author uses such as, "we observe means" and then going on to speak of the individual organisms or resources needed for the fully functional "plant, or animal body" lead to Choice B, "material resources."

2. The correct choice is **B.**

   Explanation: Again, context clues help with the selection of the proper meaning as used in the passage. The author tells us that "means" are "adjusted with the nicest artifice to the ends which they are intended to produce." While one definition of "artifice" is to trick, this has little relevance to this passage. We are then looking for something that describes an action to produce an intended result. Remember, "means" are adjusted with "artifice," leading us to Choice B, "ingenuity."

3. The correct choice is **C.**

   Explanation: The article states, "every thing is contrived for advancing the two great purposes of nature, the support of the individual, and propagation of the species." Choice C, "the individual and furtherance of the species" best qualifies.

4. The correct choice is **D.**

   Explanation: All selections other than D indicate that the there is a need or desire to totally understand the intricacies of the individual component wherein the author states we never look at circulation or food digestion for example, as an entity unto itself but only for the support and completion of the whole body.

5. The correct choice is **A.**

   Explanation: Although all answer choices have some modicum of truth and could be as a correlative, the best reasoning is Choice A because it delineates each component in the watch as the functions of the body and relates the purpose to the telling of time with the natural function of survival of the individual or propagation thereof.

6. The correct choice is **B.**

   Explanation: We need to first determine what "them" refers back to. Tracing back two sentences, we see that "them" refers to "The wheels of the watch." Substituting, the sentence reads, in essence, 'We never ascribe any such importance to the wheels of the watch, but to the watchmaker, and we know the wheels are put in motion by a spring, which only releases tension as do the wheels only move, not considering they tell time." This substitution makes it clear that Choice B, "the spring of the watch has no greater individual purpose in telling time than any of the component wheels" is correct.

7. The correct choice is **C.**

   Explanation: Although Choice E is tempting to capture the literary universality of God, Choice C, "the watch-maker who utilizes each component to accomplish the whole," is correct. The author tells us that while we often think of the "sentiments and actions" of understanding about the intricacies of the component parts of the whole as "wisdom of man" it "in reality is wisdom of God."

8. The correct choice is **D.**

   Explanation: The logic of this thought is an extension from the prior question. The author explains that when human nature is understood as a simple principle that "all its different operations" are "deduced from a single principle" or from a singular source of intent, making Choice D correct.

9. The correct choice is **E.**

   Explanation: Following and extending the logic of the prior two questions, this question asks that you draw a logical conclusion or inference as to the rationale for its writing. As we deduced that the passage supports the idea that when complex mechanisms generate from a single source of intent, all component parts work in uniform harmony, it follows that the passage is written to "present the idea that nature serves common goals due to singleness of design" or Choice E.

10. The correct choice is **E.**

Explanation: This is another inference question in that it asks you to analyze the passage, come up with an understanding of its concepts, and extend the meaning into another area of application. This is one of those questions that directly tests higher-order thinking. It is easier if you have followed the progression of thought over the last few questions. It would be significantly more difficult if you tackled this question out of order. This is something to think about when you attack difficult passages—sometimes taking the questions in order, rather than skipping a difficult one, can help you better dissect following questions, particularly if the thought process is a progression. Having said that, any choice that causes or presents any of the individual components to predicate their actions based on the whole would be incorrect. Remember, the passage related that the individual components do not consider that they tell time but rather that the spring simply does what a spring does. Toward this end, Choice E best represents the meaning of the passage when applied commercially; "pay attention to the task at hand and the common goal will be met."

Long Reading Comprehension Skill Set Two

Note: Skill sets may contain more questions than the actual SAT to show the potential range of questioning.

The passages below are followed by questions based on their content; questions following a pair of related passages may also be based on the relationship between the paired passages. Answer the questions on the basis of what is *stated* or *implied* in the passages and in any introductory material that may be provided.

Questions 1–10 are based on the following passage.

The following passage is taken from an article concerning Knowledge and Virtue.

Knowledge is one thing, virtue is another; good sense is not conscience, refinement is not humility, nor is largeness and justness of view faith. Philosophy, however enlightened, however profound, gives no command over the passions, no influential motives, no vivifying principles. Liberal Education makes not the Christian, not the Catholic, but the gentleman. It is well to be a gentleman, it is well to have a cultivated intellect, a delicate taste, a candid,
(5) equitable, dispassionate mind, a noble and courteous bearing in the conduct of life—these are the connatural qualities of a large knowledge; they are the objects of a University; I am advocating, I shall illustrate and insist upon them; but still, I repeat, they are no guarantee for sanctity or even for conscientiousness, they may attach to the man of the world, to the profligate, to the heartless, pleasant, alas, and attractive as he shows when decked out in them. Taken by themselves, they do but seem to be what they are not; they look like virtue at a distance, but they are detected by
(10) close observers, and on the long run; and hence it is that they are popularly accused of pretense and hypocrisy, not, I repeat, from their own fault, but because their professors and their admirers persist in taking them for what they are not, and are officious in arrogating for them a praise to which they have no claim. Quarry the granite rock with razors, or moor the vessel with a thread of silk; then may you hope with such keen and delicate instruments as human knowledge and human reason to contend against those giants, the passion and the pride of man.

1. What is the overall purpose of this passage?

   A. to convince the reader that knowledge can be virtuous if reasonably applied

   B. to evidence that virtue is a trait often extended following training in the University

   C. to present a real and observable difference between knowledge and virtue

   D. to show the how application of knowledge is affected when virtue is overriding

   E. to obviate the need for both virtue and knowledge

2. Which statement best describes the author's values as they relate to knowledge and virtue?

   A. Knowledge is its own reward and a precursor to virtue.

   B. Knowledge, while of the greatest importance, serves to create the necessity of the application of that knowledge toward the attainment of virtue.

   C. Knowledge is that stuff made of man through studies in places like universities wherein virtue is extolled by God.

   D. Knowledge, while of paramount importance, cannot presume to extend virtue which, in the overall measure, is to be considered of greater value.

   E. Knowledge is that which is apparent through refinement whereas virtue is that element gained through the application of that knowledge.

3. Which selection best describes the word "vivifying" as used in line (3)?

    A. cohesive

    B. life-giving

    C. validating

    D. concomitant

    E. universal

4. Which selection best describes the word "connatural" as used in line (5)?

    A. presumed

    B. expected

    C. warranted

    D. cognate

    E. heralded

5. Notwithstanding the author's predilection about virtue, which selection best describes his position on knowledge?

    A. Because knowledge can be gained by any person regardless of their position or personal virtue, knowledge is not worthy of seeking.

    B. Virtue comes through knowledge which creates the understanding of virtue making it possible for discourse.

    C. While virtue stands paramount, acquisition of knowledge is greatly desired notwithstanding its inability to attach conscientiousness.

    D. Given what we know to be the drawbacks of knowledge and the overall applications ascribed to professors and their admirers, virtue should be the only desire of man.

    E. Because knowledge cannot aid in one making positive discernment regarding virtue and the applications therein, it should not be of any primary focus.

6. Which selection best describes the word "profligate" as used in line (8)?

    A. ultra conservative

    B. uneducated

    C. boorish

    D. shamelessly immoral

    E. plebian

7. Why does the author state that the qualities of large knowledge taken by themselves, "seem to be what they are not; they look like virtue at a distance, but they are detected by close observers" lines (9–10)?

    A. Because those who possess large knowledge confuse knowledge with virtue and expound they possess both.

    B. Because people with large knowledge can disguise themselves as being virtuous.

    C. Because professors believe that knowledge is the precursor to virtue.

    D. Because to a commoner, the benefits of knowledge look like those attending virtue.

    E. Because the educated believe they are superior and convince others that they are virtuous.

8. What does the author mean by saying that professors and their admirers are, "officious in arrogating for them a praise to which they have no claim" line (12)?

    A. Professors of knowledge and their admirers in their official capacity promote praise for students that they don't possess.

    B. They claim to understand the difference between those who officially obtain a large knowledge and those who claim knowledge but didn't attend a university.

    C. They claim to have an exclusive on virtue because of their education, but, in fact, they do not.

    D. They claim that universal truths about virtue come from attaining a large knowledge from professors and admirers of that large knowledge.

    E. Professors of knowledge and their admirers volunteer unnecessarily to claim without justification praise that is, in fact, unwarranted.

9. What is the author's purpose in using the phrases, "Quarry the granite rock with razors" and "moor the vessel with a thread of silk" lines (12–13)?

   A. to delineate with figurative language the similarities between virtue and knowledge

   B. to metaphorically represent the extreme dichotomy between virtue and knowledge

   C. to represent the virtue and knowledge such that the common uneducated man could understand

   D. to convey to the reader that granite is solid like virtue and the vessel is less stable like knowledge

   E. to create a picture in the mind of the reader instead of abstract philosophical representations

10. Which statement best represents the main idea of the passage?

   A. Although knowledge is greatly to be sought, virtue is of greater value for it has the power to manipulate the passion and pride of man.

   B. While knowledge is of greatest importance, virtue is of necessity a series of qualities that augment that large knowledge gained in a university.

   C. Notwithstanding the value of virtue as it relates to the passions and pride of man, knowledge makes it possible to understand virtue and is, therefore, of superior value.

   D. Given that virtue is a much desired attribute, it becomes even more so when taking into account that virtue is what stimulates an appreciation of knowledge.

   E. Virtue is necessary to offset the knowledge gained through the fall of man which was the act that established the division between knowledge and virtue in the first place.

Answers and Explanations for Skill Set Two

1. The correct choice is **C**.

   Explanation: The simplicity of this answer if that the author opens with the phrase that tells the reader the purpose as directly as possible, "Knowledge is one thing, virtue is another," making Choice C correct. If considering the entire article, the purpose could get more bogged down in philosophical detail, but in this case, the simple direct statement is best.

2. The correct choice is **D**.

   Explanation: The author compares and separates knowledge and virtue by presenting knowledge as that which is gained through studies at universities. He compares those elements of knowledge as desired, even greatly to be sought, but something that can be obtained by the heartless or the man of the world whereas virtue controls the passions of man, the pride of man, making Choice D correct.

3. The correct choice is **B**.

   Explanation: This is a rather difficult vocabulary to figure out based on context clues although some are given in the logical sequencing of the passage. Note that the author is listing virtues that are not accompanied by knowledge or philosophy so we know that the adjective describing principles must be one that attends virtue. Of the choices, universal and life-giving are the only two that rise to that level. Recognizing the detail with which the author is presenting the differences between knowledge and virtue, the term *universal* would seem more out of sync than *life-giving* so Choice B would be the better choice.

4. The correct choice is **D**.

   Explanation: While all choices effectively make sense given the author is talking about the natural extensions of a large knowledge, only Choice D, "cognate," follows the style of writing used by the author. By presenting the benefits of a large knowledge as such a given, it can best be understood that a word meaning inborn or innate as it relates to the acquisition thereof would be used.

5. The correct choice is **C**.

   Explanation: Even though the author ascribes greater significance to virtue over knowledge, he gives great importance to a large knowledge gained through a university. Any answer choice that indicates that the pursuit of knowledge should not be made cannot, therefore, be correct. This only leaves Choices B and C as possibilities. Choice B holds that virtue comes through knowledge which is not suggested anywhere in the passage leaving Choice C as the best choice.

6. The correct choice is **D**.

   Explanation: What the author is saying is that the qualities of large knowledge may be gained by anyone and does not convey any virtue as a result of that acquisition. We can extrapolate then, that the samples given might not be those of whom we would normally associate with virtue. This line of thought leads us to two possible choices. Choice C, "boorish," and Choice D, "shamelessly immoral," fit within our reasoning. Of the two, boorish, which means rude, while not a good quality, hardly rises to the same level of *not* virtuous as does, "shamelessly immoral," making Choice D correct.

7. The correct choice is **A**.

   Explanation: The author states that the qualities of large knowledge—being a gentleman; having a cultivated intellect; having a delicate taste; having a candid, equitable, and dispassionate mind; and having a noble and courteous bearing in the conduct of life—look like virtues but fall woefully short of being offsets to the passions and pride of man, making Choice A correct.

8. The correct choice is **E**.

Explanation: Although disguised, this is really a vocabulary question for the terms "officious" and "arrogating." By reading the passage closely, one can determine the correct choice based on the information surrounding the terms that may not be known to the test-taker. In other words, by reading the passage carefully, one can determine that those who possess an education don't, according to the author, automatically possess virtue. Because professors and their admirers often profess they do, Choice E, "professors of knowledge and their admirers volunteer unnecessarily to claim without justification praise that is, in fact, unwarranted," can be determined to be correct.

9. The correct choice is **B**.

Explanation: The author proposes that someone cannot obtain the grandness of virtue through the obtaining of knowledge. He uses comparatives to show the grandness of virtue and the smallness of knowledge when gotten for knowledge sake. A grand feat represented by the granite and the vessel cannot be controlled with something that pales by comparison; in this case, knowledge represented by the razor and the silk thread. Choice B makes this comparison.

10. The correct choice is **A**.

Explanation: Although all of the answer selections are thought-provoking in their own rights, only one is based totally upon information derived from the passage. The last sentence in the passage reads, "Quarry the granite rock with razors, or moor the vessel with a thread of silk; then may you hope with such keen and delicate instruments as human knowledge and human reason to contend against those giants, the passion and the pride of man." Choice A is based entirely on this information, which is what makes it correct.

Long Reading Comprehension Skill Set Three

Note: Skill sets may contain more questions than the actual SAT to show the potential range of questioning.

The passages below are followed by questions based on their content; questions following a pair of related passages may also be based on the relationship between the paired passages. Answer the questions on the basis of what is *stated* or *implied* in the passages and in any introductory material that may be provided.

Questions 1-10 are based on the following passages.

Passage 1

The following is an excerpt by Lord Chesterfield in a letter to his son written in 1747.

Women have, in general, but one object, which is their beauty; upon which scarce any flattery is too gross for them to follow. Nature has hardly formed a woman ugly enough to be insensible to flattery upon her person; if her face is so shocking that she must, in some degree, be conscious of it, her figure and air, she trusts, make ample amends for it. If her figure is deformed, her face, she thinks, counterbalances it. If they are both bad, she comforts
(5)   herself that she has graces, a certain manner, a je ne sais quoi still more engaging than beauty. This truth is evident from the studied and elaborate dress of the ugliest woman in the world. An undoubted, uncontested, conscious beauty is, of all women, the least sensible of flattery upon that head; she knows it is her due, and is therefore obliged to nobody for giving it her. She must be flattered upon her understanding; which, though she may possibly not doubt of herself, yet she suspects that men may distrust.
(10) Do not mistake me, and think that I mean to recommend to you abject and criminal flattery: no; flatter nobody's vices or crimes: on the contrary, abhor and discourage them. But there is no living in the world without a complaisant indulgence for people's weaknesses, and innocent, though ridiculous vanities. If a man has a mind to be thought wiser, and woman handsomer, than they really are, their error is a comfortable one to themselves, and an innocent one with regard to other people; and I would rather make them my friends by indulging them in it, than
(15) my enemies by endeavoring (and that to no purpose) to undeceive them.

Passage 2

The following is an excerpt by Samuel Clemens in a lecture given in 1882 on advice to youth.

Now as to the matter of lying. You want to be very careful about lying; otherwise you are nearly sure to get caught. Once caught, you can never again be, in the eyes of the good and the pure, what you were before. Many a young person has injured himself permanently through a single clumsy and ill-finnished lie, the result of carelessness born of incomplete training. Some authorities hold that the young ought not to lie at all. That, of course, is
(20) putting it rather stronger than necessary; still, while I cannot go quite so far as that, I do maintain, and I believe I am right, that the young ought to be temperate in the use of this great art until practice and experience shall give them that confidence, elegance, and precision which alone can make attention to detail – these are the requirements; these, in time, will make the student perfect; upon these, and upon these only, may he rely as the sure foundation for future eminence.

1. What is the general tone of the letter in Passage (1)?

    A. humorous

    B. deleterious

    C. sincere

    D. laudable

    E. foreboding

2. What information suggests that the statement in Passage (1), line (1), "Women have, in general, but one object, which is their beauty" might make the author to consider this to be an appropriate position?

    A. because the letter says that ugly women have to rely upon dress

    B. because the letter was written during a period when women didn't have rights

    C. because the letter was written by a father to a son in order to help the son find a suitable mate

    D. because the letter says that sensible flattery is appreciated by all women unless they know they are pretty

    E. because the letter indicates that flattery about a woman's beauty is universally acceptable

3. What is inferred in the sentences, "An undoubted, uncontested, conscious beauty is, of all women, the least sensible of flattery upon that head; she knows it is her due, and is therefore obliged to nobody for giving it her. She must be flattered upon her understanding; which, though she may possibly not doubt of herself, yet she suspects that men may distrust" Passage (1), lines (6–9)?

    A. Establish trust by reassurance when a woman is actually pretty.

    B. Even a pretty woman has doubts, so flattery is still warranted.

    C. Because a truly pretty woman will distrust your sincerity, restate you flattery so she can understand.

    D. Flatter a woman's intelligence if she is actually pretty.

    E. Truly pretty women are not as intelligent as others, so it may take more compliments to gain their favor.

4. What does the author in Passage (1) caution his son relative to this practice of flattery?

    A. Only use flattery when you are sincere and totally objective.

    B. It is alright to use flattery when it is an obvious lie if the situation warrants.

    C. Flattery should not be given to the extent it qualifies as criminal or a lie.

    D. Flattery is a tool that, when used properly, may be perfected such as to convince the recipient of even greater, more abject flattery.

    E. Flattery should not be given meritoriously but for the gaining of some advantage on the recipient.

5. What writing style is employed by the author in Passage (2)?

    A. extended metaphor

    B. sardonic

    C. lofty

    D. metaphysical

    E. satire

6. What advice does the author give to our youth about lying in Passage (2)?

    A. Lying is evil and should be avoided whenever possible.

    B. There are various gradations of lies, and the harshest should be reserved when possible.

    C. Lying should be used in moderation until perfected and for personal gains.

    D. Lying to authorities is less acceptable than to acquaintances.

    E. Once perfected, the art of lying may be used only occasionally so as not to get caught.

7. By suggesting that perfection in lying is the only path to eminence, as the author does in Passage (2), what can we infer about leadership in government?

    A. After a position of eminence is achieved, the benefit of lying ceases.

    B. All government leaders are liars of superior accomplishment.

    C. Leadership has the responsibility to teach others the ills of lying since they are the experts.

    D. They may be trusted to speak the truth now that they have taken an oath of office.

    E. Lying leaders is an appropriate and just extension given that they represent the people.

8. Regarding both Passage (1) and Passage (2), what is the relational ironic element considering each of these very differently presented passages independently?

  A. Passage (1) supports lying and Passage (2) dissuades lying.

  B. Passage (1) dissuades lying and Passage (1) supports lying.

  C. Both Passage (1) and Passage (2) support lying.

  D. Both Passage (1) and Passage (2) dissuade lying.

  E. Both Passage (1) and Passage (2) leave the moral position of lying up to the discretion of the reader.

9. On the sheer face of what is written, which position in Passage (1) would Clemens support?

  A. Women all appreciate being flattered.

  B. A truly pretty woman will have to be flattered for her intelligence.

  C. Abject and criminal flattery is objectionable.

  D. Flattery lying is something to be condoned.

  E. Any flattery contains an element of untruth.

10. In what way are Passage (1) and Passage (2) most parallel?

  A. Although using different styles, both endorse the adage that the ends justify the means.

  B. Both passages agree that the intellect of the recipient of a lie is less than the teller of the lie.

  C. Arguably, both passages condone any conduct necessary to gain prominence.

  D. Although in differing ways, both are giving advice to youth.

  E. Both passages agree that prominence and eminence are the ultimate goals of lying.

Answers and Explanations for Skill Set Three

1. The correct choice is **C**.

   Explanation: There is nothing in the letter to suggest anything other than the sincerity of a father instructing his son on matters in life, making Choice C correct.

2. The correct choice is **B**.

   Explanation: Actually, here is one of those times when more information can be derived by the introduction to the passage than in the passage itself. As noted, this letter was written in 1747. Women of that time were not emancipated, couldn't own land, were considered in large measure to be chattel, and, therefore, couldn't be complimented on hardly any other matter than looks or beauty. Although the letter isn't meant to demean women, it can't hold them up in many categories other than their looks. Choice B is correct.

3. The correct choice is **D**.

   Explanation: When the author states, of a truly pretty woman, "She must be flattered upon her understanding," he means that as she knows she is pretty, it is better to flatter her intelligence. Although she will already believe she is intelligent, she suspects that men don't think so, making your flattery of her intelligence accomplish the same benefits as complimenting a less pretty woman on her good looks, which makes Choice D correct.

4. The correct choice is **C**.

   Explanation: The letter reads, "Do not mistake me, and think that I mean to recommend to you abject and criminal flattery," making Choice C correct.

5. The correct choice is **E**.

   Explanation: Here again, information given about the text, namely the author, may give you some clue. Clemens is known for his satire and wit, although you wouldn't have to know that in order to identify the writing style. Clearly, Choice E is correct.

6. The correct choice is **C**.

   Explanation: The author states, "I do maintain, and I believe I am right, that the young ought to be temperate in the use of this great art until practice and experience shall give them that confidence, elegance, and precision, which alone can make the accomplishment graceful and profitable," making Choice C correct.

7. The correct choice is **B**.

   Explanation: Although Choice E may represent poetic justice, the passage supports Choice B in that the author represents that only with adequate training and practice can lying be perfected to the point where the liar can expect to reach future eminence.

8. The correct choice is **A**.

   Explanation: The ironic element to Passage (1) is that Chesterfield is writing a sincere instruction to his son where he wished to extol virtuous behavior but, in reality, actually gives permission to tell little white lies in the form of flattery. The ironic element in Passage (2) is that through satire and wit, while Clemens is telling youth to lie with expertise, he is actually extolling the virtue of always telling the truth. Choice A supports this irony.

9. The correct choice is **D**.

   Explanation: As Clemens satirically takes the position that lying is acceptable, on the surface, he would agree that flattery lying should be condoned making Choice D correct.

10. The correct choice is **D**.

    Explanation: Passage (1) is written as a letter to a son, and Passage (2) is written for advice to youth, qualifying Choice D as the correct selection.

Long Reading Comprehension Skill Set Four

Note: Skill sets may contain more questions than the actual SAT to show the potential range of questioning.

The passages below are followed by questions based on their content; questions following a pair of related passages may also be based on the relationship between the paired passages. Answer the questions on the basis of what is *stated* or *implied* in the passages and in any introductory material that may be provided.

Questions 1–4 are based on the following passage.

The following is from Aesop: The Frogs Desiring a King written in the 3rd century C.E.

The frogs always had lived a happy life in the marshes. They had jumped and splashed about with never a care in the world. Yet some of them were not satisfied with their easygoing life. They thought they should have a king to rule over them and to watch over their morals. So they decided to send a petition to Jupiter asking him to appoint a king.

Jupiter was amused by the frogs' plea. Good-naturedly he threw down a log into the lake, which landed with
(5)   such splash that it sent all the frogs scampering for safety. But after a while, when one venturesome frog saw that the log lay still, he encouraged his friends to approach the fallen monster. In no time at all the frogs, growing bolder and bolder, swarmed over the log Jupiter had sent and treated it with the greatest contempt.

Dissatisfied with so tame a ruler, they petitioned Jupiter a second time, saying: "We want a real king, a king who will really rule over us." Jupiter, by this time, had lost some of his good nature and was tired of the frogs'
(10) complaining.

So he sent them a stork, who proceeded to gobble up the frogs right and left. After a few days the survivors sent Mercury with a private message to Jupiter, beseeching him to take pity on them once more.

"Tell them," said Jupiter coldly, "that this is their own doing. They wanted a king. Now they will have to make the best of what they asked for."

1. Which of the following devices does Aesop use in relation to the frogs?

   A. hyperbole

   B. onomatopoeia

   C. alliteration

   D. personification

   E. allegory

2. What can be inferred from the story about the frogs' initial beliefs regarding the character of a king?

   A. A king would set down just rules and create order in the swamp.

   B. A king would understand the needs peculiar to a frog.

   C. A king would necessarily be superior to them and therefore a benefit.

   D. Kings must be inherently moral as this was the rationale for requesting one.

   E. Kings sent from gods must possess all necessary powers to maintain order and rule.

3. Jupiter's initial response to the frogs' plea was ironic in all of the following except?

   A. Jupiter sends a nonliving object as a king to rule living would-be subjects.

   B. The primary responsibility desired from the frogs could not have been supplied by the king.

   C. The log caused a great disturbance as delivered such that no pomp or circumstance was possible.

   D. Jupiter's response is a default endorsement of a form of idolatry.

   E. The entrance of the new god causes all subjects to hide rather than welcome.

4. Which of the following might be the best moral for this story?

   A. Beware kings with long beaks.

   B. The concerns of a few can serve the masses.

   C. Let well enough alone.

   D. Be careful what you ask unless detailed in the request.

   E. Asking for a change may anger the one asked.

Questions 5–10 are based on the following passage.

The following is from a moral treatment about a spider and a bee by Jonathan Swift.

Things were at this crisis, when a material accident fell out. For, upon the highest corner of a large window, there dwelt a certain spider, swollen up to the first magnitude by the destruction of infinite number of flies, whose spoils lay scattered before the gates of his palace, like human bones before the cave of some giant. The avenues of his castle were guarded with turnpikes and palisades, all after the modern way of fortification. After you had passed
(5) several courts, you came to the center, wherein you might behold the constable himself in his own lodgings, which had windows fronting to each avenue, and ports to sally out upon all occasions of prey or defense. In this mansion he had for some time dwelt in peace and plenty, without danger to his person by swallows from above, or to his palace by brooms from below, when it was the pleasure of fortune to conduct thither a wandering bee, to whose curiosity a broken pane in the glass had discovered itself, and in he went; where expatiating a while, he at last hap-
(10) pened to alight upon one of the outward walls of the spider's citadel; which, yielding to the unequal weight , sunk down to the very foundation. Thrice he endeavored to force his passage, and thrice the center shook. The spider within, feeling the terrible convulsion, supposed at first that nature was approaching to her final dissolution; or else Beelzebub, with all his legions, was come to revenge the death of many thousands of his subjects, whom his enemy had slain and devoured. However, he at length valiantly resolved to issue forth, and meet his fate. Meanwhile the
(15) bee had acquitted himself of his toils, and posted securely at some distance, was employed in cleansing his wings, and disengaging them from the ragged remnants of the spiderweb. By this time the spider was adventured out, when beholding the chasms and ruins, and dilapidations of his fortress, he was very near at his wit's end; he stormed and swore like a madman, and swelled till he was ready to burst.

5. Which of the following accurately identifies the literary device used in the following phrase, "like human bones before the cave of some giant" line (3)?

   A. metaphor
   B. personification
   C. simile
   D. litote
   E. hyperbole

6. Which term best describes the word "sally" as used in line (6)?

   A. a rushing attack
   B. walk
   C. venture
   D. cautiously observe from
   E. watch with interest

7. Which term best describes the word "expatiating" as used in line (9)?

   A. resting
   B. wandering freely
   C. observing curiously
   D. relaxing
   E. plotting ardently

8. All of the following are revealed by the author in the phrase, "nature was approaching to her final dissolution; or else that Beelzebub with all his legions, was come to revenge the death of many thousands of his subjects whom his enemy had slain and devoured" lines (12–14) EXCEPT:

   A. the author believes that at some appointed time the end of the world will come.
   B. flies are considered to be of a lower order than spiders.
   C. there is a supreme creator and ruler of the universe.
   D. there is a supremely evil spirit who will extract revenge.
   E. the author understands that the food chain of life is established by evil.

9. The phrase, "he was very near at his wit's end; he stormed and swore like a madman, and swelled till he was ready to burst" best exemplifies which of the following literary devices?

    A. descriptive speech

    B. figurative language

    C. juxtaposition

    D. personification

    E. anaphora

10. What moral lesson might be inferred from the evidence presented in the story about the characterizations of the spider and the bee, respectively?

    A. the spider is a good worker to keep his palace but the bee is clumsy to destroy part of it.

    B. the spider is fairly lazy waiting for his food but the bee works to collect his.

    C. the spider tricks the bee hoping to eat him but the bee is too smart to be caught.

    D. the spider is angry because of the broken window and the bee should not have entered if not invited.

    E. the spider should worry about the end of nature but the bee can fly to safety unharmed.

Answers and Explanations for Skill Set Four

1. The correct choice is **D.**

   Explanation: As the frogs are given human-like qualities, Choice D, "personification" is correct.

2. The correct choice is **D.**

   Explanation: The story states that some frogs "thought they should have a king to rule over them and to watch over their morals." Although we don't know how far the frogs had fallen into a state of moral degradation, it can be inferred that a king must be of good moral fiber if one of their charters would be to watch over the frogs' morals making Choice D correct.

3. The correct choice is **C.**

   Explanation: One of the nice parts about a fable is that convention is left open in large measure. Fortunately, this allows for some unusually rich writing. In this fable, much presented is ironic, generally situational. Choice A has Jupiter sending an inanimate, dead tree to rule as king over living subjects. Choice B furthers that dilemma in that a dead tree has no morals and would be unqualified to rule over the frogs' morals. Choice D continues with the same difficulty in that an inanimate object being revered as a king is tantamount to idolatry. Choice E relates that since the log "landed with such a splash that it sent all the frogs scampering for safety" instead of welcoming the arrival of their newly appointed king. Choice C may seem ironic and close to Choice E on the surface, but there is no irony in the fact that a log hurled from the heavens would cause a great splash and generally disturb the otherwise peaceful lake. This non-ironic disturbance causes there to be no opportunity for pomp and circumstance, which again, is not ironic as it is grounded in a natural physical occurrence.

4. The correct choice is **C.**

   Explanation: Remember that a moral must teach, be universal in application, and foster good. The only choice qualifying as a moral, by default, is Choice C.

5. The correct choice is **C.**

   Explanation: The author compares the flies' carcasses to human bones and connects the two with "like" qualifying as a simile, making Choice C correct.

6. The correct choice is **A.**

   Explanation: Although difficult to determine strictly from the sentence, looking at a broader context for clues might help. We know that the spider is an accomplished slayer, and his being swollen is a testimonial to that fact. We also know as a universal truth that defending cannot be passive by nature. With these two facts, we can determine that Choice A, "a rushing attack" is correct.

7. The correct choice is **B.**

   Explanation: The line where the term is used is, "where expatiating a while, he at last happened to alight upon one of the outward walls of the spider's citadel." Based on available clues, we know there was some physical action involved in order for the bee to get from where he went in, to when he alighted upon the outward walls of the spider's citadel. The only selection involving any physical action is Choice B.

8. The correct choice is **E.**

   Explanation: Let's take these one at a time. Choice A, "the author believes that at some appointed time the end of the world will come" is supported by "nature was approaching to her final dissolution." Choice B, "flies are considered to be of a lower order than spiders" is supported by the fact that dominion over the flies was given to the spiders for food. Choice C, "there is a supreme creator and ruler of the universe" is supported by the established order of dominion and by the fact that the author invokes the name Beelzebub who represents Satan. Choice D, "there is a supremely evil spirit who will extract revenge," is supported by "Beelzebub, with all his legions, was come to revenge the death of many thousands of his subjects." Only Choice E, "the author understands that the food chain of life is established by evil" cannot be directly support by the passage. If there were to be support, it would be that the supreme being established the chain, not evil.

9. The correct choice is **D.**

Explanation: Although Choices A and B, "descriptive speech" and "figurative language," may appear good possibilities, the best choice is the one that represents giving human characteristics to a nonhuman subject like the author gives in this example to the spider in his rant.

10. The correct choice is **B.**

Explanation: Remember that lessons of morality must teach. In this regard, Choice B presents a better work ethic for the bee and is the correct choice.

Long Reading Comprehension Skill Set Five

Note: Skill sets may contain more questions than the actual SAT to show the potential range of questioning.

The passages below are followed by questions based on their content; questions following a pair of related passages may also be based on the relationship between the paired passages. Answer the questions on the basis of what is *stated* or *implied* in the passages and in any introductory material that may be provided.

Questions 1–10 are based on the following passage.

The following is an excerpt from a moral piece titled The War Prayer as dictated by Samuel Clemens.

The stranger touched his arm, motioned him to step aside—which the startled minister did—and took his place. During some moments he surveyed the spellbound audience with solemn eyes in which burned an uncanny light; then in a deep voice he said:

"I come from the Throne—bearing a message from Almighty God!" The words smote the house with a shock; if
(5)   the stranger perceived it he gave no attention. "He has heard the prayer of His servant your shepherd and will grant it if such shall be your desire after I, His Messenger, shall have explained to you its import—that is to say, its full import. For it is like unto many prayers of men, in that it asks for more than he who utters it is aware of – except he pause and think.

"God's servant and yours has prayed his prayer. Has he paused and taken thought? Is it one prayer? No, it is
(10)   two—one uttered, the other not. Both have reached the ear of Him Who heareth all supplications, the spoken and the unspoken. Ponder this—keep it in mind. If you would beseech a blessing upon yourself, beware! lest without intent you invoke a curse upon a neighbor at the same time. If you pray for the blessing of rain upon your crop which needs it, by that act you are possibly praying for a curse upon some neighbor's crop which may not need rain and can be injured by it.

(15)   "You have heard your servant's prayer—the uttered part of it. I am commissioned of God to put into words the other part of it—that part which the pastor, and also you in your hearts, fervently prayed silently. And ignorantly and unthinkingly? God grant that it was so! You heard these words: 'Grant us the victory, O Lord our God!' That is sufficient. The *whole* of the uttered prayer is compact into those pregnant words. Elaborations were not necessary. When you have prayed for victory you have prayed for many unmentioned results which follow victory—*must* fol-
(20)   low it, cannot help but follow it. Upon the listening spirit of God the Father fell also the unspoken part of the prayer. He commandeth me to put it into words. Listen!

"O Lord our Father, our young patriots, idols of our hearts, go forth to battle—be Thou near them! With them, in spirit, we also go forth for the sweet peace of our beloved firesides to smite the foe. O Lord our God, help us to tear their soldiers to bloody shreds with our shells; help us to cover their smiling fields with the pale forms of their
(25)   patriot dead; help us to drown the thunder of the guns with the shrieks of their wounded, writhing in pain; help us to lay waste their humble homes with a hurricane of fire; help us to wring the hearts of their unoffending widows with unavailing grief; help us to turn them out roofless with their little children to wander unfriended the wastes of their desolated land in rags and hunger and thirst, sports of the sun flames of summer and icy winds of winter, broken in spirit, worn with travail, imploring Thee for the refuge of the grave and denied it—for our sakes who adore
(30)   Thee, Lord, blast their hopes, blight their lives, protract their bitter pilgrimage, make heavy their steps, water their way with their tears, stain the white snow with blood of their wounded feet! We ask it, in the spirit of love, of Him Who is the Source of Love, and Who is the ever-faithful refuge and friend of all that are sore beset and seek His aid with humble and contrite hearts. Amen."

"Ye have prayed it: if ye still desire it, speak! The messenger of the Most High waits."

1. All of the following might explain the author having given the speaker a "deep voice" EXCEPT:

   A. it commands attention when heard.

   B. it extracts a great degree of seriousness.

   C. it establishes a belief that the possessor has authority.

   D. it reinforces the idea that the speaker speaks in jest.

   E. it supports the notion that a messenger from God will be heard.

2. Which of the following choices best describes the word, "smote" as used in line (4)?

   A. strongly affected

   B. curiously aroused

   C. simultaneously confused

   D. guardedly feared

   E. brought to attention

3. Which of the following best describes the situational irony in the following quote, "He has heard the prayer of His servant your shepherd and will grant it if such shall be your desire after I, His Messenger, shall have explained to you its import" lines (5–6)?

   A. A messenger from God has visited their church.

   B. God has chosen them from all the churches to receive a message.

   C. God has affirmed that their pastor is indeed His servant.

   D. The crowd would need an explanation to a prayer they just uttered.

   E. The messenger informs the crowd that their prayer will in fact be answered.

4. Which selection might best summate the mini-moral in paragraph (3), lines (9–14)?

   A. Reflect upon what you ask that you ask for yourself.

   B. Clarify what you ask such that you will always receive your request.

   C. Determine the importance of your need before you ask.

   D. Consider that your supplication bring not curse with answer.

   E. Pray that you pray for what you really need so as not to waste requests.

5. Which selection best relates the meaning of, "Is it one prayer? No, it is two—one uttered, the other not" lines (9–10)?

   A. When someone prays, they also utter another.

   B. When the pastor prays, the crowd utters another prayer.

   C. The crowd and the pastor sometimes utter two different prayers.

   D. There is always an unspoken prayer with each spoken one.

   E. Because there are two prayers, only one can be answered.

6. What best relates the inference from the messenger to the crowd?

   A. Because the eyes of the crowd were open watching him enter, the prayer is invalid.

   B. Because the crowd had their eyes open during the prayer, they didn't agree with the prayer.

   C. Because the pastor nor the crowd did "pause and take thought" the prayer wouldn't be answered.

   D. The crowd and the pastor are joined in their common failing to think about what they were praying.

   E. The crowd bears the full responsibility for the erroneous prayer they demanded of the pastor.

7. What choice best describes the author's purpose in using figurative language in paragraph (5), lines (22–33)?

   A. Keeps the tone of the story the same throughout.

   B. Effectively changes the mood by describing the gore of the unspoken prayer in detail.

   C. Plays an important role in evidencing the author's abilities in word choice.

   D. Creates an opportunity for the author to present varied syntax for effect.

   E. Challenges the reader to remain actively engaged with the plot.

8. The phrase, "hurricane of fire" is a good example of what device?

   A.   onomatopoeia

   B.   oxymoron

   C.   double entendre

   D.   assonance

   E.   alliteration

9. What selection could best qualify the quote, "Ye have prayed it: if ye still desire it, speak!"

   A.   The messenger did as charged by God and now requires an answer as to which message he delivers back to God.

   B.   The pastor and the crowd prayed and it will be granted just as soon as the messenger delivers their decision to God.

   C.   Now that you understand what you really prayed for, do you still consider it appropriate?

   D.   Now that I have explained the offsetting curse you would bring about, do you still want your soldiers to be victorious?

   E.   Tell me that you want the offsetting prayer answered as well as your spoken one and I'll deliver that message to God.

10. The primary focus of the passage is to

   A.   expose the lunacy of war.

   B.   present the full scope of prayer.

   C.   attest to the fact that God is just.

   D.   confirm the ideology that God is alive.

   E.   convey the parishioners desire to protect their soldiers.

Answers and Explanations for Skill Set Five

1. The correct choice is **D**.

Explanation: All choices except D are basic universal truths. In fact, the only information needed from the passage for this question was that the speaker did indeed have a deep voice.

2. The correct choice is **A**.

Explanation: This is a fairly straightforward vocabulary question. Choices A, B, and E, "strongly affected," "curiously aroused," and "brought to attention" are the only viable choices given the ending of the phrase, "with a shock." Given the gravity of the situation in the tone of the passage, having just heard someone profess he is a messenger from God would likely extol the most egregious response, which is what makes Choice A correct.

3. The correct choice is **D**.

Explanation: Why would someone need to have a prayer as simple as, "Grant us the victory, O Lord our God," explained to them? Herein lay the situational irony. A messenger directly from the Throne takes over a church meeting to explain to the crowd the meaning of such a simple prayer. Choice D is correct.

4. The correct choice is **D**.

Explanation: Given the seriousness of the subject, we are looking for some moral lesson as the question states. In this regard, the cited paragraph clearly tells us to be mindful that we don't accidentally ask for another to be cursed as we are blessed qualifying Choice D as the correct selection.

5. The correct choice is **D**.

Explanation: This type question is one of those literal questions that simply require a reading and rephrasing into different words. While not quoted, the restatement of the quote without altering meaning is Choice D.

6. The correct choice is **D**.

Explanation: Inference questions rely firstly upon the facts given. The messenger addresses the entire crowd, not just the pastor. The messenger's admonishment is to all who hear his deep voice. The messenger addresses the crowd as "you" such as to enjoin them in whatever errors or omissions suffered by the pastor. As this infraction was not thinking about the totality of what was meant by the prayer offered, Choice D is best.

7. The correct choice is **B**.

Explanation: It is important to keep in mind that this is a moral piece wherein the author is conveying some universal lesson of good. One of the best ways to do this for a writer is to really detail the error or the negative of the actions that create a need for change. In this case, it is the unspoken prayer that offsets the spoken prayer. In order to expose the error of the spoken prayer, it is important to descriptively relate the horror of the negative consequences. This is why the author employs figurative language making Choice E appropriate.

8. The correct choice is **B**.

Explanation: Choice B is the only selection qualifying as an "oxymoron" in the use of seemingly dichotomous terms. We normally think of a hurricane as a tropical storm with tremendous amounts of water coupled with high winds, not of fire.

9. The correct choice is **C**.

Explanation: To qualify something is to establish a set of criteria against which the merits will be compared. The quote was, "Ye have prayed it: if ye still desire it, speak!" Keeping in mind that this is teaching a moral, we can qualify the quote as follows: you are a church; you believe in the powers of a God of love; you now know that if God grants your spoken prayer, he must grant your unspoken prayer as they both have been equally asked; given what you now know, speak your answer and it shall be done as soon as I communicate your decision to God. Choice D seems plausible, but poses an unqualified question wherein having been given the information from the messenger about the horrid devastation that would accompany their answered spoken prayer, they have been asked to now sacrifice their own soldiers—this doesn't actually teach a moral. Choice C however simply asks that they now make a moral decision based upon their full understanding of the attendant consequences.

10. The correct choice is **A.**

Explanation: Choice B, "present the full scope of prayer," represents the vehicle used by the author to expose the tragedies of war. Choices C and D "attest to the fact that God is just" and "confirm the ideology that God is alive," respectively, relate to the vehicle as well. Choice E, "convey the parishioners desire to protect their soldiers," simply restates the original prayer and accomplishes nothing in terms of teaching any moral values. Choice A, "expose the lunacy of war," follows the title given in the informational section, teaches the moral counterpoints of war, and furthers the position that if the purpose were to simply teach the silent sides to spoken prayers, the author could have furthered the example of rain helping one farmer while ruining the other.

Long Reading Comprehension Skill Set Six

Note: Skill sets may contain more questions than the actual SAT to show the potential range of questioning.

The passages below are followed by questions based on their content; questions following a pair of related passages may also be based on the relationship between the paired passages. Answer the questions on the basis of what is *stated* or *implied* in the passages and in any introductory material that may be provided.

Questions 1–10 are based on the following passage.

The following is an excerpt from Life on the Mississippi by Mark Twain. Twain spent considerable time on the Mississippi River and was well versed in the perils of navigating this body of water.

Now on very dark nights, light is a deadly enemy to piloting; you are aware that if you stand in a lighted room, on such a night, you cannot see things in the street to any purpose; but if you put out the lights and stand in the gloom you can make out objects in the street pretty well. So, on very dark nights, pilots do not smoke; they allow no fire in the pilot-house stove if there is a crack which can allow the least ray to escape; they order the furnaces to
(5)   be curtained with huge tarpaulins and the sky-lights to be closely blinded. Then no light whatever issues from the boat. The undefinable shape that now entered the pilot-house had Mr. X.'s voice. This said—

'Let me take her, George; I've seen this place since you have, and it is so crooked that I reckon I can run it my-self easier than I could tell you how to do it.'

'It is kind of you, and I swear—I—am willing. I haven't got another drop of perspiration left in me. I have been
(10)   spinning around and around the wheel like a squirrel. It is so dark I can't tell which way she is swinging till she is coming around like a whirligig.'

So Ealer took a seat on the bench, panting and breathless. The black phantom assumed the wheel without saying anything, steadied the waltzing steamer with a turn or two, and then stood at ease, coaxing her a little to this side and then to that, as gently and as sweetly as if the time had been noonday. When Ealer observed this marvel of
(15)   steering, he wished he had not confessed! He stared, and wondered, and finally said—

'Well, I thought I knew how to steer a steamboat, but that was another mistake of mine.'

X. said nothing, but went serenely on with his work. He rang for the leads; he rang to slow down the steam; he worked the boat carefully and neatly into invisible marks, then stood at the center of the wheel and peered blandly out into the blackness, fore and aft, to verify his position; as the leads shoaled more and more, he stopped the en-
(20)   gines entirely, and the dead silence and suspense of 'drifting' followed when the shoalest water was struck, he cracked on the steam, carried her handsomely over, and then began to work her warily into the next system of shoal marks; the same patient, heedful use of leads and engines followed, the boat slipped through without touching bottom, and entered upon the third and last intricacy of the crossing; imperceptibly she moved through the gloom, crept by inches into her marks, drifted tediously till the shoalest water was cried, and then, under a tremendous
(25)   head of steam, went swinging over the reef and away into deep water and safety!

Ealer let his long-pent breath pour out in a great, relieving sigh, and said—

'That's the sweetest piece of piloting that was ever done on the Mississippi River! I wouldn't believed it could be done, if I hadn't seen it.'

There was no reply, and he added—
(30)   'Just hold her five minutes longer, partner, and let me run down and get a cup of coffee.'

A minute later Ealer was biting into a pie, down in the 'texas,' and comforting himself with coffee. Just then the night watchman happened in, and was about to happen out again, when he noticed Ealer and exclaimed—

'Who is at the wheel, sir?'

'X.'
(35)   'Dart for the pilot-house, quicker than lightning!'

The next moment both men were flying up the pilot-house companion way, three steps at a jump! Nobody there! The great steamer was whistling down the middle of the river at her own sweet will! The watchman shot out of the place again; Ealer seized the wheel, set an engine back with power, and held his breath while the boat reluctantly swung away from a 'towhead' which she was about to knock into the middle of the Gulf of Mexico!

131

(40)   By and by the watchman came back and said—
        'Didn't that lunatic tell you he was asleep, when he first came up here?'
        'NO.'
        'Well, he was.
        I found him walking along on top of the railings just as unconcerned as another man would walk a pavement;
(45)   and I put him to bed; now just this minute there he was again, away astern, going through that sort of tight-rope
        deviltry the same as before.'
        'Well, I think I'll stay by, next time he has one of those fits. But I hope he'll have them often. You just ought to
        have seen him take this boat through Helena crossing. I never saw anything so gaudy before. And if he can do such
        gold-leaf, kid-glove, diamond-breastpin piloting when he is sound asleep, what COULDN'T he do if he was dead!'

1. What is the primary purpose for the first paragraph lines (1–6)?

A. to explain what lengths pilots go to keep the pilot-house

B. to explain that even though freezing, no furnace is burned at night in the pilot-house

C. to explain that pilots do not even smoke in the pilot-house to keep it dark

D. to explain the dangers of piloting at night

E. to explain that it was difficult to identify anyone entering the pilot-house at night

2. What can the reader infer by the comment of Mr. X., "I've seen this place since you have" line (7)?

A. It was simply a nice way to take over the wheel of the boat.

B. It implies it had been a very long time since George had seen this part of the river.

C. It suggests that due to the current, the river shifts with some frequency.

D. It is simply a form of boasting by Mr. X. that he pilots more frequently than George.

E. It means that Mr. X. has been in the pilot-house more recently than George and can better pilot.

3. Which statement best summarizes George's statements in lines (9–11)?

A. He is upset at the suggestion and swears at Mr. X. albeit he acquiesces in the end.

B. He has fought the darkness and over-steered such that he has sweat to the point of dehydration.

C. The currents are so strong that the wheel was very difficult to turn making him sweat profusely.

D. He is disgusted that it is so dark in the pilot-house that he over-steers because he can't see the instruments.

E. He has been spinning around the wheel like a squirrel runs around a tree getting nowhere.

4. Why does the phrase, "It is so dark I can't tell which way she is swinging" line (10) seem strange?

A. because a dark pilot-house is supposed to help pilot the boat, not confuse the pilot

B. because darker is supposed to be better, so it could not be too dark

C. because at first glance you don't know he is speaking of the outside and it doesn't match with the desire for total darkness in the pilot-house

D. because you would initially think that darkness was a friend to the pilot in the pilot-house and now he is saying it was too dark to know which way the boat was turning

E. because of the discussions about it being dark in the pilot-house and it being very dark at night and that if light is deadly, why is it now a problem

5. Which device is evidenced with the phrase, "waltzing steamer" in line (13)?

   A. symbolism
   B. anachronism
   C. anaphora
   D. assonance
   E. personification

6. What can be inferred by the phrase "he wished he had not confessed" line (15)?

   A. He felt childish for having not been tougher during a tense situation and thought that Mr. X. would think less of him as a comrade.
   B. Given the ease with which Mr. X. traversed the river, George was more than a little embarrassed with his confession that he could not do nearly so well.
   C. Because Mr. X. was not engaged in conversation with him, George thought he was upset that his companion could not have managed this piece of the river, particularly given the ease with which it obviously could be done.
   D. He felt like since he so easily relinquished the wheel to Mr. X. that now Mr. X. would think that he was unwilling to pull his own weight aboard the boat.
   E. He was fearful the Mr. X. would share his confession and inadequacy with the other hands or even the captain.

7. Which of the following would not be a reasonable deduction as a result of Mr. X. not speaking to George the whole of the relief piloting episode lines (12–29)?

   A. Mr. X. was fully focused on the task at hand and did not wish to engage in conversation.
   B. Mr. X. was offended by the readiness George demonstrated by giving up the wheel so readily.
   C. George was a less tendered mate and Mr. X. did not choose to engage in social conversation with someone of lesser position.
   D. Mr. X. had a hearing impairment and simply didn't hear George.
   E. Mr. X. was answering George but George was hearing impaired.

8. What literary device is used when it is disclosed that Mr. X. was asleep?

   A. twist of fate
   B. dénouement
   C. surprise ending
   D. flashback
   E. foreshadowing

9. In line (48), the word "gaudy" most nearly means

   A. professional.
   B. expertly done.
   C. flawlessly.
   D. showy.
   E. amazing.

10. What is most likely the main purpose for writing the story?

   A. to inform
   B. to argue a point
   C. to persuade
   D. to entertain
   E. to dissuade

Answers and Explanations for Skill Set Six

1. The correct choice is **D**.

    Explanation: Although all choices are correct statements, all but D and E deal with the lengths undertaken to make the pilot-house dark rather than the purpose for darkness. Choice E simply identifies a result of that darkness, leaving only Choice D "to explain the dangers of piloting at night," which is the correct selection.

2. The correct choice is **C**.

    Explanation: River pilots are not likely given to formality, making Choice A wrong. Although it is possible that some time had passed since George had navigated this part of the river, if it was that treacherous, pilots remember those areas and commit them to memory notwithstanding navigational maps, so Choice B can't be correct. Mr. X. boasting is a possibility, but there was no hint of that in the words used. The tone of his voice did not suggest any boasting, making Choice D erroneous. The remainder of the sentence about it being "crooked" eliminates Choice E, leaving only Choice C as correct.

3. The correct choice is **B**.

    Explanation: In summary type questions, the trick is to look for matching information. Remember that the answer choices may be restated, reworded, or reverse-worded but still convey the same meaning. In this case, we are looking for an answer that conveys that it was very dark outside, creating the need for much attention to steering in this very treacherous area of the river and that the physical demands of the pilot, possibly coupled with raw nerves, causes such perspiration as to be on the brink of dehydration. Choice B fulfills this need.

4. The correct choice is **C**.

    Explanation: The strangeness of the phrase is set up in the information presented previously in the passage. In speaking of the darkest of nights, a goodly portion of text is then presented to demonstrate what great efforts the crew performs to make the pilot-house completely dark. Naturally, the reader is left with the notion and belief that the more darkness, the better—but this is only true of the pilot-house. . .not outside. This then, is what seems strange. Until the reader realizes George is speaking of how dark it is outside, the phrase can seem strange, making Choice C correct.

5. The correct choice is **E**.

    Explanation: Giving a steamer humanlike traits such as waltzing is clearly personification, making Choice E correct.

6. The correct choice is **B**.

    Explanation: Sometimes the timing of when something is said is as important as what they say. In this case, George has just watched a display in piloting such as he has never before seen and his confession previously about how tremendously difficult this piece of the river was seems totally errant at this time. Clearly, Choice B is correct.

7. The correct choice is **E**.

    Explanation: At this point in the story, all choices are reasonable deductions except for Choice E. This might have made for a good twist had it not been for the fact that George heard Mr. X. clearly when he asked whether he could take over the wheel.

8. The correct choice is **C**.

    Explanation: A surprise ending is what happens when you simply don't see coming what is actually presented. The element of surprise in Mr. X. being asleep certainly qualifies as a surprise ending for this passage, making Choice C correct.

9. The correct choice is **D**.

    Explanation: Although a number of choices might fit the situation, we can acquire some context clues with the tone and expressions used by George in the next line. Terms such as "gold-leaf" and "diamond-breastpin" are flashy, showy items leading to Choice D, which is correct.

10. The correct choice is **D**.

    Explanation: Here is a case in which there is no real useable information, no instruction, no one trying to convince you of one thing or another, but simply to entertain the reader, making Choice D correct.

Long Reading Comprehension Skill Set Seven

Note: Skill sets may contain more questions than the actual SAT to show the potential range of questioning.

The passages below are followed by questions based on their content; questions following a pair of related passages may also be based on the relationship between the paired passages. Answer the questions on the basis of what is *stated* or *implied* in the passages and in any introductory material that may be provided.

Questions 1–10 are based on the following passage.

This is an excerpt from The Stolen White Elephant.

     You know in what reverence the royal white elephant of Siam is held by the people of that country. You know it is sacred to kings, only kings may possess it, and that it is, indeed, in a measure even superior to kings, since it receives not merely honor but worship. Very well; five years ago, when the troubles concerning the frontier line arose between Great Britain and Siam, it was presently manifest that Siam had been in the wrong. Therefore every repa-
(5) ration was quickly made, and the British representative stated that he was satisfied and the past should be forgotten. This greatly relieved the King of Siam, and partly as a token of gratitude, partly also, perhaps, to wipe out any little remaining vestige of unpleasantness which England might feel toward him, he wished to send the Queen a present —the sole sure way of propitiating an enemy, according to Oriental ideas. This present ought not only to be a royal one, but transcendently royal. Wherefore, what offering could be so meet as that of a white elephant? My
(10) position in the Indian civil service was such that I was deemed peculiarly worthy of the honor of conveying the present to Her Majesty. A ship was fitted out for me and my servants and the officers and attendants of the elephant, and in due time I arrived in New York harbor and placed my royal charge in admirable quarters in Jersey City. It was necessary to remain awhile in order to recruit the animal's health before resuming the voyage.

     All went well during a fortnight - then my calamities began. The white elephant was stolen! I was called up at
(15) dead of night and informed of this fearful misfortune. For some moments I was beside myself with terror and anxiety; I was helpless. Then I grew calmer and collected my faculties. I soon saw my course - for, indeed, there was but the one course for an intelligent man to pursue. Late as it was, I flew to New York and got a policeman to conduct me to the headquarters of the detective force. Fortunately I arrived in time, though the chief of the force, the celebrated Inspector Blunt was just on the point of leaving for his home. He was a man of middle size and compact
(20) frame, and when he was thinking deeply he had a way of knitting his brows and tapping his forehead reflectively with his finger, which impressed you at once with the conviction that you stood in the presence of a person of no common order. The very sight of him gave me confidence and made me hopeful. I stated my errand. It did not flurry him in the least; it had no more visible effect upon his iron self-possession than if I had told him somebody had stolen my dog. He motioned me to a seat, and said, calmly:
(25)   "Allow me to think a moment, please."

     So saying, he sat down at his office table and leaned his head upon his hand. Several clerks were at work at the other end of the room; the scratching of their pens was all the sound I heard during the next six or seven minutes. Meantime the inspector sat there, buried in thought. Finally he raised his head, and there was that in the firm lines of his face which showed me that his brain had done its work and his plan was made. Said he - and his voice was
(30) low and impressive:

     "This is no ordinary case. Every step must be warily taken; each step must be made sure before the next is ventured. And secrecy must be observed - secrecy profound and absolute. Speak to no one about the matter, not even the reporters. I will take care of them; I will see that they get only what it may suit my ends to let them know." He touched a bell; a youth appeared.

(35)   "Alaric, tell the reporters to remain for the present." The boy retired. "Now let us proceed to business - and systematically. Nothing can be accomplished in this trade of mine without strict and minute method."

     He took a pen and some paper. "Now - name of the elephant?"

     "Hassan Ben Ali Ben Selim Abdallah Mohammed Moist Alhammal Jamsetjejeebhoy Dhuleep Sultan Ebu Bhudpoor."

(40)   "Very well. Given name?"

     "Jumbo."

     "Very well. Place of birth?"

"The capital city of Siam."

"Parents living?"

(45)   "No - dead."

"Had they any other issue besides this one?"

"None. He was an only child."

"Very well. These matters are sufficient under that head. Now please describe the elephant, and leave out no particular, however insignificant—that is, insignificant from your point of view. To me in my profession there are no

(50)   insignificant particulars; they do not exist."

1. What is the mood throughout the story?

    A. raucous

    B. solemn

    C. dire

    D. giddy

    E. reverent

2. All of the following presented in the first paragraph, lines (1–13) might indicate that the author is foreshadowing some dire event as it relates to the delivery of this great gift EXCEPT?

    A. The gift was one that was even more than royal.

    B. The gift was to completely appease a head of state after the offending faux pas.

    C. The gift was to be entrusted to only one man.

    D. There was a requisite stop-over in New York of all places.

    E. There was only one other gift of this kind as a safeguard.

3. In line (8) "propitiating" most nearly means

    A. conquering.

    B. placating.

    C. wooing.

    D. regaining favor.

    E. artificially apologizing.

4. In line (9) "transcendently" most nearly means

    A. rise above.

    B. extend to.

    C. encapsulate.

    D. marginally.

    E. effectively.

5. Which of the following would likely not convey why the term "fearful" line (15) was used?

    A. It was likely a fearful situation for the elephant.

    B. It created fear in he who was in charge of the gift.

    C. It is fearful because of how the King of Siam would likely react

    D. It would create ear for the well-being of the gift

    E. It would cause fear that they wouldn't find the gift in time to set sail for Great Britain

6. All of the following questions asked by Inspector Blunt qualify as ironic EXCEPT:

    A. name of the elephant.

    B. given name.

    C. place of birth.

    D. parents living.

    E. color.

7. What linguistic modification is utilized in, "Said he—and his voice was low and impressive" line (29–30)?

    A. characterization

    B. anthropomorphism

    C. exposition

    D. syntax

    E. foil

8. When the author has Inspector Blunt state, "This is no ordinary case," in line (31), he accomplishes all of the following EXCEPT:

   A. stating the obvious.

   B. qualifying an unknown.

   C. set up the ironic treatment of this as anything but an exceptional case.

   D. establish Inspector Blunt as a comic relief figure as it took "six or seven" minutes to receive this revelation.

   E. establish that the messenger is absolutely gullible when it comes to dealing with the inspector.

9. From the readers' perspective, which is the best choice to describe the entire question and answer sequence between Inspector Blunt and the messenger, lines (37–50)?

   A. informative

   B. ludicrous

   C. appalling

   D. absurd

   E. raucous

10. What is the overriding factor in making this piece qualify as irony?

   A. The most precious gift, one greater than royalty was lost.

   B. The most qualified person in all of Siam to deliver the gift lost it.

   C. Inspector Blunt was caught in the nick of time, and he was the most qualified to work the case.

   D. The details of a white elephant are so painstakingly needed to start looking.

   E. None of the servants, officers, or attendants of the elephant were posted as guards.

Answers and Explanations for Skill Set Seven

1. The correct choice is **B.**

   Explanation: The situation between Siam and Great Britain is solemn. The charge to deliver this token of great importance is solemn. The theft is solemn. And even Inspector Blunt was solemnly performing his duties albeit humorous to us. Therefore, Choice B is correct.

2. The correct choice is **E.**

   Explanation: All of the selections could be considered to foreshadow some dire event except Choice E, which was never mentioned in the passage but would be highly unlikely anyway.

3. The correct choice is **D.**

   Explanation: The object and direction of the paragraph have not changed and is still sincere in its goal; to give an extraordinarily priceless gift to the targeted country. As they had only recently been at odds with Great Britain and the purpose of the gift was to make final appeasement for an awkward situation, Choice D, "regaining favor," is correct.

4. The correct choice is **A.**

   Explanation: To transcend is to rise above so this is a fairly straightforward vocabulary question. You know from the context it will need to be something that indicates the best or better than royal because of the language leading up to the word in question, "This present ought not only to be a royal one, but transcendently royal." Choice A, "rise above," is the only choice meeting this criterion.

5. The correct choice is **E.**

   Explanation: The only fear not supported in the passage is E, "fear that they wouldn't find the gift in time to set sail for Great Britain."

6. The correct choice is **E.**

   Explanation: Although we are not told specifically that the messenger informed Inspector Blunt when he stated his errand that the elephant was indeed white (making it extremely rare. . .not to mention noticeable), we do know that the inspector did not ask that question directly in the text, making Choice E correct. Of course, the author speaks tongue-in-cheek when the inspector follows a meticulously set and laid out "minute method" of questioning as if he were looking for an abducted child.

7. The correct choice is **D.**

   Explanation: Although Choice A looks like a candidate because the voice of Inspector Blunt is being identified as "low and impressive," which does give character to him, this is not a deviation or modification, making it an incorrect choice. Rather, Choice D, "syntax," is correct as the normal placement of word order has been changed or modified for effect.

8. The correct choice is **B.**

   Explanation: Clearly, a great deal can be established with few words. All choices except B, "qualifying and unknown," happen almost simultaneously with this singular comment. Although hoping for some actual revelation from the inspector given his pre-established notoriety as a great and wondrous detective, we get something so academic, it needn't have even been said. All the while, the messenger remains awestruck by the "greatness" before him.

9. The correct choice is **B.**

   Explanation: Choice A, "informative," is actually kind of tricky. It was informative from the readers' perspective, but not in terms of learning about the elephant. It was informative to the reader as to identifying the humor and irony being presented by the author. This question is actually asking for a qualification upon the actual questioning in the sequence rather than the imparting of any specific devices being used by the author. Toward this end, Choice D, "absurd," looks good as it relates to being ridiculous or unreasonable were it not for the fact that "absurd" does not take into account the humor involved from "the readers' perspective." Choice B, however, "ludicrous" describes the sequence from the readers' perspective perfectly—comically ridiculous.

10. The correct choice is **D**.

Explanation: Although all of the choices contain their own bits of irony, the classic and overriding qualifier is the fact that we're looking for a huge white elephant. This isn't a pocket-watch easily hidden under someone's coat; it's an elephant, which leads to the obvious choice of D. The turning point and revelation of this is the following: "I stated my errand. It did not flurry him in the least; it had no more visible effect upon his iron self-possession than if I had told him somebody had stolen my dog. He motioned me to a seat, and said, calmly:

"Allow me to think a moment, please."

I invite you to do the same on the SAT.

Long Reading Comprehension Skill Set Eight

Note: Skill sets may contain more questions than the actual SAT to show the potential range of questioning.

The passages below are followed by questions based on their content; questions following a pair of related passages may also be based on the relationship between the paired passages. Answer the questions on the basis of what is *stated* or *implied* in the passages and in any introductory material that may be provided.

Questions 1–10 are based on the following passage.

The following is an excerpt from Persuasion by Jane Austen.

Vanity was the beginning and the end of Sir Walter Elliot's character; vanity of person and of situation. He had been remarkably handsome in his youth; and, at fifty-four, was still a very fine man. Few women could think more of their personal appearance than he did, nor could the valet of any new made lord be more delighted with the place he held in society. He considered the blessing of beauty as inferior only to the blessing of a baronetcy; and the Sir
(5)   Walter Elliot, who united these gifts, was the constant object of his warmest respect and devotion.

His good looks and his rank had one fair claim on his attachment; since to them he must have owed a wife of very superior character to any thing deserved by his own. Lady Elliot had been an excellent woman, sensible and amiable; whose judgement [sic] and conduct, if they might be pardoned the youthful infatuation which made her Lady Elliot, had never required indulgence afterwards. She had humoured [sic], or softened, or concealed his fail-
(10)   ings, and promoted his real respectability for seventeen years; and though not the very happiest being in the world herself, had found enough in her duties, her friends, and her children, to attach her to life, and make it no matter of indifference to her when she was called on to quit them. Three girls, the two eldest sixteen and fourteen, was an awful legacy for a mother to bequeath, an awful charge rather, to confide to the authority and guidance of a conceited, silly father. She had, however, one very intimate friend, a sensible, deserving woman, who had been
(15)   brought, by strong attachment to herself, to settle close by her, in the village of Kellynch; and on her kindness and advice, Lady Elliot mainly relied for the best help and maintenance of the good principles and instruction which she had been anxiously giving her daughters.

This friend, and Sir Walter, did not marry, whatever might have been anticipated on that head by their acquaintance. Thirteen years had passed away since Lady Elliot's death, and they were still near neighbours [sic] and intimate
(20)   friends, and one remained a widower, the other a widow.

That Lady Russell, of steady age and character, and extremely well provided for, should have no thought of a second marriage, needs no apology to the public, which is rather apt to be unreasonably discontented when a woman does marry again, than when she does not; but Sir Walter's continuing in singleness requires explanation. Be it known then, that Sir Walter, like a good father, (having met with one or two private disappointments in very unrea-
(25)   sonable applications), prided himself on remaining single for his dear daughters' sake. For one daughter, his eldest, he would really have given up any thing, which he had not been very much tempted to do. Elizabeth had succeeded, at sixteen, to all that was possible, of her mother's rights and consequence; and being very handsome, and very like himself, her influence had always been great, and they had gone on together most happily. His two other children were of very inferior value. Mary had acquired a little artificial importance, by becoming Mrs. Charles Musgrove;
(30)   but Anne, with an elegance of mind and sweetness of character, which must have placed her high with any people of real understanding, was nobody with either father or sister; her word had no weight, her convenience was always to give way—she was only Anne.

To Lady Russell, indeed, she was a most dear and highly valued god-daughter, favourite [sic], and friend. Lady Russell loved them all; but it was only in Anne that she could fancy the mother to revive again.
(35)   A few years before, Anne Elliot had been a very pretty girl, but her bloom had vanished early; and as even in its height, her father had found little to admire in her (so totally different were her delicate features and mild dark eyes from his own), there could be nothing in them, now that she was faded and thin, to excite his esteem. He had never indulged much hope, he had now none, of ever reading her name in any other page of his favourite [sic] work. All equality of alliance must rest with Elizabeth, for Mary had merely connected herself with an old country family of
(40)   respectability and large fortune, and had therefore given all the honour [sic] and received none: Elizabeth would, one day or other, marry suitably.

1. What is the author's purpose in the first paragraph, lines (1–5)?

   A. to establish a time frame for the story
   B. to establish a setting for the story
   C. to establish an overall tone in the story
   D. to establish the character of Sir Elliot in the story
   E. to establish the financial condition of Sir Elliot in the story

2. Which selection properly identifies the "fair claim" in line (6)?

   A. His wealth stemmed from looks and rank.
   B. His birthright gave him looks and rank attainable.
   C. His possession of looks and rank commanded respect.
   D. He got his wife because of looks and rank.
   E. He was held high in society because of looks and rank.

3. What does "his own" refer to as used in line (7)?

   A. his own wife
   B. his own looks
   C. his own character
   D. his own rank
   E. his own claim

4. The device evidenced in line (7) by eliminating the word "character" after "his own" is known as

   A. parasynthesis.
   B. mythopoetics.
   C. monosemy.
   D. ellipsis.
   E. interpolation.

5. Which statement best defines the meaning of the phrase "attach her to life" line (11), as used in this passage?

   A. Make her feel alive due to all the social activities resulting from her husband's rank.
   B. Her duties, friends, and children were constantly attached to her demanding attention.
   C. She found reason to live in her duties, friends, and children.
   D. Her entire life was relegated to her duties, friends, and children.
   E. Ensure that she lived well when she could not attend to her duties or be with her friends or children.

6. The phrase "no matter of indifference" lines (11–12) is best represented as an example of

   A. hyperbole.
   B. understatement.
   C. exaggeration.
   D. assonance.
   E. litotes.

7. The phrase "called on to quit them" line (12) qualifies as

   A. a metaphor.
   B. a simile.
   C. hyperbole.
   D. anaphora.
   E. ellipses.

8. Which selection best represents the dichotomous views of Anne as demonstrated in lines (35–38)?

   A. Elliot believes she will marry one day—Russell believes she does not.
   B. Elliot believes she is still fair—Russell believes she has inward qualities.
   C. Elliot believes she has nothing to offer—Russell believes she has her mother's qualities.
   D. Elliot believes she had worth—Russell believes she had no worth.
   E. Elliot believes she resembles his looks—Russell believes she does not.

9. What is the author telling us that Elliot believes of his daughters as it concerns marriage in lines (25–41)?

   A. Anne will eventually marry to good stock; Elizabeth will stay and attend estate needs; Mary married for convenience.

   B. Anne married, but not well; Elizabeth will marry well; Mary will never marry as she is too thin.

   C. Anne won't marry; Elizabeth married, but not well; Mary will marry well.

   D. Anne lost what little looks she had so will marry into a bad alliance; Elizabeth will marry a good alliance; Mary married into a lower level family.

   E. Anne was too thin and homely so won't marry; Elizabeth is best suited and will marry with good alliance; Mary married into a family that adds nothing to the Elliot alliance.

10. Which selection best describes the relationship between the first and last paragraphs?

   A. Information presented in paragraph one is contradictory to the last paragraph.

   B. Information presented in paragraph one is opposite to what is presented in the last paragraph.

   C. Information presented in paragraph one is validated in the final paragraph.

   D. Information presented in paragraph one is similar to that in the final paragraph.

   E. Information presented in paragraph one is basically the same as that in the final paragraph.

Answers and Explanations for Skill Set Eight

1. The correct choice is **D.**

Explanation: Although the first paragraph addresses some of the choices, it most importantly establishes the character of Sir Walter Elliot and even states, "Vanity was the beginning and the end of Sir Walter Elliot's character," making Choice D correct.

2. The correct choice is **D.**

Explanation: This is one of those, "Go figure out the syntax" questions. So, if we look at the sentence, it basically says he owes his good looks and rank for the gaining of the one prize of worth, his wife, Lady Elliot. This is the "fair claim" then, that he could claim that his looks and rank won him his wife.

3. The correct choice is **C.**

Explanation: If test-makers only selected passages that were more formulaically written, we wouldn't have questions like this, but they don't, so we do. Now to the task at hand; looking at the entire sentence, we know that he owed his looks and rank for landing him a wife. We also know that his wife had a superior character, which was one of the qualities he didn't deserve based on his own character, making Choice C correct.

4. The correct choice is **D.**

Explanation: There are those who will tell you that it is not important to know the device terminology to pass the SAT. I agree; but I do not agree that you can score your best if you aren't familiar enough with them to know them by name, because if you don't know them by name, you likely can't master them, and many of the questions on the SAT utilize the structure and detail of a device as a basis for a question. So, I make no apologies for asking these types of questions as a study guide for improving SAT scores, which this book will do. Having said that, an ellipses, Choice D is the device that omits one or more words that might be essential grammatically, but easily supplied for meaning.

5. The correct choice is **C.**

Explanation: Effectively, we are told that in spite of her husband's failings creating hardships on her and in spite of her basically making him what he was perceived to be in society, she found enough reason to live in her positive duties, friends, and her children, making Choice C, "she found reason to live in her duties, friends, and children," correct.

6. The correct choice is **E.**

Explanation: Although Choice B, "understatement," is correct, it is not the selection that is the best representative. Litotes is a form of understatement in which something is affirmed by stating the negative of its opposite. To say "no matter of indifference" qualifies as that form of understatement called litotes, making Choice E correct.

7. The correct choice is **A.**

Explanation: The phrase "called on to quit them" is simply a metaphor for dying. Certainly, if understatement would have been a choice, that would have been correct also. Choice A is correct.

8. The correct choice is **C.**

Explanation: Sometimes, the best way to handle a question like this is to employ that old strategy used when there were two blanks in the Sentence Completion Section. If you remember, verifying one side of the equation will help eliminate some choices immediately. Then work through the other side until all the conditions match. In this case, Choice C, "Elliot believes she has nothing to offer—Russell believes she has her mother's qualities," is supported by the text.

9. The correct choice is **E.**

Explanation: This is just another follow-the-trail question. Similar to multiple blank sentence completion questions, it is sometimes better to work through the first qualifier crossing off the selections that don't comply. Systematically work through the second (and third if necessary), qualifier until the correct selection literally presents itself. In this case, Choice E is the only selection left standing.

10. The correct choice is **C.**

Explanation: Choice D, "information presented in paragraph one is similar to that in the final paragraph," seems feasible but similar would indicate a repetition of sorts of the same information, which is not correct. Choice C, "information presented in paragraph one is validated in the final paragraph," is the best selection as the character flaws attributed to Sir Elliot are realized in the final paragraph.

Long Reading Comprehension Skill Set Nine

Note: Skill sets may contain more questions than the actual SAT to show the potential range of questioning.

The passages below are followed by questions based on their content; questions following a pair of related passages may also be based on the relationship between the paired passages. Answer the questions on the basis of what is *stated* or *implied* in the passages and in any introductory material that may be provided.

Questions 1–10 are based on the following passage.

The following is an excerpt from Dracula by Bram Stoker.

I shuddered as I bent over to touch him, and every sense in me revolted at the contact, but I had to search, or I was lost. The coming night might see my own body a banquet in a similar way to those horrid three. I felt all over the body, but no sign could I find of the key. Then I stopped and looked at the Count. There was a mocking smile on the bloated face which seemed to drive me mad. This was the being I was helping to transfer to London, where,

(5)   perhaps, for centuries to come he might, amongst its teeming millions, satiate his lust for blood, and create a new and ever-widening circle of semi-demons to batten on the helpless.

The very thought drove me mad. A terrible desire came upon me to rid the world of such a monster. There was no lethal weapon at hand, but I seized a shovel which the workmen had been using to fill the cases, and lifting it high, struck, with the edge downward, at the hateful face. But as I did so the head turned, and the eyes fell upon me,

(10) with all their blaze of basilisk horror. The sight seemed to paralyze me, and the shovel turned in my hand and glanced from the face, merely making a deep gash above the forehead. The shovel fell from my hand across the box, and as I pulled it away the flange of the blade caught the edge of the lid which fell over again, and hid the horrid thing from my sight. The last glimpse I had was of the bloated face, blood-stained and fixed with a grin of malice which would have held its own in the nethermost hell.

(15) I thought and thought what should be my next move, but my brain seemed on fire, and I waited with a despairing feeling growing over me. As I waited I heard in the distance a gipsy song sung by merry voices coming closer, and through their song the rolling of heavy wheels and the cracking of whips. The Szgany and the Slovaks of whom the Count had spoken were coming. With a last look around and at the box which contained the vile body, I ran from the place and gained the Count's room, determined to rush out at the moment the door should be opened. With

(20) strained ears, I listened, and heard downstairs the grinding of the key in the great lock and the falling back of the heavy door. There must have been some other means of entry, or some one had a key for one of the locked doors.

Then there came the sound of many feet tramping and dying away in some passage which sent up a clanging echo. I turned to run down again towards the vault, where I might find the new entrance, but at the moment there seemed to come a violent puff of wind, and the door to the winding stair blew to with a shock that set the dust from

(25) the lintels flying. When I ran to push it open, I found that it was hopelessly fast. I was again a prisoner, and the net of doom was closing round me more closely.

As I write there is in the passage below a sound of many tramping feet and the crash of weights being set down heavily, doubtless the boxes, with their freight of earth. There was a sound of hammering. It is the box being nailed down. Now I can hear the heavy feet tramping again along the hall, with many other idle feet coming behind them.

(30) The door is shut, the chains rattle. There is a grinding of the key in the lock. I can hear the key withdrawn, then another door opens and shuts. I hear the creaking of lock and bolt.

Hark! In the courtyard and down the rocky way the roll of heavy wheels, the crack of whips, and the chorus of the Szgany as they pass into the distance.

I am alone in the castle with those horrible women. Faugh! Mina is a woman, and there is nought in common.

(35) They are devils of the Pit!

I shall not remain alone with them. I shall try to scale the castle wall farther than I have yet attempted. I shall take some of the gold with me, lest I want it later. I may find a way from this dreadful place.

And then away for home! Away to the quickest and nearest train! Away from the cursed spot, from this cursed land, where the devil and his children still walk with earthly feet!

(40) At least God's mercy is better than that of those monsters, and the precipice is steep and high. At its foot a man may sleep, as a man. Goodbye, all. Mina!

1. What of these selections is not one of the sensations of the narrator in this excerpt?

   A. levity
   B. hesitation
   C. terror
   D. fear
   E. trepidation

2. Which of the following best describes "satiate" line (5) as used in the excerpt?

   A. spur
   B. spread
   C. furnish
   D. overindulge
   E. create

3. The combination "blaze of basilisk horror" line (10) is an example of what device?

   A. anadiplosis
   B. anaphora
   C. alliteration
   D. assonance
   E. repetition

4. The quote, "The sight seemed to paralyze me," line (10) seems to be necessary because

   A. it helps explain the definition of basilisk.
   B. it explains why the shovel struck only a glancing blow.
   C. it establishes a change of pace in the story slowing it down for effect.
   D. it helps explain why, even though it would appear there was a perfect opportunity, he didn't finish what he started.
   E. it helps explain why as he drew the shovel away the flange of the blade caught the edge of the lid causing it to close.

5. What can we determine of the physical setting related in lines (18–26)?

   A. There is a passageway from the Count's room, which is on the main floor, to a vault below where the boxes reside; an alternative entrance to the vault exists or the villagers have key access to it.
   B. The Count's room is on the second floor and the boxes are kept on the main floor in a vault where the villagers gain entry through a side door or have a key to the main door.
   C. The vault is on the main floor and there is a passageway from the main floor to the Count's room where the villagers gain entry with a key or alternative entrance.
   D. The boxes are in the vault on the second floor and the Count's room is on the first floor; the villagers gain access through an alternative route or door.
   E. There is an entrance to the Count's room through the passageway to where the boxes are stored on the second floor; the vault is on the first floor and the villagers gain access through a different entrance.

6. Which of the following best describes "lintels" line (25) as used in the excerpt?

   A. lamp shades
   B. firebox supports
   C. chandelier bobbles
   D. door framing
   E. curving banister

7. Which selection should the reader NOT infer in lines (30–31)?

   A. The villagers attendance was pre-planned.
   B. The villagers had previously visited the castle.
   C. The villagers were unaware of the narrator's presence in the castle.
   D. The entry used by the villagers was infrequently used.
   E. The villagers recently frequented the castle.

8. Which of the selections provide the least support for the inference that the boxes the villagers removed were believed by them to have been filled with corpses?

   A. Line (28) refers to the boxes as "freight of earth."

   B. Line (2) says "The coming night might see my own body a banquet in a similar way to those horrid three."

   C. Lines (34–35) reads "I am alone in the castle with those horrible women. Faugh! Mina is a woman, and there is nought in common. They are devils of the Pit!"

   D. Lines (25–26) says "I was again a prisoner, and the net of doom was closing round me more closely."

   E. Lines (38–39) state "Away from the cursed spot, from this cursed land, where the devil and his children still walk with earthly feet!"

9. Which device is best represented by "They are devils of the Pit" line (35)?

   A. alliteration
   B. allusion
   C. allegory
   D. assonance
   E. anaphora

10. Which word best describes the overall tone of the entire passage?

   A. frustrating
   B. eerie
   C. nerve racking
   D. foreboding
   E. anticipatory

Answers and Explanations for Skill Set Nine

1. The correct choice is **A.**

   Explanation: The narrator experiences all of these feelings during the passage except A, "levity," making it the correct choice.

2. The correct choice is **D.**

   Explanation: All choices save for D have something to do with furthering the lust for blood so all of these might fit if that were the condition. Ironically, the only way for Dracula to pass his lust or craving for blood to others is to drink their blood himself. Since "overindulge" would only be possible by his drinking of blood, Choice D is correct.

3. The correct choice is **C.**

   Explanation: The repetition of the initial consonant sound like "blaze of basilisk" is alliteration, making Choice C correct.

4. The correct choice is **D.**

   Explanation: This is a tough question. All of the answer choices are correct, but only Choice D is the best choice. Choice A is correct because it does provide context clues for the definition of "basilisk," which is a legendary reptile with a fatal glare and breath. Choices B, C, and E are all correct because someone with even partial paralysis would have difficulty performing mostly routine physical tasks. Choice D provides the best answer to the question as it relates to necessity. The necessity for the partial paralysis is that it is the only factor given to answer the unspoken question, "Why don't you finish the job you started with the shovel?" If not for the paralysis, a flaw in the development of the plot is born.

5. The correct choice is **A.**

   Explanation: Dare I say that these are the times that try men's souls? A question like this won't appear often, thank goodness, but you may see one at some time to test your ability to remain active in your reading. If you follow the story, or go back and "follow the yellow brick road," you will see that Choice A is correct.

6. The correct choice is **D.**

   Explanation: Upon close review, we see that the wind did not cause the dust to fly, but rather the door that blew to with a shock. So the door is actually what caused the flying dust. The closest thing to the door is obviously the door framing, which makes Choice D correct, and once again shows how context clues help determine the meaning of words.

7. The correct choice is **E.**

   Explanation: Choice A, "that the villagers attendance was pre-planned," is correct as they had their own key. Choice B, "that the villagers had previously visited the castle," is correct because without guidance they knew where to go and how to get there. Choice C, "that the villagers were unaware of the narrator's presence in the castle," as they didn't look for him. Choice D, "that the entry used by the villagers was infrequently used," is correct because of the grinding and creaking in the locks and bolt, evidencing limited use. Choice E, "that the villagers recently frequented the castle," does not seem likely as they did not know of the narrator's presence, and the locks creaked, making it the best choice.

8. The correct choice is **D.**

   Explanation: We'll need to walk through these to see how they all provide better support than Choice D. Choice A, "freight of earth," supports that the boxes were weighted with earth to replicate corpses so the villagers would not miss the three women who had become semi-demons. Choice B, "The coming night might see my own body a banquet in a similar way to those horrid three," supports that the three women are in fact now semi-demons and as such couldn't be in the boxes because semi-demons are children of the devil and still walk with earthly feet. Choice C, "I am alone in the castle with those horrible women. Faugh! Mina is a woman, and there is nought in common. They are devils of the Pit!" supports again that the three women are still wandering about. Choice E, "Away from the cursed spot, from this cursed land, where the devil and his children still walk with earthly feet!"

support that the Count and the three women are in position to make the narrator's body the banquet of the evening. Choice D, "I was again a prisoner, and the net of doom was closing round me more closely," conveys a concern but does not provide as good support to the inference as the other choices, making it the best choice for this question.

9. The correct choice is **B.**

Explanation: Choice B, "allusion," is the best selection. "Pit" alludes to Hell, ergo, allusion.

10. The correct choice is **B.**

Explanation: Certainly, it was frustrating, Choice A, when the narrator couldn't get back in the passage. Certainly, it was nerve racking, Choice C, knowing that if things didn't change, tonight would be his night. Certainly, it was foreboding to hear the villagers leaving without attracting their attention. And, certainly, it was anticipatory in that the narrator anticipated what would befall him at next nightfall. But, the overall tone, at every turn and during each of the previous examples, was "eerie," Choice B.

Long Reading Comprehension Skill Set Ten

Note: Skill sets may contain more questions than the actual SAT to show the potential range of questioning.

The passages below are followed by questions based on their content; questions following a pair of related passages may also be based on the relationship between the paired passages. Answer the questions on the basis of what is *stated* or *implied* in the passages and in any introductory material that may be provided.

Questions 1–10 are based on the following passage.

The following is an excerpt from Oliver Twist by Charles Dickens.

Among other public buildings in a certain town, which for many reasons it will be prudent to refrain from mentioning, and to which I will assign no fictitious name, there is one anciently common to most towns, great or small: to wit, a workhouse; and in this workhouse was born; on a day and date which I need not trouble myself to repeat, inasmuch as it can be of no possible consequence to the reader, in this stage of the business at all events; the item
(5) of mortality whose name is prefixed to the head of this chapter.

For a long time after it was ushered into this world of sorrow and trouble, by the parish surgeon, it remained a matter of considerable doubt whether the child would survive to bear any name at all; in which case it is somewhat more than probable that these memoirs would never have appeared; or, if they had, that being comprised within a couple of pages, they would have possessed the inestimable merit of being the most concise and faithful specimen
(10) of biography, extant in the literature of any age or country.

Although I am not disposed to maintain that the being born in a workhouse, is in itself the most fortunate and enviable circumstance that can possibly befall a human being, I do mean to say that in this particular instance, it was the best thing for Oliver Twist that could by possibility have occurred. The fact is, that there was considerable difficulty in inducing Oliver to take upon himself the office of respiration, - a troublesome practice, but one which
(15) custom has rendered necessary to our easy existence; and for some time he lay gasping on a little flock mattress, rather unequally poised between this world and the next: the balance being decidedly in favour of the latter. Now, if, during this brief period, Oliver had been surrounded by careful grandmothers, anxious aunts, experienced nurses, and doctors of profound wisdom, he would most inevitably and indubitably have been killed in no time. There being nobody by, however, but a pauper old woman, who was rendered rather misty by an unwonted al-
(20) lowance of beer; and a parish surgeon who did such matters by contract; Oliver and Nature fought out the point between them. The result was, that, after a few struggles, Oliver breathed, sneezed, and proceeded to advertise to the inmates of the workhouse the fact of a new burden having been imposed upon the parish, by setting up as loud a cry as could reasonably have been expected from a male infant who had not been possessed of that very useful appendage, a voice, for a much longer space of time than three minutes and a quarter.

(25) As Oliver gave this first proof of the free and proper action of his lungs, the patchwork coverlet which was carelessly flung over the iron bedstead, rustled; the pale face of a young woman was raised feebly from the pillow; and a faint voice imperfectly articulated the words, "Let me see the child, and die."

The surgeon had been sitting with his face turned towards the fire: giving the palms of his hands a warm and a rub alternately. As the young woman spoke, he rose, and advancing to the bed's head, said, with more kindness
(30) than might have been expected of him:

"Oh, you must not talk about dying yet."

"Lor bless her dear heart, no!" interposed the nurse, hastily depositing in her pocket a green glass bottle, the contents of which she had been tasting in a corner with evident satisfaction.

"Lor bless her dear heart, when she has lived as long as I have, sir, and had thirteen children of her own, and all
(35) on 'em dead except two, and them in the wurkus with me, she'll know better than to take on in that way, bless her dear heart! Think what it is to be a mother, there's a dear young lamb do."

Apparently this consolatory perspective of a mother's prospects failed in producing its due effect. The patient shook her head, and stretched out her hand towards the child.

The surgeon deposited it in her arms. She imprinted her cold white lips passionately on its forehead; passed her
(40) hands over her face; gazed wildly round; shuddered; fell back - and died. They chafed her breast, hands, and temples; but the blood had stopped forever. They talked of hope and comfort. They had been strangers too long.

"It's all over, Mrs. Thingummy!" said the surgeon at last.

"Ah, poor dear, so it is!" said the nurse, picking up the cork of the green bottle, which had fallen out on the pillow, as she stooped to take up the child. "Poor dear!"

(45)   "You needn't mind sending up to me, if the child cries, nurse," said the surgeon, putting on his gloves with great deliberation. "It's very likely it WILL be troublesome. Give it a little gruel if it is." He put on his hat, and, pausing by the bed-side on his way to the door, added, "She was a good-looking girl, too; where did she come from?"

"She was brought here last night," replied the old woman, "by the overseer's order. She was found lying in the street. She had walked some distance, for her shoes were worn to pieces; but where she came from, or where she

(50) was going to, nobody knows."

The surgeon leaned over the body, and raised the left hand. "The old story," he said, shaking his head: "no wedding-ring, I see. Ah! Good night!"

The medical gentleman walked away to dinner; and the nurse, having once more applied herself to the green bottle, sat down on a low chair before the fire, and proceeded to dress the infant.

(55)   What an excellent example of the power of dress, young Oliver Twist was! Wrapped in the blanket which had hitherto formed his only covering, he might have been the child of a nobleman or a beggar; it would have been hard for the haughtiest stranger to have assigned him his proper station in society. But now that he was enveloped in the old calico robes which had grown yellow in the same service, he was badged and ticketed, and fell into his place at once - a parish child - the orphan of a workhouse—he humble, half-starved drudge - to be cuffed and buffeted

(60) through the world—despised by all, and pitied by none.

Oliver cried lustily. If he could have known that he was an orphan, left to the tender mercies of church-wardens and overseers, perhaps he would have cried the louder.

1. The phrase "the item of mortality" line (4–5) is an example of

A.   anastrophe.
B.   synecdoche.
C.   hyperbole.
D.   metaphor.
E.   oxymoron.

2. The author is unwilling to give many details in the first paragraph because

A.   his sources are sketchy and incomplete information could harm the authenticity of the story.
B.   likely because the establishment that allowed the writer to observe conditioned that allowance on anonymity.
C.   a workhouse is not something representing community pride so the author is giving consideration.
D.   writers like to protect sources and he is protecting that privilege.
E.   orphanages records are protected so to protect all parties so little information could be given.

3. The overall purpose for the third paragraph can best be described

A.   to give the reader a first good look at the hardships facing someone born into a workhouse.
B.   to reinforce the difficulty Twist had coming into this world.
C.   to identify some of the main characters in the story.
D.   to introduce the coldness and callousness of the economy at that time.
E.   to inform the reader that in some respects, Twist is better off in the workhouse.

4. The fact that Twist, we are told, would have surely died at birth had he not been born in a place where literally only the strong survive, creates an example of

A.   an extended metaphor.
B.   an allegory.
C.   a situational irony.
D.   a foil.
E.   an altruism.

5. What season can the reader infer it is based upon the information given in the passage?

   A. early spring

   B. summer

   C. fall

   D. winter

   E. late spring

6. What was the author's purpose in referring to Twist's arrival as a "new burden" line (22)?

   A. to remind the reader that, like the nurse, an infant is not easy to care for

   B. to establish that all residents in the workhouse contribute to all duties which have now just increased

   C. to reinforce the harsh conditions in the workhouse and the declination of resources due to his arrival

   D. to qualify the notion that space in the workhouse is at a critical shortage

   E. to forward the idea that there are limited beds in the workhouse and there would be shortages

7. The phrase "imperfectly articulated" line (27) exemplifies

   A. assonance.

   B. synecdoche.

   C. parataxis.

   D. oxymoron.

   E. ellipses.

8. What of the following does not qualify as irony presented by the nurse's speech to the new mother in paragraph 8 lines (34–36)?

   A. All the new mother wants to do is see her baby, and the nurse launches a soliloquy.

   B. The new mother is hanging onto life by a thread with the first child, and the nurse is encouraging her to hold on so she can experience this festive occasion multiples of times.

   C. The nurse, in trying to console her, likely makes her feel even more miserable in that all but two of the nurses children have died and a new mother likely does not wish to face that prospect.

   D. The workhouse overseer did accept her, even with child, into the workhouse.

   E. Understanding that the only hope you might have for your newborn is that you can spend life together, albeit in a workhouse living from hand-to-mouth daily in a cold, overcrowded, under-rationed facility should be the one piece of information to brighten any new mother.

9. Which of the following best describes what the inner voice of the surgeon likely was saying during his remarks in lines (51–52)?

   A. It's another shame that the parish couldn't have helped before now.

   B. What's wrong with our society that men are not supporting women in this condition?

   C. Why doesn't the parish open its doors to these women before it becomes a matter of life or death?

   D. She's just another loose woman who got herself into trouble and deserved what she got.

   E. She's probably addicted to drugs as well as being pregnant.

10. What does the author convey with "What an excellent example of the power of dress, young Oliver Twist was!" line (55)?

   A. His blanket was of excellent quality.

   B. In the beginning, in the very beginning, all are noble.

   C. Every newborn is dressed the same initially.

   D. All infants who are warm are happy with their clothing.

   E. Only older people are concerned with the clothes of infants.

Answers and Explanations for Skill Set Ten

1. The correct choice is **D.**

Explanation: Choice D, "metaphor," is correct as "the item of mortality" is a metaphor for the baby Twist.

2. The correct choice is **C.**

Explanation: Based on the overall tone of the piece, one might understand that workhouses were not well-thought-of and sometimes represented the back or dark side of church orphanages. Choice C captures this position.

3. The correct choice is **A.**

Explanation: Although all of the choices contribute to the overall development and understanding of the story line, Choice A best describes the totality of the purpose.

4. The correct choice is **C.**

Explanation: Choice C, "situational irony," is correct as the situation of his being born in a workhouse where there are no emergency or supplemental medical opportunities, a minimally hardly qualified staff to handle an emergency, and wherein the only ones who live are the ones that have the will and strength to fight and survive.

5. The correct choice is **D.**

Explanation: Choice D, "winter," is correct. Because the doctor warms and rubs his hands by the fire and the nurse dressed the infant by the fire indicating the coldness inside the workhouse derived likely from the winter season.

6. The correct choice is **C.**

Explanation: As the parish who ran the workhouse relied upon donations and contributions for the continuation of their services, each new arrival (particularly a newborn who would not be able to work and contribute to the efforts for years to come), became a burden and an immediate drain on extraordinarily limited resources.

7. The correct choice is **D.**

Explanation: Choice D, "oxymoron," is correct as one cannot imperfectly articulate. They are incompatible as articulation is the effective delivery which is not imperfect, ergo; oxymoron.

8. The correct choice is **D.**

Explanation: All other choices present either situational, dramatic, or verbal irony, making Choice D the one that does not.

9. The correct choice is **D.**

Explanation: The fact that the surgeon thought to look at the finger for a ring and, seeing none, the body language (shaking his head), suggest his disdain with the situation makes Choice D the best selection.

10. The correct choice is **B.**

Explanation: The author is effectively saying that at birth, all are noble creatures whether the son of a nobleman or a pauper. The distinction is thrust upon them by others, not their own merits. But, for that first moment, all experience greatness, making Choice B correct.

PART III

PRACTICE TESTS

Answer Sheet for Practice Test One

Section 1

1 Ⓐ Ⓑ Ⓒ Ⓓ Ⓔ	16 Ⓐ Ⓑ Ⓒ Ⓓ Ⓔ
2 Ⓐ Ⓑ Ⓒ Ⓓ Ⓔ	17 Ⓐ Ⓑ Ⓒ Ⓓ Ⓔ
3 Ⓐ Ⓑ Ⓒ Ⓓ Ⓔ	18 Ⓐ Ⓑ Ⓒ Ⓓ Ⓔ
4 Ⓐ Ⓑ Ⓒ Ⓓ Ⓔ	19 Ⓐ Ⓑ Ⓒ Ⓓ Ⓔ
5 Ⓐ Ⓑ Ⓒ Ⓓ Ⓔ	20 Ⓐ Ⓑ Ⓒ Ⓓ Ⓔ
6 Ⓐ Ⓑ Ⓒ Ⓓ Ⓔ	21 Ⓐ Ⓑ Ⓒ Ⓓ Ⓔ
7 Ⓐ Ⓑ Ⓒ Ⓓ Ⓔ	22 Ⓐ Ⓑ Ⓒ Ⓓ Ⓔ
8 Ⓐ Ⓑ Ⓒ Ⓓ Ⓔ	23 Ⓐ Ⓑ Ⓒ Ⓓ Ⓔ
9 Ⓐ Ⓑ Ⓒ Ⓓ Ⓔ	24 Ⓐ Ⓑ Ⓒ Ⓓ Ⓔ
10 Ⓐ Ⓑ Ⓒ Ⓓ Ⓔ	25 Ⓐ Ⓑ Ⓒ Ⓓ Ⓔ
11 Ⓐ Ⓑ Ⓒ Ⓓ Ⓔ	26 Ⓐ Ⓑ Ⓒ Ⓓ Ⓔ
12 Ⓐ Ⓑ Ⓒ Ⓓ Ⓔ	27 Ⓐ Ⓑ Ⓒ Ⓓ Ⓔ
13 Ⓐ Ⓑ Ⓒ Ⓓ Ⓔ	28 Ⓐ Ⓑ Ⓒ Ⓓ Ⓔ
14 Ⓐ Ⓑ Ⓒ Ⓓ Ⓔ	29 Ⓐ Ⓑ Ⓒ Ⓓ Ⓔ
15 Ⓐ Ⓑ Ⓒ Ⓓ Ⓔ	30 Ⓐ Ⓑ Ⓒ Ⓓ Ⓔ

Section 2

1 Ⓐ Ⓑ Ⓒ Ⓓ Ⓔ	16 Ⓐ Ⓑ Ⓒ Ⓓ Ⓔ
2 Ⓐ Ⓑ Ⓒ Ⓓ Ⓔ	17 Ⓐ Ⓑ Ⓒ Ⓓ Ⓔ
3 Ⓐ Ⓑ Ⓒ Ⓓ Ⓔ	18 Ⓐ Ⓑ Ⓒ Ⓓ Ⓔ
4 Ⓐ Ⓑ Ⓒ Ⓓ Ⓔ	19 Ⓐ Ⓑ Ⓒ Ⓓ Ⓔ
5 Ⓐ Ⓑ Ⓒ Ⓓ Ⓔ	20 Ⓐ Ⓑ Ⓒ Ⓓ Ⓔ
6 Ⓐ Ⓑ Ⓒ Ⓓ Ⓔ	21 Ⓐ Ⓑ Ⓒ Ⓓ Ⓔ
7 Ⓐ Ⓑ Ⓒ Ⓓ Ⓔ	22 Ⓐ Ⓑ Ⓒ Ⓓ Ⓔ
8 Ⓐ Ⓑ Ⓒ Ⓓ Ⓔ	23 Ⓐ Ⓑ Ⓒ Ⓓ Ⓔ
9 Ⓐ Ⓑ Ⓒ Ⓓ Ⓔ	24 Ⓐ Ⓑ Ⓒ Ⓓ Ⓔ
10 Ⓐ Ⓑ Ⓒ Ⓓ Ⓔ	25 Ⓐ Ⓑ Ⓒ Ⓓ Ⓔ
11 Ⓐ Ⓑ Ⓒ Ⓓ Ⓔ	26 Ⓐ Ⓑ Ⓒ Ⓓ Ⓔ
12 Ⓐ Ⓑ Ⓒ Ⓓ Ⓔ	27 Ⓐ Ⓑ Ⓒ Ⓓ Ⓔ
13 Ⓐ Ⓑ Ⓒ Ⓓ Ⓔ	28 Ⓐ Ⓑ Ⓒ Ⓓ Ⓔ
14 Ⓐ Ⓑ Ⓒ Ⓓ Ⓔ	29 Ⓐ Ⓑ Ⓒ Ⓓ Ⓔ
15 Ⓐ Ⓑ Ⓒ Ⓓ Ⓔ	30 Ⓐ Ⓑ Ⓒ Ⓓ Ⓔ

CUT HERE

Section 1: Sentence Completion

Each sentence below has one or two blanks, each blank indicating that something has been omitted. Beneath the sentence are five words or sets of words labeled **A** through **E.** Choose the word or set of words that, when inserted in the sentence, *best* fits the meaning of the sentence as a whole.

---

1. The _____ behavior of the demonstrators became even more apparent when they all chained themselves together when the authorities came on scene.

    A. indolent
    B. spurious
    C. individual
    D. recalcitrant
    E. cohesive

2. The _____ dress of the performers was considered _____ by the censors.

    A. matching. . .unfashionable
    B. ostentatious. . .repugnant
    C. overly revealing. . .acceptable
    D. uniform. . .haughty
    E. color of. . .errant

3. It is absolutely _____ that the individual assigned to defuse a bomb be extremely _____.

    A. essential. . .mature
    B. alright. . .nervous
    C. necessary. . .excited
    D. warranted. . .tired
    E. critical. . .dexterous

4. She was not normally invited to serve as a critic because she had a _____ toward _____.

    A. desire. . .reading
    B. bent. . .commonplace
    C. proclivity. . .castigation
    D. tendency. . .wayward
    E. philosophy. . .everything

5. The problem with scoring well on too many SAT practice tests is the tendency toward _____.

    A. success
    B. complacency
    C. burn-out
    D. supremacy
    E. celerity

6. Throughout history great civilizations including the Egyptians, Romans, and Greeks can trace their downfalls to a certain societal _____ and general failing of moral values.

    A. hierarchy
    B. bliss
    C. indifference
    D. decadence
    E. latitude

7. Had Einstein not been such a _____ mathematician, many of our engineering accomplishments may have taken many years before even reaching the drawing board.

    A. prodigious
    B. superb
    C. qualified
    D. prophetic
    E. prosaic

GO ON TO THE NEXT PAGE

8. Had it not been for his _____ prowess, Muhammad Ali, formerly known as Cassius Clay, would not be considered one of the worlds' greatest fighters of all time.

   A. elocutionary
   B. prestidigitation
   C. ponderous
   D. poetical
   E. pugilistic

9. Were I indeed _____, I likely would not still be teaching, for I would have long ago played the winning lottery numbers and be traveling the world sending postcards to the classroom.

   A. fortuitous
   B. clairvoyant
   C. prescient
   D. philanthropic
   E. perspicacious

10. Given the seeming _____ of alternatives to fossil fuels, it seems rather _____ to continue on our current path without fully directing our collective resources to develop independence from questionable suppliers.

    A. gluttony. . .reticent
    B. plethora. . .pernicious
    C. readiness. . .curious
    D. availability. . .understandable
    E. capacity. . .forgiving

Section 1: Short Reading Comprehension

The passages below are followed by questions based on their content; questions following a pair of related passages may also be based on the relationship between the paired passages. Answer the questions on the basis of what is *stated* or *implied* in the passages and in any introductory material that may be provided.

Questions 11–13 are based on the following passage.

When Rob became interested in electricity, his clear-headed father considered the boy's fancy to be instructive as well as amusing; so he heartily encouraged his son, and Rob never lacked batteries, motors, or supplies of any sort that his experiments might require.

He fitted up the little back room in the attic as his workshop, and from thence, a network of wires soon ran
(5) throughout the house. Not only had every outside door its electric bell, but every window was fitted with a burglar alarm; moreover, no one could cross the threshold of any interior room without registering the fact in Rob's workshop. The gas was lighted by an electric fob; a chime, connected with an erratic clock in the boy's room, woke the servants at all hours of the night and caused the cook to give warning; a bell rang whenever the postman dropped a letter into the box; there were bells, bells, bells everywhere, ringing at the right time, the wrong time and all the
(10) time. And there were telephones in the different rooms, too, through which Rob could call up the different members of the family just when they did not wish to be disturbed.

His mother and sisters soon came to vote the boy's scientific craze a nuisance; but his father was delighted with these evidences of Rob's skill as an electrician and insisted that he be allowed perfect freedom in carrying out his ideas.

11. Which is the best selection describing the social commentary inferred in the passage?

    A. Father knows best.

    B. Father makes the decisions as head of household.

    C. Mother provides input taken into consideration by father.

    D. Mother has half decision-making authority over the children.

    E. Sisters have a vote in the family business as do all family members.

12. The author's purpose for the second paragraph lines (4–11) is

    A. to show how ingenious Rob was.

    B. to evidence that Rob lacked for no supplies.

    C. to represent just how far Rob's experiments went.

    D. to fully develop the latitude father gave and the control he had.

    E. to show just how intrusive the experiments were, much to the chagrin of all inhabitants.

13. Paragraph three, lines (12–14), performs which of the following functions?

    A. shows that mother and sister's input is valuable and heralded

    B. shows father is willing to listen and alter decisions if warranted

    C. postulates the notion that perhaps the experiments have gone too far

    D. demonstrates the continuing grip father has over the entire household

    E. warrants a rethinking of the continuous supplying of materials to Rob

GO ON TO THE NEXT PAGE

Questions 14–17 are based on the following passage.

In conclusion, it seized first the corpse of the daughter, and thrust it up the chimney, as it was found; then that of the old lady, which it immediately hurled through the window headlong.

As the ape approached the casement with its mutilated burden, the sailor shrank aghast to the rod, and, rather gliding than clambering down it, hurried at once home—dreading the consequences of the butchery, and gladly (5) abandoning, in his terror, all solicitude about the fate of the Ourang-Outang. The words heard by the party upon the staircase were the Frenchman's exclamations of horror and affright, commingled with the fiendish jabberings of the brute.

I have scarcely anything to add. The Ourang-Outang must have escaped from the chamber, by the rod, just before the break of the door. It must have closed the window as it passed through it. It was subsequently caught by the owner (10) himself, who obtained for it a very large sum at the Jardin des Plantes. Le Don was instantly released, upon our narration of the circumstances (with some comments from Dupin) at the bureau of the Prefect of Police. This functionary, however well disposed to my friend, could not altogether conceal his chagrin at the turn which affairs had taken, and was fain to indulge in a sarcasm or two, about the propriety of every person minding his own business.

14. The word "solicitude" in line (5) most nearly means

    A. interest.

    B. curiosity.

    C. concern.

    D. anger.

    E. fear.

15. The word "brute" in line (7) refers to

    A. the fiend.

    B. the sailor.

    C. the Ourang-Outang.

    D. the party.

    E. the Frenchman.

16. Which selection best rephrases "I have scarcely anything to add" line (8)?

    A. I only have a little bit more to tell.

    B. I'm afraid of what I have left to tell.

    C. I'm concerned I can't add much more.

    D. I don't know anything else to add.

    E. I've told you everything I know.

17. Which selection best describes the action referred to by "break of the door" line (9)?

    A. The door was broken into by using a rod.

    B. The party broke down the door.

    C. The party entered through the door broken by the brute.

    D. The Ourang-Outang broke the door to gain entry.

    E. The sailor broke into the chamber allowing the Ourang-Outang to follow.

Questions 18–20 are based on the following passage.

Your knowledge of English Literature—to which I am indebted for the first faithful and intelligent translation of my novels into the Italian language—has long since informed you, that there are certain important social topics which are held to be forbidden to the English novelist (no matter how seriously and how delicately he may treat them), by a narrow-minded minority of readers, and by the critics who flatter their prejudices. You also know, having done me the
(5) honor to read my books; that I respect my art far too sincerely to permit limits to be wantonly assigned to it, which are imposed in no other civilized country on the face of the earth. When my work is undertaken with a pure purpose, I claim the same liberty which is accorded to a writer in a newspaper, or to a clergyman in a pulpit; knowing, by previous experience, that the increase of readers and the lapse of time will assuredly do me justice, if I have only written well enough to deserve it.

18. What is the overall mood of this passage?

- A. incipient
- B. witty
- C. sarcastic
- D. curious
- E. angry

19. Which statement least describes the author's feelings about English critics?

- A. They are not educated enough to understand the social implications of these writings.
- B. They think more of their artificial airs than of dealing with current social issues.
- C. They do not know how to deal with enlightened authors so they forbid the reading of them.
- D. They wish their country to remain sheltered and backward by restricting authors' freedoms.
- E. They are wont to hold others who express views in various forums to the same restrictions as literary authors.

20. Which selections best indicates how the author believes he will be vindicated?

- A. when sufficient people cry out for more liberal values
- B. when moral values deteriorate over time
- C. when well recognized enough to command acceptance
- D. when enough readers read over a prolonged period of time
- E. when the limiting country lessens its hold on literary writers

GO ON TO THE NEXT PAGE

Section 1: Long Reading Comprehension

The passages below are followed by questions based on their content; questions following a pair of related passages may also be based on the relationship between the paired passages. Answer the questions on the basis of what is *stated* or *implied* in the passages and in any introductory material that may be provided.

Questions 21–30 are based on the following passage.

The following passage is taken from Sombody's Luggage by Charles Dickens.

But the Dust-Bin was going down then, and your father took but little, excepting from a liquid point of view. Your mother's object in those visits was of a house-keeping character, and you was set on to whistle your father out. Sometimes he came out, but generally not. Come or not come, however, all that part of his existence which was unconnected with open Waitering was kept a close secret, and was acknowledged by your mother to be a close se-
(5)   cret, and you and your mother flitted about the court, close secrets both of you, and would scarcely have confessed under torture that you know your father, or that your father had any name than Dick (which wasn't his name, though he was never known by any other), or that he had kith or kin or chick or child. Perhaps the attraction of this mystery, combined with your father's having a damp compartment, to himself, behind a leaky cistern, at the Dust-Bin, a sort of a cellar compartment, with a sink in it, and a smell, and a plate-rack, and a bottle-rack, and three win-
(10)   dows that didn't match each other or anything else, and no daylight, caused your young mind to feel convinced that you must grow up to be a Waiter too; but you did feel convinced of it, and so did all your brothers, down to your sister. Every one of you felt convinced that you was born to the Waitering. At this stage of your career, what was your feelings one day when your father came home to your mother in open broad daylight, of itself an act of Madness on the part of a Waiter, and took to his bed (leastwise, your mother and family's bed), with the statement
(15)   that his eyes were devilled kidneys. Physicians being in vain, your father expired, after repeating at intervals for a day and a night, when gleams of reason and old business fitfully illuminated his being, "Two and two is five. And three is sixpence." Interred in the parochial department of the neighbouring [sic] churchyard, and accompanied to the grave by as many Waiters of long standing as could spare the morning time from their soiled glasses (namely, one), your bereaved form was attired in a white neckankecher [sic], and you was took on from motives of benevo-
(20)   lence at The George and Gridiron, theatrical and supper. Here, supporting nature on what you found in the plates (which was as it happened, and but too often thoughtlessly, immersed in mustard), and on what you found in the glasses (which rarely went beyond driblets and lemon), by night you dropped asleep standing, till you was cuffed awake, and by day was set to polishing every individual article in the coffee-room. Your couch being sawdust; your counterpane being ashes of cigars. Here, frequently hiding a heavy heart under the smart tie of your white neck-
(25)   ankecher [sic] (or correctly speaking lower down and more to the left), you picked up the rudiments of knowledge from an extra, by the name of Bishops, and by calling plate-washer, and gradually elevating your mind with chalk on the back of the corner-box partition, until such time as you used the inkstand when it was out of hand, attained to manhood, and to be the Waiter that you find yourself.

I could wish here to offer a few respectful words on behalf of the calling so long the calling of myself and fam-
(30)   ily, and the public interest in which is but too often very limited. We are not generally understood. No, we are not. Allowance enough is not made for us. For, say that we ever show a little drooping listlessness of spirits, or what might be termed indifference or apathy. Put it to yourself what would your own state of mind be, if you was one of an enormous family every member of which except you was always greedy, and in a hurry. Put it to yourself that you was regularly replete with animal food at the slack hours of one in the day and again at nine p.m., and that the
(35)   repleter [sic] you was, the more voracious all your fellow-creatures came in. Put it to yourself that it was your business, when your digestion was well on, to take a personal interest and sympathy in a hundred gentlemen fresh and fresh (say, for the sake of argument, only a hundred), whose imaginations was given up to grease and fat and gravy and melted butter, and abandoned to questioning you about cuts of this, and dishes of that, each of 'em going on as if him and you and the bill of fare was alone in the world.

21. What is being inferred by "your father took but little, excepting from a liquid point of view" line (1)?

    A. He rarely appropriated anything other than liquids.
    B. He was unable to procure anything of a substantial nature.
    C. He was only allowed to consume liquids as opposed to solids.
    D. He was not inclined to food only alcohol.
    E. He was on a restricted diet comprised of liquids only.

22. The discussion of visits to father's compartment lines (1–7) suggests that

    A. the family bonds were strong.
    B. suitable income made it possible to maintain two well-furnished homes.
    C. there was little romance between husband and wife.
    D. there was not the intention of hiding a familial relationship.
    E. the family often met to perform routine tasks as a family.

23. Overall, what is the author referring when he writes "Perhaps the attraction of this mystery" lines (7–8)?

    A. the idea that no one was to know his father's name
    B. the fact that no one knew that his father was married and apparently weren't allowed to
    C. the situation of only visiting his father instead of living together with approval from the wife
    D. the entire secrecy of the lifestyle of his family notwithstanding the compartment
    E. the compartment his father kept and lived alone in even though it didn't seem like much

24. What purpose was served by the detailed description of the compartment lines (8–10)?

    A. informs the reader of a level of economic expectation for a waiter at this time
    B. provides a window into the lifestyle the father is able to provide his family
    C. provides a rationale for the wife to come over and perform house-keeping
    D. explains why father would not want his real identity known to others
    E. allows the reader to understand more fully the mystery surrounding the desire to become a waiter

25. All of the following may indicate why the author states the father coming home is an "act of Madness" lines (13–14) EXCEPT:

    A. it is broad daylight and not a visit under the shroud of darkness.
    B. it is during the day when he should be working.
    C. he risks exposing that he has a wife and family.
    D. it is likely someone will find out who he really is.
    E. it is feasible that he will cause the son to lose his job.

26. The use of the term "expired" line (15) in lieu of "died" is an example of

    A. litotes.
    B. anaphora.
    C. hyperbole.
    D. understatement.
    E. allegory.

GO ON TO THE NEXT PAGE

27. Why does the language "Two and two is five. And three is sixpence" lines (16–17) illuminate rather than confuse the character of the father on his deathbed?

  A. It is reasonable that a father would be concerned about his family's finances following his death.

  B. It is normal for a dying person to speak of money or fortune upon their deathbed.

  C. It indicates that he wanted his wife and son to be sure to get the money from the compartment.

  D. It was the amount being communicated that should be paid for his burial.

  E. It was his practice the whole of his daily vocation.

28. What is meant by "supporting nature" line (20)?

  A. being an environmentalist

  B. giving to causes of the parish following the death of the father

  C. because the George and Gridiron was an outdoor theatrical and supper establishment

  D. staying alive on what could be scraped from plates and glasses

  E. keeping the cycle of life in balance with working and supplying his mother's needs

29. Which selection best describes the overall purpose of the author in lines (1–28)?

  A. to establish how the main character became a waiter

  B. to establish that the life of a waiter was harsh

  C. to illuminate the lifestyle of a waiter during the time of this writing

  D. to share the hardships of the wife of a waiter

  E. to offer some explanation as to the secrecy shrouding the father

30. What term best describes the overall tone toward waiters in this excerpt?

  A. satiric

  B. empathetic

  C. belittling

  D. apologetic

  E. informational

Section 2: Sentence Completion

Each sentence below has one or two blanks, each blank indicating that something has been omitted. Beneath the sentence are five words or sets of words labeled **A** through **E.** Choose the word or set of words that, when inserted in the sentence, *best* fits the meaning of the sentence as a whole.

1. Given the _____ nature of movie stars, I suppose one should not question the divorce rate among them, but question whether it is a character flaw developed in the business, or a trait necessary to enter the business.

    A. grandiose
    B. capricious
    C. ideological
    D. indulgent
    E. pernicious

2. Notwithstanding much educated _____, even as we speak, there is no _____ relationship between current levels of hydrocarbon output and ozone deterioration.

    A. speculation. . .tenuous
    B. conjecture. . .proven
    C. evidence. . .speculative
    D. argument. . .rational
    E. confusion. . .systematic

3. Jennifer liked third period best as her English professor was a most _____ fellow; so much so that there was often no time left for student input, which suited her fine.

    A. garrulous
    B. ingenious
    C. superlative
    D. felicitous
    E. facetious

4. The paparazzi received many sizeable offers for the pictures of Ferggie in the _____ act of topless bathing in Capri.

    A. embarrassing
    B. ignoble
    C. hypocritical
    D. degenerative
    E. hedonistic

5. It seems America has not lacked for presidents who as a result of their own _____ have performed acts that most considered insensitive, corrupt, and immoral.

    A. grandiloquence
    B. fortitude
    C. effluvia
    D. demagoguery
    E. hubris

6. It probably wasn't the singular _____ remark, but the _____ effect of hearing the same stories every day forced her to resign what had been a very lucrative position.

    A. off-colored. . .genuine
    B. errant. . .overall
    C. defamatory. . .cumulative
    D. encouraging. . .negative
    E. negative. . .monotonous

7. Living in a constant state of _____ is understandable given the _____ of pronouncing the CEO's name incorrectly twice during his introduction.

    A. friction. . .fact
    B. prohibition. . .intimation
    C. fear. . .irreverence
    D. consternation. . .debacle
    E. nihilism. . .onus

8. The supervisor was absolutely _____ on the issue of wearing a tie and coat in the office; I mean, she was absolutely _____.

    A. obdurate. . .implacable
    B. persistent. . .moved
    C. passionate. . .vehement
    D. malleable. . .fixated
    E. mawkish. . .impassioned

GO ON TO THE NEXT PAGE

9. The drill instructor at the Marine Corps Recruiting Depot was quick to correct the _____ recruit when he was referred to as "dude."

    A. rascal

    B. imperious

    C. impudent

    D. gregarious

    E. loquacious

10. It is indeed a social commentary that so-called reality shows top the charts in viewer counts, thus confirming the suspicion that the _____ taste of the American television viewer is easily satisfied.

    A. corrupt

    B. incorrigible

    C. indomitable

    D. plebeian

    E. incredulous

Section 2: Short Reading Comprehension

The passages below are followed by questions based on their content; questions following a pair of related passages may also be based on the relationship between the paired passages. Answer the questions on the basis of what is *stated* or *implied* in the passages and in any introductory material that may be provided.

Questions 11–16 are based on the following passage.

The main purpose of this story is to appeal to the reader's interest in a subject which has been the theme of some of the greatest writers, living and dead—but which has never been, and can never be, exhausted, because it is a subject eternally interesting to all mankind. Here is one more book that depicts the struggle of a human creature, under those opposing influences of Good and Evil, which we have all felt, which we have all known. It has been my aim (5) to make the character of "Magdalen," which personifies this struggle, a pathetic character even in its perversity and its error; and I have tried hard to attain this result by the least obtrusive and the least artificial of all means—by a resolute adherence throughout to the truth as it is in Nature. This design was no easy one to accomplish; and it has been a great encouragement to me (during the publication of my story in its periodical form) to know, on the authority of many readers, that the object which I had proposed to myself, I might, in some degree, consider as an (10) object achieved.

Round the central figure in the narrative other characters will be found grouped, in sharp contrast—contrast, for the most part, in which I have endeavored to make the element of humor mainly predominant. I have sought to impart this relief to the more serious passages in the book, not only because I believe myself to be justified in doing so by the laws of Art—but because experience has taught me (what the experience of my readers will doubtless (15) confirm) that there is no such moral phenomenon as unmixed tragedy to be found in the world around us. Look where we may, the dark threads and the light cross each other perpetually in the texture of human life.

11. What selection best identifies the device utilized as a whole in the opening lines (1–4)?

   A. allegory
   B. rhetorical question
   C. allusion
   D. epic
   E. antagonist

12. Which word best describes the meaning of "personifies" line (5)?

   A. contains the qualities of goodness
   B. represents as a human being
   C. embodies the basic evil within
   D. takes on the characteristics of a pathetic character
   E. exemplifies perversity

13. What does the author likely mean when he writes, "truth as it is in Nature" line (7)?

   A. Natural things do not always appear as they seem.
   B. Nature changes often as does the character in the story.
   C. No matter what, Magdalen will be truthful.
   D. The struggle of Good and Evil as embodied by Nature is truth.
   E. Good and Evil are presented through Magdalen in her Natural characterization.

14. Why does the author believe he is justified in using humor in the work being referenced?

   A. only because it is his artistic freedom to do so
   B. because this art must represent life and life is humorous
   C. because there are no pure lines between Good and Evil or humor and tragedy
   D. because the human characteristics of Magdalen have to show both sides of humanity to be truly representative and accepted as realistic by the reader
   E. just to show that he can master both the serious and humorous aspects of writing and to do so in a singular work is commendable

GO ON TO THE NEXT PAGE

15. Which selection best identifies the device used in the phrase "the dark threads and the light cross each other perpetually in the texture of human life" line (16)?

    A. alliteration

    B. allusion

    C. allegory

    D. simile

    E. metaphor

16. What is the overall purpose of this passage?

    A. to explain the balance in Nature between Good and Evil

    B. to identify the character of Magdalen as possessing Natural characteristics

    C. to introduce the reader to a new work and explain his artistic rationale

    D. to delineate the significance of the age-old battle between Good and Evil

    E. to dimension the similarities between humor and tragedy

Questions 17–20 are based on the following passage.

In compliance with the request of a friend of mine, who wrote me from the East, I called on good-natured, garrulous old Simon Wheeler, and inquired after my friend's friend, *Leonidas W.* Smiley, as requested to do, and I hereunto append the result. I have a lurking suspicion that *Leonidas W.* Smiley is a myth; that my friend never knew such a personage; and that he only conjectured that, if I asked old Wheeler about him, it would remind him of his (5) infamous *Jim* Smiley, and he would go to work and bore me nearly to death with some infernal reminiscence of him as long and tedious as it should be useless to me. If that was the design, it certainly succeeded.

I found Simon Wheeler dozing comfortably by the barroom stove of the old, dilapidated tavern in the ancient mining camp of Angel's, and I noticed that he was fat and bald-headed, and had an expression of winning gentleness and simplicity upon his tranquil countenance. He roused up and gave me good-day. I told him a friend of mine (10) had commissioned me to make some inquiries about a cherished companion of his boyhood named *Leonidas W.* Smiley—*Rev. Leonidas W.* Smiley—a young minister of the Gospel, who he had heard was at one time a resident of Angel's Camp. I added that, if Mr. Wheeler could tell me anything about this Rev. Leonidas W. Smiley, I would feel under many obligations to him.

17. In context, the word "garrulous" line (1–2) most nearly means

    A. rich.

    B. friendly.

    C. talkative.

    D. rotund.

    E. flamboyant.

18. What can we infer about what the author thinks of his friend from the East by the statement, "I have a lurking suspicion that *Leonidas W.* Smiley is a myth" line (3)?

    A. His friend is mistaken about the existence of Smiley.

    B. His friend may be playing a practical joke on him.

    C. He believes his friend wants revenge for some earlier misgivings.

    D. His friend knows that Smiley and he will strike a friendship.

    E. Smiley will, as a result of his friend referring him, will show him a rousing good time.

19. What information does the narrator relate prior to the retelling of the meeting of Simon Wheeler?

    A. The story likely to be heard would feasibly be boring and long.

    B. The information he might hear would be of no general interest to him.

    C. Any story he might hear from Wheeler would likely be long.

    D. It was a fact that all his suspicions regarding Wheeler proved true.

    E. Somehow there might be a story about Jim Smiley to be perhaps told by Wheeler.

20. What is the significance of the information "he was fat and bald-headed, and had an expression of winning gentleness and simplicity upon his tranquil countenance" lines (8–9) to the narrator?

    A. The narrator was hesitant about meeting someone unknown and his countenance settled his nerves.

    B. Wheeler's unassuming nature allowed the narrator to let his guard down to Wheeler's garrulous side.

    C. This made the narrator feel reassured that his friend from the East was serious.

    D. This allowed the narrator to be reassured due to Wheeler's "tranquil countenance."

    E. Wheeler's winning gentleness calmed the narrator allowing an open discussion as to his business.

GO ON TO THE NEXT PAGE

Section 2: Long Reading Comprehension

The passages below are followed by questions based on their content; questions following a pair of related passages may also be based on the relationship between the paired passages. Answer the questions on the basis of what is *stated* or *implied* in the passages and in any introductory material that may be provided.

Questions 21–30 are based on the following passage.

The following is an excerpt from Going Into Society by Charles Dickens. (Note: the original dialect is retained.)

He was a un-common small man, he really was. Certainly not so small as he was made out to be, but where IS your Dwarf as is? He was a most uncommon small man, with a most uncommon large Ed; and what he had inside that Ed, nobody ever knowed but himself: even supposin himself to have ever took stock of it, which it would have been a stiff job for even him to do.

(5)   The kindest little man as never growed! Spirited, but not proud. When he travelled with the Spotted Baby though he knowed himself to be a nat'ral Dwarf, and knowed the Baby's spots to be put upon him artificial, he nursed that Baby like a mother. You never heerd him give a ill-name to a Giant. He DID allow himself to break out into strong language respectin the Fat Lady from Norfolk; but that was an affair of the 'art; and when a man's 'art has been trifled with by a lady, and the preference giv to a Indian, he ain't master of his actions.

(10)   He was always in love, of course; every human nat'ral phenomenon is. And he was always in love with a large woman; I never knowed the Dwarf as could be got to love a small one. Which helps to keep 'em the Curiosities they are.

One sing'ler idea he had in that Ed of his, which must have meant something, or it wouldn't have been there. It was always his opinion that he was entitled to property. He never would put his name to anything. He had been
(15)   taught to write, by the young man without arms, who got his living with his toes (quite a writing master HE was, and taught scores in the line), but Chops would have starved to death, afore he'd have gained a bit of bread by putting his hand to a paper. This is the more curious to bear in mind, because HE had no property, nor hope of property, except his house and a sarser. When I say his house, I mean the box, painted and got up outside like a reg'lar six-roomer, that he used to creep into, with a diamond ring (or quite as good to look at) on his forefinger, and ring
(20)   a little bell out of what the Public believed to be the Drawing-room winder. And when I say a sarser, I mean a Chaney sarser in which he made a collection for himself at the end of every Entertainment. His cue for that, he took from me: "Ladies and gentlemen, the little man will now walk three times round the Cairawan, and retire behind the curtain." When he said anything important, in private life, he mostly wound it up with this form of words, and they was generally the last thing he said to me at night afore he went to bed.

(25)   He had what I consider a fine mind—a poetic mind. His ideas respectin his property never come upon him so strong as when he sat upon a barrel-organ and had the handle turned. Arter the wibration had run through him a little time, he would screech out, "Toby, I feel my property coming—grind away! I'm counting my guineas by thousands, Toby—grind away! Toby, I shall be a man of fortun! I feel the Mint a jingling in me, Toby, and I'm swelling out into the Bank of England!" Such is the influence of music on a poetic mind. Not that he was partial to any other
(30)   music but a barrel-organ; on the contrary, hated it.

He had a kind of a everlasting grudge agin the Public: which is a thing you may notice in many phenomenons that get their living out of it. What riled him most in the nater of his occupation was, that it kep him out of Society. He was continiwally saying, "Toby, my ambition is, to go into Society. The curse of my position towards the Public is, that it keeps me hout of Society. This don't signify to a low beast of a Indian; he an't formed for Society. This
(35)   don't signify to a Spotted Baby; HE an't formed for Society. I am."

21. Which best depicts the type of writing represented by this excerpt?

   A. informational

   B. persuasive

   C. argumentative

   D. interrogatory

   E. expository

22. For what purpose does the narrator most likely describe the Dwarf's character in lines (5–12)?

   A. establishes the character as being quite normal save for size

   B. establishes the character has a temper when it comes to love

   C. establishes the character has ability to fall in love

   D. establishes the character as a kind individual

   E. establishes the character as rather proud that his phenomenon is authentic

23. What is the likely connection with *property* and *belonging to society* from the Dwarf's perspective?

   A. Owning property establishes a certain independence and freedoms not enjoyed by a phenomenon.

   B. Belonging to society provides one the opportunity to acquire property.

   C. Gaining enough wealth allows one to acquire property and property establishes one as a member of society.

   D. Joining society is predicated upon owning or being able to acquire property and earnings derived from a phenomenon performer will provide that opportunity shortly.

   E. The *diamond ring* or look alike exemplifies the property noted which is but a beginning to becoming a member of society.

24. The phrase "He had been taught to write, by the young man without arms" lines (14–15) is an example of

   A. euphemism.

   B. allusion.

   C. rhetoric.

   D. irony.

   E. exposition.

25. Which selection best interprets "Chops would have starved to death, afore he'd have gained a bit of bread by putting his hand to a paper" lines (16–17)?

   A. He would starve before he would accept charity from anyone.

   B. He would starve before he would agree to anything.

   C. He would starve before signing a performance contract as a phenomenon.

   D. He would starve before borrowing money to buy bread.

   E. He would starve before wrapping paper around food showing distrust in the preparation of same.

26. Which of the selections is the best indicator of the closeness of Toby to the Dwarf?

   A. Toby was the grinder of the barrel-organ.

   B. The Dwarf used Toby's closing line following his performances.

   C. Toby knew of his desires to join society.

   D. Toby knew of his sarser where the Dwarf kept his collection.

   E. Toby was the last one the Dwarf spoke to before going to bed.

27. Which is the most likely reason for the author to include the paragraph concerning the barrel-organ lines (25–30)?

   A. shows a personal side of the two characters other than performers

   B. allows the reader to better understand the relationship between the two characters

   C. establishes societal qualifications of the Dwarf related to poetry and music

   D. qualifies the strength of the Dwarf's desire and preoccupation with fortune

   E. provides a comic relief from the seriousness and somberness of the rest of the excerpt

28. Which selection best represents the device displayed in the overall excerpt but especially summated in the last paragraph, lines (31–35)?

   A. allegory

   B. allusion

   C. paradox

   D. epic

   E. choral

GO ON TO THE NEXT PAGE

29. Which of the selections best describes the general commentary on society represented in this excerpt?

    A. Society supports the acceptance of those outside their established parameter.

    B. Those in a minority position may expect to be accepted into society.

    C. After the attributes of society are acquired, including property, anyone may be accepted into society.

    D. Efforts to join society, though arduous, are readily achievable to those in minority.

    E. Societal norms errantly exclude any deviation to that established norm.

30. Which of the selections would make the best alternative title for this work?

    A. Society Bound

    B. The Unworthy Society

    C. The Journey into Society

    D. The Preoccupation with Society

    E. Property and Society

Answer Key for Practice Test One

Section 1

Sentence Completion

1. D
2. B
3. E
4. C
5. B

6. D
7. A
8. E
9. C
10. B

Short Reading Comprehension

11. A
12. D
13. D
14. C
15. C

16. D
17. B
18. E
19. A
20. D

Long Reading Comprehension

21. D
22. C
23. D
24. A
25. E

26. D
27. E
28. D
29. A
30. B

Section 2

Sentence Completion

1. B	6. C
2. B	7. D
3. A	8. A
4. B	9. C
5. E	10. D

Short Reading Comprehension

11. C	16. C
12. B	17. C
13. D	18. B
14. C	19. D
15. E	20. B

Long Reading Comprehension

21. E	26. E
22. A	27. C
23. C	28. C
24. D	29. E
25. D	30. B

Answers and Explanations for Practice Test One

Section 1

Sentence Completion

1. **D.** Choices A and B indicate lazy or not genuine, respectively, which is not the case, or they wouldn't be there demonstrating. Choice C grammatically fits, but the individuality of the act becomes lost when chaining themselves together. Choice E, "cohesive," or sticking together certainly fits and is correct; however, this is not the best choice. Choice D, "recalcitrant," is the best choice as it includes "stubbornly resisting authority," which further matches the action following the arrival of the authorities.

2. **B.** We know that censors typically judge with a view to suppress so we're probably looking for two negatives in this case. Starting with that proposition, Choices B and C are the only possibilities. The second negative eliminates Choice C, making Choice B correct.

3. **E.** Here again, the strategy is to divide and conquer. Only Choices A, C, and E qualify as being suited with *absolutely.* This leaves the second blank. Now the qualities for someone to defuse a bomb are almost a given. Choice A, "mature," is not something good as it is tantamount to feeble—much shaking of the hands is not a great characteristic to have as a bomb technician. Choice C, "excited," is just as bad as too mature and shaking. This only leave Choice E, "dexterous," or someone with skillful hands.

4. **C.** The key word is *not* indicating some flawed qualification in the service of being a critic. In looking at the last blank first, we see that there is only one actual negative; Choice C, "castigation," which means to "chastise severely," which is not a particularly good quality for a critic to possess.

5. **B.** Choice E, "celerity," looks plausible and could be, but the development of speed won't be the worst thing to develop. However, Choice B, "complacency," or self-satisfaction can give a false sense of readiness and should be avoided.

6. **D.** The key word is "and" including a "failing of moral values." Choice D, "decadence" certainly fits in with the loss of moral values.

7. **A.** Actually all of the answer choices lend themselves to this question. Remember SAT is looking for the best choice and Choice A, "prodigious" or extraordinary in degree, is the only choice actually rising to the occasion to praise such an accomplished mathematician.

8. **E.** Although Ali was certainly known for his elocution, seeming prestidigitation in the ring, and his poetical ravings, he would not have reached the heights of boxing success had it not been for his "pugilistic" or boxing prowess, Choice E.

9. **C.** Choice B, "clairvoyant," seems like a shoe-in for this questions, but a clairvoyant only has greater powers of perception, not foreknowledge. Choice C, "prescient," incorporates the needed ability to know events in advance of the occurrence to properly pick winning numbers in a lottery.

10. **B.** A quick look at the first blank options doesn't yield much reduction of choices. In fact, any of them might be correct. Remembering that the tone of the sentence is bent toward the negative, we're looking for a fit for the second blank that is negative. Only Choice B, "pernicious," qualifies as it means harmful.

Short Reading Comprehension

11. **A.** Although Choice B looks accurate, there is nothing to be inferred as this is what the reader sees directly from the passage. Choice A qualifies as the best selection as it is only inferred that father knows best.

12. **D.** The author uses this paragraph to fully demonstrate the latitude given to Rob but as importantly, the control, as head of household, father has on the house.

13. **D.** Notwithstanding Rob's mother and sisters feel that the experiments are a nuisance, father still holds firm in his decision to allow things to continue, reinforcing the control father has over the entire house.

14. C. The sailor, having seen the murderous scene, lost all concern for the well-being of his animal.

15. C. The word "brute" refers back to the animal whose animal noises or "fiendish jabberings" were heard from the chamber.

16. D. "I have scarcely anything to add" is almost a euphemism but literally means, having solved the mystery, "I don't know anything else to add."

17. B. We know the Ourang-Outang did not break the door because it escaped from the window just before the door was broken. Since everyone else had already escaped or was dead, only someone from the outside could have broken the door. The party of people investigating the noises coming from the chamber had to break down the door to gain entrance.

18. E. The author is angered that he has to write for a foreign audience as the critics of the time in his homeland refuse to endorse his treatment of a social occurrence.

19. A. All of the selections represent some feelings expressed by the author in dealing with the issue of censorship with the exception of Choice A.

20. D. The author states "that the increase of readers and the lapse of time will assuredly do me justice," which is supported by Choice D.

Long Reading Comprehension

21. D. Given the tone of the article, hard times had befallen the family, which has a universal tendency to cause depression and turning to alcohol for relief. Such was the case for father.

22. C. The key here is that we are told that the "object in those visits was of a house-keeping character." Had they been of a romantic nature, the child would not have been there to summon the father out with a whistle.

23. D. Not any one element is specifically referred to prior to the statement. The entire element of shrouded secrecy that no one could know the father's real name, that no one was supposed to know that he was married or had children, that family visits had to be kept secret were all contributing factors. Because of syntax, the compartment did not enter into the mystery as the author added the compartment information following "combined."

24. A. Although most of the selections provide some tangential information as to the rationale for the description being so detailed, the result is that it informs the reader of a lifestyle that could be expected for a waiter at this time. We are not told about the lifestyle of the remainder of the family or what their living conditions are.

25. E. All of the choices indicate some risk that has been previously set out by the author in leading up to this moment. In fact, the author purposely gives us adequate information such that without it being specifically stated, we would wonder what his thinking is coming home to his family's house during broad daylight. There is no information, suggesting that the son would lose his job.

26. D. This is classic understatement in that the literal sense of what is said falls detectably short of the magnitude of what is being talked about. Litotes, another form of understatement, is not correct because there was no negative relief employed.

27. E. As a waiter, it would be his job every day to count back change to patrons at the conclusion of each meal. What is a universal truth is that upon one's deathbed, given general circumstances, during times of conscience interludes people often speak in jargon related to their vocations.

28. D. It would appear that newly hired waiters, which was the case as the George and Gridiron gave him the job out of benevolence upon his father's death, were paid so little that to literally survive, they would support "nature" by eating whatever leftovers could be scraped from plates and glasses of patrons.

29. A. The entire section identified either the mysterious lifestyle that enticed the main character into becoming a waiter, explained how he got the job following his father's death, or gave insights as to his lifestyle as a waiter. All of the information provided by the author was to establish the reasoning and experiences of this character.

30. B. Empathetic means experiencing the feelings and thoughts of another. The narrator states he was himself called to be a waiter qualifying him to empathize with the main character.

Section 2

Sentence Completion

1. **B.** Choice D, "indulgent," seems plausible, but if movie stars were truly indulgent, they wouldn't mind the indiscretions of their mate. Choice B, "capricious," or unpredictable and impulsive best describes the character flaw causing this problem.

2. **B.** Choices C, D, and E, "evidence," "argument," and "confusion," respectively, disqualify them as choices based on the first word choice. The qualifier as *much educated* doesn't match with argument or confusion. Educated folk tend to present, not argue; and if it was a much educated prospective, there likely wouldn't be confusion. Considering much educated "evidence" would pretty much settle the discussion if it is truly evidence. This leaves only Choices A and B. Choice A has "tenuous" as a second word, and "weak" doesn't fit the sentence. Choice B, "conjecture" and "proven," is the best choice.

3. **A.** Choices A and E are the only real qualifiers as to there being no time left for student input. Choice E, "facetious," means jocular, and the good professor would likely be in jeopardy of losing his job were this the case. Choice A, "garrulous" or given to prosy rambling, fits the more typical English professor.

4. **B.** Choice A, "embarrassing," certainly qualifies but may be too simplistic for an SAT question. Be guarded against picking the first factually correct choice. Choice C, "hypocritical," might qualify if we were told she typically spoke against such acts, but we aren't. Choice D, "degenerative," suggests a degraded act or a sexual perversion, and topless bathing generally would not meet such criteria, particularly in an area where such practice was commonplace. Choice E, "hedonistic," seems to fit with the exception that a singular incident does not a lifestyle devoted to pleasure make. Choice B, "ignoble," fits nicely, particularly since she represented the royal family.

5. **E.** Although many presidents are guilty of Choice A, "grandiloquence" or pompous speaking, and Choice D, "demagoguery" or politically appealing to the emotions or prejudice of a people, these acts don't typically qualify someone to perform the type acts represented. However, as pride goeth before a fall, Choice E, "hubris" or excessive pride, certainly sets one up for this type failure.

6. **C.** Any time we speak of repetition, an adding up or cumulative effect is present. As Choice C qualifies exactingly on the second word choice, we need qualify only the first blank. "Defamatory" or injurious to the reputation makes it a certain winner.

7. **D.** Alright, we need to look for something that pronouncing the CEO's name incorrectly might cause and what that error might be called (other than suicidal). Choice D, "consternation" or an intense state of fear, certainly trumps pure "fear" as in Choice C. And, most certainly, mispronouncing the CEO's name is certainly a "debacle," disaster, or fiasco.

8. **A.** We need two words that are synonymous. Choices A and C are the only two real qualifiers. Choice C, "passionate," doesn't tell us whether she was in favor of or against the wearing of a tie and coat that would be almost incongruent with "absolutely" feeling that way. . . unless you worked in a casual garment business. Choice A, "obdurate" or stubbornly resistant and "implacable" or not capable of being appeased or changed, makes it the best choice.

9. **C.** We're looking for a word that defines the recruit who misspoke to the drill instructor. Although I can think of several, let's look only at the given possibilities. Choice D, "gregarious" or social or companionable, might describe the nature of the individual, it doesn't match with the specific act. Choice E, "loquacious" or very talkative is a given, but again, lends nothing to this egregious act. Choice C, "impudent" or insolent or contemptuously rude better fits the occasion and presents the best answer.

10. **D.** Choice A, "corrupt" or 'morally debased,' is actually too strong to fit the tone of the sentence. We're not talking about Jerry Springer. Choice D, "plebian" or ordinary satisfies the simplicity of the sentence.

Short Reading Comprehension

11. C. The author is presenting an allusion to the Garden of Evil wherein the age-old battle of Good versus Evil had its origins.

12. B. "Personifies" effectively is a personification wherein someone or thing (in this case Magdalen), represents as a human being this struggle between Good and Evil.

13. D. Here, the author is saying that as the struggle was established in the beginning of time and has manifested itself throughout the ages in Nature, the struggle is a basic truth of nature.

14. C. The author tells us that he believes that "there is no such moral phenomenon as unmixed tragedy to be found in the world around us" meaning that there are no pure lines between Good and Evil or humor and tragedy.

15. E. The phrase, "the dark threads and the light cross each other perpetually in the texture of human life" is a metaphor for the mixing and intertwining of Good and Evil across the impure lines as they present themselves through Nature.

16. C. The author is taking an opportunity to explain to his readers directly as to why he has taken a particular approach to this new undertaking and explain his rationale for how he developed this main character, Magdalen.

17. C. We can look at a variety of context clues to figure out this simple vocabulary question. We are forewarned by the author that he suspects there to be a consequence of a long, drawn-out storytelling; the narrator even tells us that it did, in fact, happen as he had suspected. We know through reading that Wheeler was then talkative.

18. B. It appears from the language that our narrator has a fair amount of disbelief about what he is being told by his friend from the East. In fact, as he doubts the existence of the individual in question, it is reasonable to infer he believes his friend from the East is playing a practical joke on him.

19. D. All of the choices other than D speak of maybe or might. The narrator point-blank tells the reader that his suspicions regarding Wheeler did prove true.

20. B. We are not given to believe that the narrator was at all concerned about the character of the stranger he was to solicit, but he did have concerns regarding the outcome of their meeting. The tranquil countenance and overall good-natured presentation would allow the narrator to be less apprehensive about being lured into long, boring, irrelevant stories. . .but alas.

Long Reading Comprehension

21. E. The style is expository in that it is telling a story. Although the piece may qualify as a social commentary, so far as the excerpt is concerned, expository is the best choice.

22. A. This section of the passage established most of the selections available, but collectively they establish that save for size, the Dwarf is in every way normal, even in affairs of the heart.

23. C. The link between property and belonging to society becomes more clear later in the passage as the Dwarf interchanges property and guineas, fortun, and Mint. Clearly, his predisposition to money is established as he collects incremental monies from the crowd, places the money in a sarser in his house, and doesn't spend it on anything except an ample supply of food. As money is seen as the avenue to property, property assigns rights to societal membership.

24. D. Clearly the fact that the Dwarf was taught to write by someone without arms qualifies as irony. None of the other devices approach legitimacy.

25. D. This choice follows the overall theme of the excerpt. Given the propensity to save money by the Dwarf, it is well in keeping with his character that he would not borrow money, even if it meant going hungry. This would only put further from reach his securing sufficient property or fortune to be able to join society.

26. E. We are told "and they was generally the last thing he said to me at night afore he went to bed," which indicates that Toby was likely the last person the Dwarf was with nightly, creating a bond more significant than any other.

27. C. Each choice holds some truth and rationale for the inclusion of this paragraph. The reason Choice C is the best selection is because it matches the overall thought line of the excerpt. Every quality and motivation in all other parts of the excerpt are directed at the establishment of the Dwarf's qualifications to enter society, with the exception of property. This paragraph serves the same purpose in as much as it qualifies that the Dwarf has a poetical mind, certainly something a gentleman of society would possess. It also establishes that he enjoys music, albeit only barrel-organ music the fact of which might be overlooked given the likelihood that this was the only type music generally available to a traveling carnival.

28. C. As the title *Going Into Society* indicates, the entire motivation for saving money, obtaining property is to pave the way for joining society. The paradox is that the methodology by which he is able to over time obtain property is the very thing that keeps him out of society—his being a phenomenon.

29. E. We clearly need to look for a negative here. By virtue, the carnival of phenomenon exists is a negative commentary on society and the values established by those so-called norms. Choice E is the only negative qualifier that represents this position.

30. B. As the overall theme is the negative commentary on society and the virtues of the Dwarf, *"The Unworthy Society"* appropriately encapsulates this representation.

Answer Sheet for Practice Test Two

Section 1

1	Ⓐ Ⓑ Ⓒ Ⓓ Ⓔ	16	Ⓐ Ⓑ Ⓒ Ⓓ Ⓔ
2	Ⓐ Ⓑ Ⓒ Ⓓ Ⓔ	17	Ⓐ Ⓑ Ⓒ Ⓓ Ⓔ
3	Ⓐ Ⓑ Ⓒ Ⓓ Ⓔ	18	Ⓐ Ⓑ Ⓒ Ⓓ Ⓔ
4	Ⓐ Ⓑ Ⓒ Ⓓ Ⓔ	19	Ⓐ Ⓑ Ⓒ Ⓓ Ⓔ
5	Ⓐ Ⓑ Ⓒ Ⓓ Ⓔ	20	Ⓐ Ⓑ Ⓒ Ⓓ Ⓔ
6	Ⓐ Ⓑ Ⓒ Ⓓ Ⓔ	21	Ⓐ Ⓑ Ⓒ Ⓓ Ⓔ
7	Ⓐ Ⓑ Ⓒ Ⓓ Ⓔ	22	Ⓐ Ⓑ Ⓒ Ⓓ Ⓔ
8	Ⓐ Ⓑ Ⓒ Ⓓ Ⓔ	23	Ⓐ Ⓑ Ⓒ Ⓓ Ⓔ
9	Ⓐ Ⓑ Ⓒ Ⓓ Ⓔ	24	Ⓐ Ⓑ Ⓒ Ⓓ Ⓔ
10	Ⓐ Ⓑ Ⓒ Ⓓ Ⓔ	25	Ⓐ Ⓑ Ⓒ Ⓓ Ⓔ
11	Ⓐ Ⓑ Ⓒ Ⓓ Ⓔ	26	Ⓐ Ⓑ Ⓒ Ⓓ Ⓔ
12	Ⓐ Ⓑ Ⓒ Ⓓ Ⓔ	27	Ⓐ Ⓑ Ⓒ Ⓓ Ⓔ
13	Ⓐ Ⓑ Ⓒ Ⓓ Ⓔ	28	Ⓐ Ⓑ Ⓒ Ⓓ Ⓔ
14	Ⓐ Ⓑ Ⓒ Ⓓ Ⓔ	29	Ⓐ Ⓑ Ⓒ Ⓓ Ⓔ
15	Ⓐ Ⓑ Ⓒ Ⓓ Ⓔ	30	Ⓐ Ⓑ Ⓒ Ⓓ Ⓔ

Section 2

1	Ⓐ Ⓑ Ⓒ Ⓓ Ⓔ	16	Ⓐ Ⓑ Ⓒ Ⓓ Ⓔ
2	Ⓐ Ⓑ Ⓒ Ⓓ Ⓔ	17	Ⓐ Ⓑ Ⓒ Ⓓ Ⓔ
3	Ⓐ Ⓑ Ⓒ Ⓓ Ⓔ	18	Ⓐ Ⓑ Ⓒ Ⓓ Ⓔ
4	Ⓐ Ⓑ Ⓒ Ⓓ Ⓔ	19	Ⓐ Ⓑ Ⓒ Ⓓ Ⓔ
5	Ⓐ Ⓑ Ⓒ Ⓓ Ⓔ	20	Ⓐ Ⓑ Ⓒ Ⓓ Ⓔ
6	Ⓐ Ⓑ Ⓒ Ⓓ Ⓔ	21	Ⓐ Ⓑ Ⓒ Ⓓ Ⓔ
7	Ⓐ Ⓑ Ⓒ Ⓓ Ⓔ	22	Ⓐ Ⓑ Ⓒ Ⓓ Ⓔ
8	Ⓐ Ⓑ Ⓒ Ⓓ Ⓔ	23	Ⓐ Ⓑ Ⓒ Ⓓ Ⓔ
9	Ⓐ Ⓑ Ⓒ Ⓓ Ⓔ	24	Ⓐ Ⓑ Ⓒ Ⓓ Ⓔ
10	Ⓐ Ⓑ Ⓒ Ⓓ Ⓔ	25	Ⓐ Ⓑ Ⓒ Ⓓ Ⓔ
11	Ⓐ Ⓑ Ⓒ Ⓓ Ⓔ	26	Ⓐ Ⓑ Ⓒ Ⓓ Ⓔ
12	Ⓐ Ⓑ Ⓒ Ⓓ Ⓔ	27	Ⓐ Ⓑ Ⓒ Ⓓ Ⓔ
13	Ⓐ Ⓑ Ⓒ Ⓓ Ⓔ	28	Ⓐ Ⓑ Ⓒ Ⓓ Ⓔ
14	Ⓐ Ⓑ Ⓒ Ⓓ Ⓔ	29	Ⓐ Ⓑ Ⓒ Ⓓ Ⓔ
15	Ⓐ Ⓑ Ⓒ Ⓓ Ⓔ	30	Ⓐ Ⓑ Ⓒ Ⓓ Ⓔ

CUT HERE

Practice Test Two

Section 1: Sentence Completion

Each sentence below has one or two blanks, each blank indicating that something has been omitted. Beneath the sentence are five words or sets of words labeled **A** through **E**. Choose the word or set of words that, when inserted in the sentence, *best* fits the meaning of the sentence as a whole.

1. Each year I am reminded of our blessings as I view the _____ of food abundant at our table.

   A. mixture
   B. gluttony
   C. bounty
   D. plethora
   E. decadence

2. The depth and _____ of Lillian's performance was most noteworthy; she presented works from ragtime to jazz to classical.

   A. duration
   B. polish
   C. scope
   D. intensity
   E. articulation

3. Once the newspaper _____ their sources were flawed, they _____ the target of their article by issuing a full retraction.

   A. realized. . .exonerated
   B. suspected. . .blasted
   C. understood. . .haranged
   D. rejected. . .issued
   E. disproved. . .comforted

4. His _____ behavior toward her caused a considerable riff in the organization, partially because of the size of the company and partially because he was a married man with children.

   A. untoward
   B. snide
   C. mysterious
   D. periodic
   E. obsequious

5. He was held up to small children as an _____, one who is worthy of imitation, principally because of his self-sacrificing dedication to helping others—clearly his _____ made him deserving of such claim.

   A. enigma. . .heart
   B. exemplar. . .altruism
   C. egotist. . .devotion
   D. emancipator. . .thrift
   E. idol. . .immortality

6. His proclivity for _____ had at one time made him a suspect in every open case of vandalism, but it also made him mentally qualified for the specialized unit in the military whose job it was to reduce _____ munitions.

   A. trouble. . .reliance
   B. gang membership. . .built up
   C. extirpation. . .stockpiled
   D. intimidation. . .depleted
   E. opulence. . .droll

7. The _____ aroma of the bark of this shrub make it _____ year round whether the leaves have fallen or not.

   A. stark. . .indistinguishable
   B. subtle. . .anomalistic
   C. pungent. . .recognizable
   D. hidden. . .obtrusive
   E. sickening. . .reticent

GO ON TO THE NEXT PAGE

8. As the grass roots movement gained momentum, outside forces attempted to infiltrate and change the direction of the original purpose so the sponsor recommended we adopt a _____, making it clear to the public our motives and purpose.

   A. manifesto
   B. declaration
   C. statement
   D. mandate
   E. invocation

9. Given the research available today on how students learn differently, teachers need to have an _____ bag of tricks to successfully engage them all.

   A. enormous
   B. expansive
   C. available
   D. impromptu
   E. eclectic

10. Children today are being taught to be _____ of any abnormality including strangers, standing packages, or simply anything out of the order; not for merely their own good, but for the good of the community—such are the times we now live in.

   A. skittish
   B. wary
   C. shy
   D. impudent
   E. challenging

Section 1: Short Reading Comprehension

The passages below are followed by questions based on their content; questions following a pair of related passages may also be based on the relationship between the paired passages. Answer the questions on the basis of what is *stated* or *implied* in the passages and in any introductory material that may be provided.

Questions 11–12 are based on the following passage.

The next morning a message came from Lady Berrick, to say that she would see her nephew after breakfast. Left by myself, I walked toward the pier, and met with a man who asked me to hire his boat. He had lines and bait, at my service. Most unfortunately, as the event proved, I decided on occupying an hour or two by sea fishing.

The wind shifted while we were out, and before we could get back to the harbor, the tide had turned against us.
(5) It was six o'clock when I arrived at the hotel. A little open carriage was waiting at the door. I found Romayne impatiently expecting me, and no signs of dinner on the table. He informed me that he had accepted an invitation, in which I was included, and promised to explain everything in the carriage.

Our driver took the road that led toward the High Town. I subordinated my curiosity to my sense of politeness, and asked for news of his aunt's health.

11. What selection best depicts the reason for the narrator's fishing episode as being "unfortunate?"

- A. The wind turned against them.
- B. The tide turned against them.
- C. There was obviously no catch due to the weather.
- D. No catch and having to pay extra for the additional hours.
- E. He missed his appointment with Romayne causing a late dinner.

12. In context, the word "subordinated" line (8) most nearly means

- A. lowered the level of importance.
- B. left.
- C. ensured it was stifled.
- D. made certain to ignore.
- E. forgot about.

GO ON TO THE NEXT PAGE

Questions 13–20 are based on the following passage.

In the year 1860, the reputation of Doctor Wybrow as a London physician reached its highest point. It was reported on good authority that he was in receipt of one of the largest incomes derived from the practice of medicine in modern times.

(5) One afternoon, towards the close of the London season, the doctor had just taken his luncheon after a specially hard morning's work in his consulting-room, and with a formidable list of visits to patients at their own houses to fill up the rest of his day—when the servant announced that a lady wished to speak to him.

"Who is she?" the Doctor asked. "A stranger?"

"Yes, sir."

"I see no strangers out of consulting-hours. Tell her what the hours are, and send her away."

(10) "I have told her, sir."

"Well?"

"And she won't go."

"Won't go?" The doctor smiled as he repeated the words. He was a humorist in his way; and there was an absurd side to the situation which rather amused him. "Has this obstinate lady given you her name?" he inquired.

(15) "No, sir. She refused to give any name—she said she wouldn't keep you five minutes, and the matter was too important to wait till to-morrow. There she is in the consulting-room; and how to get her out again is more than I know."

Doctor Wybrow considered for a moment. His knowledge of women (professionally speaking) rested on the ripe experience of more than thirty years; he had met with them in all their varieties—especially the variety which knows nothing of the value of time, and never hesitates at sheltering itself behind the privileges of its sex. A glance

(20) at his watch informed him that he must soon begin his rounds among the patients who were waiting for him at their own houses. He decided forthwith on taking the only wise course that was open under the circumstances. In other words, he decided on taking to flight.

"Is the carriage at the door?" he asked.

"Yes, sir."

(25) "Very well. Open the house-door for me without making any noise, and leave the lady in undisturbed possession of the consulting-room. When she gets tired of waiting, you know what to tell her. If she asks when I am expected to return, say that I dine at my club, and spend the evening at the theatre. Now then, softly, Thomas! If your shoes creak, I am a lost man."

---

13. What may be inferred in the opening paragraph lines (1–3)?

  A. Physicians didn't get much money in those days.

  B. Somehow a reputation makes you a good physician.

  C. The physician that made the most money was the best physician.

  D. The physician with the best reputation earned the most money.

  E. The physician earning the most money would have the best reputation.

14. Correlating irony, what type of humor is found in lines (13–16)?

  A. raucous

  B. blatant

  C. dramatic

  D. verbal

  E. situational

15. What literary device is being used with "(professionally speaking)" line (17)?

  A. influx

  B. aside

  C. machination

  D. derisive

  E. satire

16. What was the female characteristic that was most often observed by Doctor Wybrow?

  A. Once their mind was committed to something, it was impossible to change.

  B. They were all at the same a most peculiarly stubborn species.

  C. Notwithstanding their generally good nature, if cornered, they could become reticent.

  D. When set upon a mission or no, the element of an appreciation of time is escaped.

  E. When it comes to determination, there is no creature on earth so prepared to fixate .

17. What is meant by "and never hesitates at sheltering itself behind the privileges of its sex" lines (19)?

A. Because it is a known fact that women take time, members of the opposite sex need to simply accept the fact and deal with it accordingly.

B. Women know that a gentlemen, such as a physician, would never be so rude as to not allow a lady the time requested lest they be considered offensive.

C. Females have certain inherent rights and privileges, not the least of which is to take their time in all manners.

D. People of class expect that women of breeding need extra allowances and that exercising the grace of slowness is a virtue.

E. Certain appurtenances come with being a female, one of which is the ability and expectation of taking your time.

18. Why does the decision made by the physician in lines (22–23) strike the reader as unusual?

A. It is unusual that an unidentified patient would attend the consultation room and refuse to leave when told the physician could not see them.

B. It is not normally the case that physicians find themselves in a position of helping one at the expense of another.

C. It seems incongruent that a physician whose job consists of listening to patients suggesting that the only wise course is to run away.

D. Since the physician did not know the seriousness or the nature of the situation with the stranger, it seems strange that he didn't at least find out.

E. It is unusual because we know that a woman would take her time and that, unless the physician were to be considered rude, he would have to hear her complete story.

19. Which is the best restatement of "leave the lady in undisturbed possession of the consulting-room" lines (25–26)?

A. Don't tell her I'm leaving, just leave her in there behind the closed door until I'm gone.

B. Allow her to remain comfortably in the consulting-room until she feels well enough to depart.

C. Ensure that she stays in the room until I'm safely out the door and when she sufficiently tires of waiting, explain to her I had no alternative but to call upon a pressing appointment.

D. Be careful not to disturb the lady as we leave in case her condition is such that noise would bother her.

E. If we make too much noise leaving, it could worsen her condition and then we could have to treat her for free.

20. What device is being employed in "If your shoes creak, I am a lost man" lines (27–28)?

A. litotes
B. hyperbole
C. understatement
D. allusion
E. paradox

GO ON TO THE NEXT PAGE

Section 1: Long Reading Comprehension

The passages below are followed by questions based on their content; questions following a pair of related passages may also be based on the relationship between the paired passages. Answer the questions on the basis of what is *stated* or *implied* in the passages and in any introductory material that may be provided.

Questions 21–30 are based on the following passage.

This excerpt is from The Dead Secret by Wilkie Collins.

Mathew ascended three flights of stairs—passed half-way down a long arched gallery—and knocked at another old-fashioned oak door. This time the signal was answered. A low, clear, sweet voice, inside the room, inquired who was waiting without? In a few hasty words Mathew told his errand. Before he had done speaking the door was quietly and quickly opened, and Sarah Leeson confronted him on the threshold, with her candle in her hand.

(5)   Not tall, not handsome, not in her first youth—shy and irresolute in manner—simple in dress to the utmost limits of plainness—the lady's-maid, in spite of all these disadvantages, was a woman whom it was impossible to look at without a feeling of curiosity, if not of interest. Few men, at first sight of her, could have resisted the desire to find out who she was; few would have been satisfied with receiving for answer, She is Mrs. Treverton's maid; few would have refrained from the attempt to extract some secret information for themselves from her face and manner;

(10)   and none, not even the most patient and practiced of observers, could have succeeded in discovering more than that she must have passed through the ordeal of some great suffering at some former period of her life. Much in her manner, and more in her face, said plainly and sadly: I am the wreck of something that you might once have liked to see; a wreck that can never be repaired—that must drift on through life unnoticed, unguided, unpitied—drift till the fatal shore is touched, and the waves of Time have swallowed up these broken relics of me forever.

(15)   This was the story that was told in Sarah Leeson's face—this, and no more.

No two men interpreting that story for themselves, would probably have agreed on the nature of the suffering which this woman had undergone. It was hard to say, at the outset, whether the past pain that had set its ineffaceable mark on her had been pain of the body or pain of the mind. But whatever the nature of the affliction she had suffered, the traces it had left were deeply and strikingly visible in every part of her face.

(20)   Her cheeks had lost their roundness and their natural color; her lips, singularly flexible in movement and delicate in form, had faded to an unhealthy paleness; her eyes, large and black and overshadowed by unusually thick lashes, had contracted an anxious startled look, which never left them and which piteously expressed the painful acuteness of her sensibility, the inherent timidity of her disposition. So far, the marks which sorrow or sickness had set on her were the marks common to most victims of mental or physical suffering. The one extraordinary personal

(25)   deterioration which she had undergone consisted in the unnatural change that had passed over the color of her hair. It was as thick and soft, it grew as gracefully, as the hair of a young girl; but it was as gray as the hair of an old woman. It seemed to contradict, in the most startling manner, every personal assertion of youth that still existed in her face. With all its haggardness and paleness, no one could have looked at it and supposed for a moment that it was the face of an elderly woman. Wan as they might be, there was not a wrinkle in her cheeks. Her eyes, viewed

(30)   apart from their prevailing expression of uneasiness and timidity, still preserved that bright, clear moisture which is never seen in the eyes of the old. The skin about her temples was as delicately smooth as the skin of a child. These and other physical signs which never mislead, showed that she was still, as to years, in the very prime of her life. Sickly and sorrow-stricken as she was, she looked, from the eyes downward, a woman who had barely reached thirty years of age. From the eyes upward, the effect of her abundant gray hair, seen in connection with her face,

(35)   was not simply incongruous—it was absolutely startling; so startling as to make it no paradox to say that she would have looked most natural, most like herself if her hair had been dyed. In her case, Art would have seemed to be the truth, because Nature looked like falsehood.

What shock had stricken her hair, in the very maturity of its luxuriance, with the hue of an unnatural old age? Was it a serious illness, or a dreadful grief that had turned her gray in the prime of her womanhood? That question

(40)   had often been agitated among her fellow-servants, who were all struck by the peculiarities of her personal appearance, and rendered a little suspicious of her, as well, by an inveterate habit that she had of talking to herself. Inquire as they might, however, their curiosity was always baffled. Nothing more could be discovered than that Sarah Leeson was, in the common phrase, touchy on the subject of her gray hair and her habit of talking to herself, and that Sarah Leeson's mistress had long since forbidden every one, from her husband downward, to ruffle her maid's

(45)   tranquility by inquisitive questions.

21. What can the reader infer about the setting from the limited information in paragraph one, lines (1–4)?

   A. The house is in the country.

   B. The house is located in a city.

   C. It is a rather small house with ornate architecture.

   D. It is a large, old house.

   E. It is a large house with up-to-date modifications.

22. What was the overall purpose of this excerpt?

   A. to explain that Sarah was a privileged maid

   B. to describe the setting of the house and those living there

   C. to give a detailed account of the character of Sarah

   D. to establish the unique relationship Sarah had with the other servants

   E. to present her individual relation to her mistress

23. In context, the word "ineffaceable" lines (17–18) most nearly means

   A. inescapable.

   B. horrible.

   C. devastating.

   D. ugly.

   E. inerasable.

24. Why does the author end paragraph four with "But whatever. . .visible in every part of her face" lines (18–19)?

   A. to impart that there was nowhere on her face you could not see the pain

   B. to indicate to the reader just how significant the damage to her face was

   C. to reaffirm to the reader that there was massive damage that was immediately noticeable

   D. to introduce the subject matter for the next paragraph

   E. to summate the previous writing in the passage to this point

25. What makes the term "unnatural" ironic as used in line (25)?

   A. We know her to be only around 30 with all these marks.

   B. It was unusual that someone so young would have such markings.

   C. The markings would be visible in every part of her face.

   D. The gray hair was any more unnatural than any other markings was apparent.

   E. For a young girl in every other aspect, this pain caused graying hair.

26. In context, the word "wan" line (29) most nearly means

   A. pretty.

   B. pink.

   C. round.

   D. shapely.

   E. pale.

27. The phrase "Sickly and sorrow-stricken" line (33) is an example of which literary device?

   A. assonance

   B. repetition

   C. parallelism

   D. alliteration

   E. intonation

28. What does the author mean with the statement "In her case, Art would have seemed to be the truth, because Nature looked like falsehood" lines (36–37)?

   A. Usually women would have been presented in Art as natural as possible but in the case of Sarah, Art would have made improvements to Nature.

   B. Normally Art is perceptibly copying that which is natural (Nature), and this is reversed in the case of Sarah.

   C. Artists would not have used Sarah for a pose unless it was from the eyes downward.

   D. Artists would have had to modify Nature by painting her hair a different color than gray.

   E. Nature made Sarah look like a falsehood rather like Art.

GO ON TO THE NEXT PAGE

29. In context, the word "inveterate" line (41) most closely means

    A. a particularly bad.

    B. occurring over a prolonged period.

    C. something only present in vertebrates.

    D. positively unacceptable.

    E. rude.

30. What may the reader infer from "and that Sarah Leeson's mistress. . .by inquisitive questions" lines (43–45)?

    A. Sarah had a close bond with her mistress, even to the extent that the mistress might have some involvement with her pain.

    B. Sarah is a valuable servant and the mistress does not want the action of other servants to cause her distress.

    C. The mistress does not want to train another servant and does not want anything to upset Sarah and cause her to leave.

    D. Sarah is protected by her mistress, even when it comes to her husband, inasmuch as no one is allowed to disturb Sarah.

    E. Sarah knows something that the mistress does not want to get out and so she doesn't want Sarah upset.

Section 2: Sentence Completion

Each sentence below has one or two blanks, each blank indicating that something has been omitted. Beneath the sentence are five words or sets of words labeled **A** through **E**. Choose the word or set of words that, when inserted in the sentence, *best* fits the meaning of the sentence as a whole.

1. In general, new breakthroughs in scientific and biological research allow us to identify origins of many viruses of formerly _____ origins.

    A. escapable
    B. mysterious
    C. abstract
    D. useful
    E. memorable

2. Hitherto impossible research has been made _____ by the new technology recently engineered by her company with greatly enhanced scope and depth of mapping the core of the earth.

    A. commonplace
    B. controversial
    C. problematic
    D. feasible
    E. resolute

3. The dissimilarities are absolutely striking; even though she is _____, she has few friends, and even though she is a _____ stylist, few customers ask for her when booking.

    A. cute. . .fair
    B. amiable. . .consummate
    C. professional. . .haphazard
    D. nice. . .radical
    E. magnificent. . .futuristic

4. Sales literature that provide excessively complex and irrelevant numbers tend to _____ the real facts and generate sales by causing buyers to accept _____ data in lieu of the real and truthful information so hidden.

    A. obscure. . .spurious
    B. hide. . .rational
    C. confuse. . .representational
    D. elucidate. . .faulty
    E. define. . .questionable

5. Only his truest and most _____ fans remained faithful followers following the news of his steroid use.

    A. reticent
    B. vocal
    C. demonstrative
    D. boisterous
    E. ardent

6. It was her need to _____ that caused her to become an _____; the belief that the government was corrupt and the constant censorship being the two principal causes for move.

    A. express. . .outcast
    B. release. . .icon
    C. expose. . .outsider
    D. expatiate. . .expatriate
    E. control. . .anarchist

7. Not desirous of meeting his Maker in the middle of a poker game, Doc Holiday _____ placed an ace inside his vest as Bat Masterson shuffled the remaining cards.

    A. suspiciously
    B. coyly
    C. overtly
    D. furtively
    E. brazenly

8. Given _____ politicians can generally raise campaign financing easier than challengers, Lt. Governor James should have the advantage.

    A. honest
    B. incumbent
    C. entrepreneurial
    D. opulent
    E. gregarious

GO ON TO THE NEXT PAGE

9. Following the completion of an unusually arduous day at the office, Sue happily enjoyed the _____ experience of relaxing in the hot tub while watching television learning that she just won the state lottery.

   A. erratic

   B. superfluous

   C. halcyon

   D. untoward

   E. geriatric

10. I trust a proposal for matrimony would seem more _____ were it written in the sky, or written on a scoreboard, or written in a test question for the SAT prep; which is what I am formally doing now in asking Teressa for her hand in marriage.

   A. aggrandized

   B. sincere

   C. appreciated

   D. honorable

   E. cherished

Section 2: Short Reading Comprehension

The passages below are followed by questions based on their content; questions following a pair of related passages may also be based on the relationship between the paired passages. Answer the questions on the basis of what is *stated* or *implied* in the passages and in any introductory material that may be provided.

Questions 11–14 are based on the following passage.

Sir Giles's irritating reserve, not even excused by a word of apology, reached the limits of his endurance. He respectfully protested.

"I regret to find, sir," he said, "that I have lost my place in my employer's estimation. The man to whom you confide the superintendence of your clerks and the transaction of your business has, I venture to think, some claim
(5)   (under the present circumstances) to be trusted."

The banker was now offended on his side.

"I readily admit your claim," he answered, "when you are sitting at your desk in my office. But, even in these days of strikes, co-operations, and bank holidays, an employer has one privilege left—he has not ceased to be a Man, and he has not forfeited a man's right to keep his own secrets. I fail to see anything in my conduct which has
(10)   given you just reason to complain."

Dennis, rebuked, made his bow in silence, and withdrew.

Did these acts of humility mean that he submitted? They meant exactly the contrary. He had made up his mind that Sir Giles Mountjoy's motives should, sooner or later, cease to be mysteries to Sir Giles Mountjoy's clerk.

11. In context, the words "irritating reserve" line (1) is best represented by the word

A.   anguish.
B.   tolerance.
C.   perturbation.
D.   patience.
E.   level of resistance.

12. Which selection best describes the overall feeling expressed by Sir Giles in paragraph four lines (7–10)?

A.   He appreciates that as a valued employee, Dennis has a right to question his employer.
B.   Because of the right to strike, Dennis is perfectly justified in his query.
C.   Just because the employer/employee relationship has deteriorated due to employee rights, an employee still does not have the right to know all that is in an employers mind even if it doesn't have to do with work specifically.
D.   He is very upset that business is not run as it used to be what with all the changes to appease the employee such as the right to strike, form unions, and have holidays from work.
E.   He is appalled that Dennis would even question him because he is not behind his desk at work.

13. In context, the word "rebuked" line (11) is best represented by

A.   courteously disagreed.
B.   genuinely dissuaded.
C.   promptly challenged.
D.   cautiously opposed.
E.   sharply reprimanded.

14. Which selection identifies the device exemplified with "Did these acts of humility mean that he submitted?" line (12)?

A.   curio
B.   query
C.   submission
D.   rhetorical question
E.   obviate information

GO ON TO THE NEXT PAGE

Questions 15–17 are based on the following passage.

   The spring is fairly with us now. Outside my laboratory window the great chestnut-tree is all covered with the big, glutinous, gummy buds, some of which have already begun to break into little green shuttlecocks. As you walk down the lanes you are conscious of the rich, silent forces of nature working all around you. The wet earth smells fruitful and luscious. Green shoots are peeping out everywhere. The twigs are stiff with their sap; and the moist, heavy English air is laden with a faintly resinous perfume. Buds in the hedges, lambs beneath them—everywhere the work of reproduction going forward!

(5)

   I can see it without, and I can feel it within. We also have our spring when the little arterioles dilate, the lymph flows in a brisker stream, the glands work harder, winnowing and straining. Every year nature readjusts the whole machine. I can feel the ferment in my blood at this very moment, and as the cool sunshine pours through my window I could dance about in it like a gnat. So I should, only that Charles Sadler would rush upstairs to know what was the matter. Besides, I must remember that I am Professor Gilroy. An old professor may afford to be natural, but when fortune has given one of the first chairs in the university to a man of four-and-thirty he must try and act the part consistently.

(10)

15. In context, the word "glutinous" line (2) most nearly means

   A.   hungry.
   B.   fertile.
   C.   sticky.
   D.   large.
   E.   bloated.

16. In line (5), the word "lambs" is an example of which device?

   A.   allusion
   B.   foreshadowing
   C.   flashback
   D.   metaphor
   E.   simile

17. What can be inferred by the narrator's choice of words, "gnat" line (10) to describe his dance?

   A.   He is a man small in stature representing the size of a gnat.
   B.   He is agile as are the physical characteristics of a gnat.
   C.   He feels new as a gnat that has just been born in the spring.
   D.   His dance would replicate the giddy, erratic flight pattern of the gnat.
   E.   As a gnat is drawn to light, so is he drawn to the sunlight pouring through his window.

Questions 18–20 are based on the following passage.

Also the Emperor became more and more excited with curiosity, and with great suspense one awaited the hour, when according to mask-law, each masked guest must make himself known. This moment came, but although all other unmasked; the secret knight still refused to allow his features to be seen, till at last the Queen driven by curiosity, and vexed at the obstinate refusal; commanded him to open his Vizier. He opened it, and none of the high
(5) ladies and knights knew him. But from the crowded spectators, two officials advanced, who recognized the black dancer, and horror and terror spread in the saloon, as they said who the supposed knight was. It was the executioner of Bergen. But glowing with rage, the King commanded to seize the criminal and lead him to death, who had ventured to dance, with the queen; so disgraced the Empress, and insulted the crown. The culpable threw himself at the Emperor, and said—
(10) "Indeed I have heavily sinned against all noble guests assembled here, but most heavily against you my sovereign and my queen. The Queen is insulted by my haughtiness equal to treason, but no punishment even blood, will not be able to wash out the disgrace, which you have suffered by me. Therefore oh King! allow me to propose a remedy, to efface the shame, and to render it as if not done. Draw your sword and knight me, then I will throw down my gauntlet, to everyone who dares to speak disrespectfully of my king."

18. The phrase "and horror and terror spread in the saloon" line (6) qualifies as what device?

A. mockery
B. allusion
C. metaphor
D. hyperbole
E. litotes

19. All of the following would qualify to support the secret knight being labeled a "criminal" line (7) EXCEPT:

A. he was executioner of Bergen.
B. he disobeyed the mask-law.
C. he was physically in the saloon.
D. he represented himself as a knight.
E. he danced and fraternized with royalty.

20. In context, the word "culpable" line (8) is best represented by

A. faker.
B. imposter.
C. scoundrel.
D. offender.
E. criminal.

GO ON TO THE NEXT PAGE

Section 2: Long Reading Comprehension

The passages below are followed by questions based on their content; questions following a pair of related passages may also be based on the relationship between the paired passages. Answer the questions on the basis of what is *stated* or *implied* in the passages and in any introductory material that may be provided.

Questions 21–30 are based on the following passage.

The following is an excerpt from The Gold Bug by Edgar Allan Poe.

Here my friend, about whose madness I now saw, or fancied that I saw, certain indications of method, removed the peg which marked the spot where the beetle fell, to a spot about three inches to the westward of its former position. Taking, now, the tape measure from the nearest point of the trunk to the peg, as before, and continuing the extension in a straight line to the distance of fifty feet, a spot was indicated, removed, by several yards, from the
(5)   point at which we had been digging.

Around the new position a circle, somewhat larger than in the former instance, was now described, and we again set to work with the spades. I was dreadfully weary, but, scarcely understanding what had occasioned the change in my thoughts, I felt no longer any great aversion from the labor imposed. I had become most unaccountably interested—nay, even excited. Perhaps there was something, amid all the extravagant demeanor of Legrand—some
(10)   air of forethought, or of deliberation, which impressed me. I dug eagerly, and now and then caught myself actually looking, with something that very much resembled expectation, for the fancied treasure, the vision of which had demented my unfortunate companion. At a period when such vagaries of thought most fully possessed me, and when we had been at work perhaps an hour and a half, we were again interrupted by the violent howlings of the dog. His uneasiness, in the first instance, had been, evidently, but the result of playfulness or caprice, but he now
(15)   assumed a bitter and serious tone. Upon Jupiter's again attempting to muzzle him, he made furious resistance, and, leaping into the hole, tore up the mould frantically with his claws. In a few seconds he had uncovered a mass of human bones, forming two complete skeletons, intermingled with several buttons of metal, and what appeared to be the dust of decayed woolen. One or two strokes of a spade upturned the blade of a large Spanish knife, and, as we dug farther, three or four loose pieces of gold and silver coin came to light.
(20)   At sight of these the joy of Jupiter could scarcely be restrained, but the countenance of his master wore an air of extreme disappointment he urged us, however, to continue our exertions, and the words were hardly uttered when I stumbled and fell forward, having caught the toe of my boot in a large ring of iron that lay half buried in the loose earth.

We now worked in earnest, and never did I pass ten minutes of more intense excitement. During this interval we
(25)   had fairly unearthed an oblong chest of wood, which, from its perfect preservation and wonderful hardness, had plainly been subjected to some mineralizing process—perhaps that of the Bi-chloride of Mercury. This box was three feet and a half long, three feet broad, and two and a half feet deep. It was firmly secured by bands of wrought iron, riveted, and forming a kind of open trelliswork over the whole. On each side of the chest, near the top, were three rings of iron—six in all—by means of which a firm hold could be obtained by six persons. Our utmost united
(30)   endeavors served only to disturb the coffer very slightly in its bed. We at once saw the impossibility of removing so great a weight. Luckily, the sole fastenings of the lid consisted of two sliding bolts. These we drew back—trembling and panting with anxiety. In an instant, a treasure of incalculable value lay gleaming before us. As the rays of the lanterns fell within the pit, there flashed upwards a glow and a glare, from a confused heap of gold and of jewels, that absolutely dazzled our eyes.
(35)   I shall not pretend to describe the feelings with which I gazed. Amazement was, of course, predominant. Legrand appeared exhausted with excitement, and spoke very few words. Jupiter's countenance wore, for some minutes, as deadly a pallor as it is possible, in nature of things, for any negro's visage to assume. He seemed stupified—thunderstricken. Presently he fell upon his knees in the pit, and, burying his naked arms up to the elbows in gold, let them there remain, as if enjoying the luxury of a bath.
(40)   It became necessary, at last, that I should arouse both master and valet to the expediency of removing the treasure. It was growing late, and it behooved us to make exertion, that we might get every thing housed before daylight. It was difficult to say what should be done, and much time was spent in deliberation—so confused were the ideas of all. We, finally, lightened the box by removing two thirds of its contents, when we were enabled, with some trouble, to raise it from the hole. The articles taken out were deposited among the brambles, and the dog left to guard them, with
(45)   strict orders from Jupiter neither, upon any pretence, to stir from the spot, nor to open his mouth until our return.

21. Which selection best represents the phrase "Here my friend, about whose madness I now saw, or fancied that I saw, certain indications of method" line (1)?

   A. The narrator finally realized his friend has gone mad.

   B. The narrator discovered the method or cause of his friend's madness.

   C. The narrator realizes that his friend went mad only temporarily.

   D. The narrator understood his friend's methods as not mad.

   E. The narrator only believes his friend has gone mad.

22. What can be inferred by "removed, by several yards, from the point at which we had been digging" lines (4–5)?

   A. The point for digging had been changed by several yards.

   B. The measurement of the tape had been incorrect initially.

   C. The previous diggings were failures.

   D. The digging mark was moved from the initial point.

   E. The exact spot to dig was not easy to measure.

23. At what point in the excerpt was there a marked mood change?

   A. between paragraphs 1 and 2

   B. between paragraphs 2 and 3

   C. between paragraphs 3 and 4

   D. between paragraphs 4 and 5

   E. between paragraphs 5 and 6

24. The sentence "Perhaps there was something, amid all the extravagant demeanor of Legrand—some air of forethought, or of deliberation, which impressed me" lines (9–10) is best an example of

   A. figurative language.

   B. characterization.

   C. foreshadowing.

   D. aside.

   E. cause and effect.

25. In context, the word "mould" line (16) is best described as

   A. cast.

   B. broken soil.

   C. carved woodwork.

   D. box.

   E. wooden container.

26. What was the likely origin of the "three or four loose pieces of gold and silver coin" line (19)?

   A. a buried treasure

   B. coins from the buried box

   C. a portion of the treasure

   D. coins previously on the corpses

   E. a marker to indicate where the treasure was buried

27. Presuming the author ascribed an alternative meaning to "confused" other than jumbled, which selection best identifies the literary device used with "confused" line (33)?

   A. assonance

   B. personification

   C. alliteration

   D. onomatopoeia

   E. allusion

28. Considering that an alternative meaning other than jumbled was used for the term "confused" line (33), select the best rationale for the phenomenon of the treasure's confusion as related in lines (32–34).

   A. The gold and jewels were in a state of disarray.

   B. The treasure was shocked to see people after so long.

   C. The treasure didn't think anyone would be able to open the box.

   D. The lamps casting a shadowy light would have caused distorted images.

   E. The dog having just uncovered the remains of the treasure's last owners was confusion.

GO ON TO THE NEXT PAGE

29. In context, the word "behooved" line (41) most nearly means

   A. was necessary.

   B. was expedient.

   C. was convenient.

   D. was smart.

   E. was expeditious.

30. Which selection represents the best alternative title for this passage?

   A. From Here to There

   B. Almost Unfound

   C. Never Give Up—Never Give In

   D. From Madness to Millionaires

   E. Where There are Pieces, There is More

Answer Key for Practice Test Two

Section 1

Sentence Completion

1. D
2. C
3. A
4. E
5. B

6. C
7. C
8. A
9. E
10. B

Short Reading Comprehension

11. E
12. A
13. C
14. E
15. B

16. D
17. B
18. C
19. C
20. B

Long Reading Comprehension

21. D
22. C
23. E
24. D
25. D

26. E
27. D
28. B
29. B
30. A

Section 2

Sentence Completion

1. B
2. D
3. B
4. A
5. E

6. D
7. D
8. B
9. C
10. A

Short Reading Comprehension

11. D
12. D
13. E
14. D
15. C

16. D
17. D
18. D
19. A
20. E

Long Reading Comprehension

21. D
22. C
23. A
24. E
25. B

26. D
27. B
28. B
29. A
30. D

Answers and Explanations for Practice Test Two

Section 1

Sentence Completion

1. **D.** Although Choices B and C, "gluttony" and "bounty," seem plausible, gluttony has to do with over-consumption and bounty relates to generosity. Choice D "plethora" means excess and is the best fit for the sentence.

2. **C.** Although Choice E, "articulation," appears to fit, it is more appropriately used with speaking, and the examples are clearly musical, making Choice C, "scope," correct.

3. **A.** The key word here is the opening "Once" which sets up a change. This should clue you to look for companions for the action in question; in this case the printing of a retraction. We know newspapers don't like to do this, and so something must have forced them into it. Choice C, "understood," could match the first blank, but only Choice A exonerated matches both the first and second blanks.

4. **E.** Given the response of the organization, the only adjective rising to the level to stimulate such action is Choice E, "obsequious," or excessively attentive, particularly given his marital status.

5. **B.** Clearly we are looking for two positives, the first of which must be exemplary. Only Choices B and D, "exemplar" and "emancipator" qualify. The second blank need also be positive, and only Choice B "altruism" or concern for others qualifies.

6. **C.** We're looking for a first word match that would align with the crime of destruction or vandalism. Choices A, B, and C "trouble," "gang membership," and "extirpation" all qualify. The second blank should relate to the destruction of a certain type of munitions. Again, Choices B and C "built up" and "stockpiled" are possible. Now we're down to making a choice between two possible choices. Since "extirpation" means destruction and is more specific to the crime of vandalism than simply belonging to a gang, Choice C is correct.

7. **C.** We're looking for a complementary pair; either two negatives or two positives and given the overall tone of the sentence, try positive first. In this case, only "pungent" meaning strong and "recognizable" meaning recognizing makes Choice C correct.

8. **A.** A "manifesto" is a public declaration of policy or views and matches exactly what the sponsor recommended. Choices B and D, "declaration" and "statement," respectively, don't carry the specific meaning delineating policy or views as does "manifesto."

9. **E.** Although the teacher's bag of tricks certainly needs to be A "enormous," B "expansive," C "available," and D "impromptu," none of these relate to the diversity of learning styles mentioned in the sentence. Choice E, "eclectic," means drawing on or from varied sources, which is the best choice for this question.

10. **B.** Given the tone of the sentence, only one choice meets the demands of the blank. Choice B, "wary," which means to be careful in guarding against danger or deception is the only selection that fully complies with the demand of the sentence.

Short Reading Comprehension

11. **E.** Although all the elements of nature contrived against him, the unfortunate aspect of the episode was that he was detained from keeping a scheduled appointment, which made for a delay in dinner for all parties concerned.

12. **A.** He purposefully, albeit out of some feelings of guilt, lessened the importance of his curiosity as to their dinner partner so that he might elevate the concern for his colleague's mother.

13. **C.** Although not stated, it seems the author would have us infer that the best qualified physician was the one who made the most money and that would give him the best reputation.

14. **E.** The type of humor presented is based upon what is happening—that is, the situation that a woman has planted herself and will not leave despite the pleadings of Thomas, the servant.

15. **B.** Normally used in drama, when a speaker (or narrator) turns to let the audience know some information not openly represented, it is called an aside or small digression.

16. **D.** The good narrator tells us that "his knowledge of women," and he had met with all kinds, "especially the variety which knows nothing of the value of time," making Choice D correct.

17. **B.** During the time of this writing, women were treated with the utmost respect, and one way to respect a lady is to give her the time and attention requested without rushing her and being rude. Choice B best matches this historical persuasion.

18. **C.** Yes, it is also strange that the physician didn't at least ensure that there was not a real emergency with the case of the woman stranger, but, had this been the case, it surely would have presented itself as such. That being the case, the unusual element in the actions of the physician is the choice to run instead of professionally and determinately informing the woman she must return at another time.

19. **C.** Choice C best restates the situation as the physician and his accomplice attempt to smuggle the physician out the door without disturbing the stranger awaiting in the consulting room.

20. **B.** Although Choice E, "paradox," seems likely in that a shoe creaking being the cause of a catastrophe seems contrary to common sense yet true (the definition of a paradox), it does not explain the last phrase, "I am a lost man." Choice B, "hyperbole," best fits the need as it is an overstatement that a creak of the shoe would alert the enemy, but even if that were the case, it is an overstatement (hyperbole) that the physician would be a "lost man."

Long Reading Comprehension

21. **D.** The house is large as Mathew had to ascend three flights of stairs and pass down a long arched gallery. It is also old as he knocked on another old-fashioned oak door and was met with someone lighting the way with a candle.

22. **C.** This entire passage is dedicated to presenting the smallest detail, including the thick eyelashes of Sarah.

23. **E.** Inerasable or not capable of being erased. The past pain had marked Sarah's face permanently.

24. **D.** The author uses the last line of the preceding paragraph to introduce the topic of the entire next paragraph where he describes, in minute detail, each mark left by the mysterious pain.

25. **D.** It is ironic that all of the detail after sordid detail of the pain evidenced on this woman's face and the unusual markings and features should now be considered natural, but her gray hair is "unnatural."

26. **E.** Given all of the unusual features of Sarah's face, only Choice E is congruent with what we know.

27. **D.** The repetition of the first consonant sound of a series of words qualifies as alliteration.

28. **B.** There is a saying that Art imitates Life (or Nature). The author is saying that due to the extreme and unusual effects of this trauma on the woman, Life or that which was real; Nature looks more of the imitation rather than Art.

29. **B.** An inveterate habit is one occurring over a prolonged period of time. This is an important detail as it delineates a time frame for Sarah's life-changing event.

30. **A.** The author is quite revealing in this statement. Not only does the mistress forbid the other servants from disturbing Sarah, but she forbids her husband from doing so. This is an extremely bold posture for a woman during these times and may indicate some hidden relationship yet to be disclosed about just how much the mistress does know, or is even somehow involved with the cause or misfortune that befell Sarah.

Section 2

Sentence Completion

1. **B.** Choice B, "mysterious," indicates that the origin of many viruses are discovered now only through new research methods.

2. **D.** Given that the technology is new, it would hardly be Choice A, "commonplace," and since we're looking for a positive word—remembering that important tool of monitoring the tone of the sentence—Choice D, "feasible," is the best choice.

3. **B.** We're clearly looking for two qualifiers here: one regarding her ability to make friends as an offset to having few of them; two regarding her profession as a stylist and an offset to her having few requesting customers. Remembering the clue phrase "even though" is telling us that the word we're looking for is again, an offset to the conditions that follow that phrase. In the first blank, all choices are possible, although Choice B, "amiable," means easy to get along with, a really good match to the friendship issue. The second blank is the easier to eliminate bad choices and since "consummate" means complete or perfect, it is a good fit to her professional qualifications notwithstanding her lack of requesting customers.

4. **A.** Since the conditions set are "excessively complex and irrelevant," we are going to looking for two negatives. Looking at the first blank, only Choices A, B, and C are negative. Looking for a negative in the second blank, only "spurious" in that group of three qualify, making Choice A, "obscure," which means dim, hazy, or vague and "spurious," which means not genuine the best choice.

5. **E.** Only Choice E represents something other than volume or noise. "Ardent," or characterized by warmth of feeling is the stand-alone qualifier.

6. **D.** We're looking for a cause-and-effect relationship here, and that relationship has to do with the beliefs about the corrupt government and the fact that she is constantly censored. Someone who is censored has a need to present, and toward that end, Choices A, B, C, and D all qualify. Since we also know that her action involved moving, we can reduce the choices based on the second blank to Choices C and D. Further looking at the result of her actions and the subtleties of the sentence, we find that the censorship is recurring. So, in fine-tuning the first blank, we look for the word that best indicates a repetitive action. That choice is D, "expatiate," which means to speak or write at length indicating often, making Choice D the best selection.

7. **D.** Clearly, we're looking for a word that suggests not drawing attention to oneself or causing a distraction away from the shuffling. Choice B, "coyly," might look like a possibility, but there is nothing shy or pretending shyness about hiding an ace in your vest opposite Bat Masterson. Choice D, "furtively," which means slyly or secretly done is the best choice.

8. **B.** Choice E, "gregarious," is an excellent distractor as it means social or companionable; a good trait for a politician to be sure, especially if he is raising money. But the gist of the sentence is not about qualifying a politician except in light of him or her being in office as opposed to a challenger. Choice B, "incumbent," best qualifies for this distinction.

9. **C.** We're looking for a word that describes a most pleasant experience that causes much joy and is an offset to a difficult day. Choice C, "halcyon," meaning prosperous or most pleasant certainly fits the bill on both counts— pleasant hot tub and prosperous winning of the lottery.

10. **A.** While all of the choices should apply, the best selection for the test question is Choice A, "aggrandized," which means to make great or greater, which is certainly my greatest hope.

Short Reading Comprehension

11. **D.** When Dennis' patience ran out, he protested.

12. **D.** It is clear that as a business owner, Sir Giles is not pleased with the current state of affairs as it relates to all of the concessions yielded by employers to employees. Employees now have the right to strike, form unions, and they are given holidays from work, clearly felt by Sir Giles to be the early stages of the absolute decline of commerce as it was once known.

13. E. To "rebuke" someone is to sharply reprimand them. Although the language used would not be considered particularly cutting today, the language and diction used place this excerpt some years back when conversation was more genteel, and the affront by Sir Giles to Dennis would have been scathing.

14. D. The question asked that there is already a known answer to is considered rhetorical as it is unnecessary and usually used in literature for effect.

15. C. The context clue here is just next door. "Gummy buds" is a continuation of the description began with "glutinous" and as we are generally given to know that something "gummy" is sticky, Choice C best fits.

16. D. This is a fairly straightforward metaphor wherein "lambs" refers not to the literal ewe under one year of age, but a young plant.

17. D. Here, the narrator is metaphorically speaking. As gnats don't dance *per se,* they do fly erratically, and his dance would be just as unpredictable in form and grace.

18. D. The device of "hyperbole" or overstatement is the device used here by the writer to give a sense of the egregious affront made to the court.

19. A. The job of executioner was not criminal; in fact it was a position required to obey the execution of the law.

20. E. Context clues are found in the preceding sentence as the command was given to seize the "criminal." In context then, "culpable" means criminal.

Long Reading Comprehension

21. D. By adding the phrase that he saw, "certain indications of method" indicates the narrator finally saw reason where before he had seen only madness. Because the author modifies usual syntax, the reader must remain actively engaged to follow the train of thought.

22. C. Although not directly stated, if any previous diggings would have been successful, there would not have been reason to continue marking and digging; ergo, previous diggings were failures.

23. A. The mood clearly changes between paragraphs 1 and 2. The narrator clearly explains he was tired, but "scarcely understanding what had occasioned the change in my thoughts."

24. E. The cause is the "extravagant demeanor of Legrand," and the effect is the narrator not feeling "any great aversion from labor imposed" as Legrand "impressed me."

25. B. The context clues to help determine meaning follows the sentence of use, which is common. If the dog could tear it up with his claws and in so doing uncover human bones, it is most likely broken soil given the provided selections.

26. D. As these were but a few coins and there had been two corpses disturbed, it is reasonable to believe that the two had these coins on their persons at the time of death.

27. B. Giving a human-like quality to a nonhuman is called personification. If 'jumbled' was not the definition intended by the author when he used the word 'confused' then he gave an inanimate object (a heap of gold and jewels), the human-like quality of being confused. Provided the author meant other than jumbled when he used the term "confused," giving the treasure the human-like quality of being confused is personification.

28. B. Provided the author meant other than 'jumbled' when he used the term "confused," the treasure would have been confused to see people again after lying idle for so many years.

29. A. "Behooved" in context means necessary. It was late, and it was necessary for us to make exertion, that we might get every thing housed before daylight. By using the checking method of plugging in your selection in the place of the queried word, you improve your chances of success.

30. D. Given the opening paragraph describing the previous madness and the conclusion in becoming millionaires, "From Madness to Millionaires," is the best fit.